CONSTRUCTING THE PATH TO EASTERN ENLARGEMENT

Manchester University Press

ULRICH SEDELMEIER

CONSTRUCTING THE PATH TO EASTERN ENLARGEMENT

The uneven policy impact of EU identity

MANCHESTER UNIVERSITY PRESS
Manchester and New York

distributed exclusively in the USA by Palgrave

Published by Manchester University Press
Oxford Road, Manchester M13 9NR, UK
and Room 400, 175 Fifth Avenue, New York, NY 10010, USA
www.manchesteruniversitypress.co.uk

Distributed exclusively in the USA by
Palgrave, 175 Fifth Avenue, New York, NY 10010, USA

Distributed exclusively in Canada by
UBC Press, University of British Columbia, 2029 West Mall, Vancouver, BC, Canada V6T 1Z2

British Library Cataloguing-in-Publication Data
A catalogue record for this book is available from the British Library

Library of Congress Cataloging-in-Publication Data applied for

ISBN   0 7190 7008 2 *hardback*
EAN   978 0 7190 7008 2

First published 2005

14 13 12 11 10 09 08 07 06 05   10 9 8 7 6 5 4 3 2 1

Typeset in Minion with Lithos
by Action Publishing Technology Ltd, Gloucester
Printed in Great Britain
by Biddles Ltd, King's Lynn

Sabini,

koju volim najviše na svijetu

Contents

Boxes and tables

Boxes

Tables

$\mathcal{A}$CKNOWLEDGEMENTS

I am deeply grateful to all those who made it possible to finally see the publication of this book on which I have worked for far too long. First and foremost, I would like to thank Helen Wallace, who has not only supervised the thesis on which this book is based, but also afterwards never tired to remind me to 'hit the print button'.

I am grateful to the institutions and individuals who enabled me to carry out the research for this book. The University of Sussex Research Fund provided funding for my PhD thesis and the Sussex European Institute – where I feel privileged to have been during its founding years - provided a supportive and stimulating research environment. I am indebted to the over 100 practitioners who generously agreed to be interviewed. A number of institutions and colleagues provided a base and assistance for my fieldwork and very kindly looked after me: Heinz Kramer and the Stiftung für Wissenschaft und Politik, Ebenhausen; Barbara Lippert and the Institut für Europäische Politik, Bonn; Fernando Rodrigo and the Centro Español de Relaciones Internacionales, Madrid; Christian Lequesne and the Centre d'Etudes et de Recherches Internationales/Fondation Nationale des Sciences Politiques, Paris; and Anita Popescu and David Blackman at the European Parliament, Brussels. I am also most grateful to the friends who put me up and put up with me during my stays at these places.

My home institution, Central European University in Budapest, generously granted me research leave to write the book. I am grateful for the opportunity to spend my sabbatical in the excellent working environment of the Max-Planck-Institut für Gesellschaftsforschung in Cologne, and for a Jean Monnet Fellowship from the European University Institute and a visiting fellowship from the Mannheimer Zentrum für Europäische Sozialforschung.

I would also like to thank the series editors and the efficient team at Manchester University Press for doing their best for a speedy publication process (and for not losing patience with me even when it might have seemed that I was not doing mine) and Jelena Stojanović for the index.

Finally, many thanks to the colleagues and friends who have commented on aspects of this work: Jeff Checkel, Heather Grabbe, Stefano Guzzini, Dora Husz, Erin Jenne, Rachel Jones, Mary Kaldor, Zdenek Kavan, Jeremy Kempton, Nicole Lindstrom, Michael Merlingen, Thomas Risse, Paul Roe, Frank Schimmelfennig, Alasdair Smith, Ed Smith, Paul Taggart, Helen

Wallace, Antje Wiener, Cornelia Woll and Alasdair Young. Last but quite obviously not least, I would like to thank my wife, Sabina Avdagić, who read most of this manuscript (if everybody with only marginally more interest in the EU read anywhere near as much of this book as she did, it surely would become the best-read book in EU studies!) and has been a constant source of support, encouragement and happiness.

*A*BBREVIATIONS

ACP	African, Caribbean, and Pacific countries
APs	Accession Partnerships
BDI	Bundesverband der Deutschen Industrie
Bull-EC	Bulletin of the European Community
Bull-EPC	EPC Documentation Bulletin
CAP	Common Agricultural Policy
CEECs	central and eastern European countries
CFSP	Common Foreign and Security Policy
CMEA	Council for Mutual Economic Assistance
CNPF	Conseil National du Patronat Français
COREPER	Committee of Permanent Representatives
COREU	Correspondance Européenne (EPC/CFSP communication network)
CSCE	Conference on Security and Cooperation in Europe
CSFR	Czechoslovak Federal Republic
DG	Directorate General (of the European Commission)
DIHT	Deutscher Industrie und Handelstag
EA	Europe Agreement
EBRD	European Bank for Reconstruction and Development
EC	European Community
ECJ	European Court of Justice
ECSC	European Coal and Steel Community
EEA	European Economic Area
EEWG	Council Working Group on Eastern Europe
EFTA	European Free Trade Association
EMU	Economic and Monetary Union
EP	European Parliament
EPA	European Political Area
EPC	European Political Cooperation
ETUC	European Trade Union Congress
EU	European Union
EUROFER	European Steel Producer Association
G7	Group of 7 (western economic powers)
G24	Group of 24 (member states of the OECD)
GAC	General Affairs Council
GATT	General Agreement on Tariffs and Trade

GDP	Gross Domestic Product
GDR	German Democratic Republic
GNP	Gross National Product
GSP	General System of Preferences
IGC	Intergovernmental Conference
IR	International Relations
JHA	Justice and Home Affairs
MFA	Multi-Fibre Arrangement
MSA	Multilateral Steel Agreement
NATO	North Atlantic Treaty Organisation
NGO	Non-Governmental Organisation
NTBs	Non-Tariff Barriers
OECD	Organisation for Economic Cooperation and Development
PHARE	Pologne et Hongrie: assistance à la restructuration économique
QMV	qualified majority voting
QRs	quantitative restrictions
RPR	Rassemblement pour la République
SEA	Single European Act
SGCI	Secrétariat Général du Comité Interministériel pour les questions de coopération économique européenne
TAIEX	Technical Assistance Information Exchange Office
TCA	Trade and Cooperation Agreement
TENs	Trans-European Networks
TEU	(Maastricht) Treaty on European Union
UDF	Union pour la Démocratie Française
UNICE	Union of Industrial and Employers' Confederations of the European Communities
USSR	Union of the Socialist Soviet Republics
VRAs	Voluntary Restraint Agreements
WEU	Western European Union
WP	White Paper

Part I

Analytical framework

1

Introduction: the puzzle(s) of the EU's eastern enlargement

The European Union (EU) has completed the first wave of its eastern enlargement. On 1 May 2004, eight central and eastern European countries (CEECs) – the Czech Republic, Estonia, Hungary, Latvia, Lithuania, Poland, Slovakia, and Slovenia – joined the EU.[1] For the new members, accession presented the achievement of one of the central foreign policy goals that their governments had formulated more than a decade earlier, after the political transformations of the late 1980s. As with many historical events, it might appear now that the EU's eastern enlargement was always inevitable. However, while the process still took much longer than many CEEC governments initially had hoped, we should not forget that not too long ago, it was far from taken for granted that enlargement would happen at all, let alone that it would happen when it did. Practitioners and academics alike were sceptical about the likelihood of eastern enlargement, or at least expected the whole process to take considerably longer. For example, in early 1991, then French President François Mitterrand commented that EU membership for the CEECs would take 'tens and tens of years' (Vernet 1992: 660). In 1994, a leading political economist studying eastern enlargement argued that it would take 'at least [another] two decades' (Baldwin 1994: 157), since it would be 'at least two decades before the leading CEECs can be full members without threatening incumbents' special interests' (1994: 196). Thus, while eastern enlargement looked a certainty at least since the start of this decade, it was far from obvious that we would get there at all.

More generally, the EU member states' agreement on the accession of the CEECs appears to present a puzzle for rationalist approaches in International Relations (IR) theory. Most rationalist approaches and in particular their main proponent in EU studies, liberal intergovernmentalism (Moravcsik 1993, 1998), are based on materialist assumptions. From this perspective, EU policy-making is thus the outcome of a bargaining process between actors who maximise given material preferences. On the basis of these assumptions, the collective agreement of the incumbent member states to enlarge is difficult to explain. To be sure, aggregate benefits for the EU – the economic opportunities of a larger market and gains in terms of stability and security – are high (e.g. Baldwin et al. 1997; Grabbe 2001; Grabbe and Hughes 1998; Mayhew 1998). However, the costs and benefits from eastern enlargement are unevenly distributed among the incumbent members. Why was the process – which required a unanimous decision – not vetoed by any of the member state governments that cannot expect their gains from enlargement to outweigh the costs?

The decision to enlarge as such is not the only dimension of the EU's eastern enlargement that poses a puzzle. The EU's decision to enlarge does not tell us much about the terms of enlargement. The terms of enlargement are expressed in specific provision of the accession treaties, but also in the content of the EU's policies towards the CEECs in the pre-accession phase. These substantive policies are the other dimension of eastern enlargement that constitutes a puzzle. More precisely, the (uneven) pattern of the EU's accommodation of the CEECs' preferences in the various substantive policies is difficult to explain purely on the basis of material interest-maximisation and bargaining power. Liberal intergovernmentalist approaches identify domestic interest group pressure as a central factor shaping government preferences, which they then defend in inter-state bargaining. Given the inferior bargaining power of the CEECs, the preferences of EU interest groups should then restrict the extent to which EU policies accommodate the preferences of the CEEC governments. Why, then, did the EU accommodate the CEECs' preferences in certain sectoral policies despite strong countervailing interest group pressure?

This book seeks to answer the central questions that respectively underpin these two dimensions of the EU's eastern enlargement: (1) Why did the European Union decide to enlarge to the CEECs? (2) How can we explain the (uneven) patterns of interest accommodation in substantive policies that are part of the EU's enlargement policy? These questions are not simply of historical interest. First, enlargement will remain on the EU's agenda for some time to come: Bulgaria, Romania, Turkey and Croatia are officially recognised as accession candidates and the membership perspective has been extended to the remaining countries of south-eastern Europe. Second, a better understanding of the dynamics that led to eastern enlargement enables us to appreciate better the dynamics underpinning the enlarged EU. Finally, by addressing a central theoretical debate in IR theory, EU studies and comparative politics, the book offers broader insights into EU politics and policy-making in international organisations more generally.

Thus, a central puzzle of eastern enlargement concerns the EU's (uneven) accommodation of the CEECs preference, both with regard to their general membership preference and their particular preferences in specific policy areas. Of course, preference accommodation as such is not necessarily a problem for rationalist and materialist approaches. The following section briefly examines in a counterfactual analysis how rationalist approaches – and liberal intergovernmentalist approaches specifically – would explain, first, the EU's decision to enlarge,[2] and second, the likelihood of accommodation in substantive policies towards the CEECs.

Rationalist explanations of the EU's decision to enlarge

The assumption of rational, selfish actors of course does not preclude the possibility of interest accommodation. While rationalist approaches generally assume interest-maximisation according to a narrow utility function, this does not necessarily imply a complete disregard for the interests of other actors. Indeed, as Keohane (1991) pointed out, only a very crude, 'myopic' notion of self-interest implies indifference to the welfare of others. Actors' behaviour might accommodate the interests of others if their relationship is characterised by either 'instrumental interdependence' or 'situational inter-dependence' (1991: 229). The former implies that actors are able to retaliate against actions that negatively affect them, while the latter means that improvements in others' welfare improve one's own welfare.

However, in the case of eastern enlargement, the relationship between the EU and the CEECs is characterised by asymmetrical, rather than instrumental, interdependence. The CEECs depend far more on market access to the EU than vice versa. In other words, the bargaining power of CEEC governments is not sufficient to extract concessions from the EU member states. On the other hand, there is indeed a degree of situational interdependence. Prosperous and politically stable, democratic eastern neighbours (and members) are beneficial to incumbent member states: as markets and invest-ment opportunities, and as reduced security risks. Indeed, as Moravcsik and Vachudova (2003: 50) argue, the EU can expect sizeable economic and geopo-litical benefits from enlargement while the economic costs can be considered marginal (see also Vachudova 2005: 245–6). Furthermore, these benefits are also particularly salient for some of the most powerful member states, notably Germany. However, the economic benefits and the risks of instability are unevenly distributed among the incumbents. Crucially, not all member states can expect their individual benefits from enlargement to outweigh the cost.

Potential economic and security gains vary with geographical proximity. The member states on the southern and western periphery that stand to gain least from enlargement have to fear that enlargement will leave them worse off than the status quo. Ireland, Portugal, or Spain, for example, are neither particularly vulnerable to political instability in the CEECs, nor best placed to exploit the economic opportunities of enlargement.[3] By contrast, enlarge-ment entails significant risks for them, most obviously the loss of substantial receipts from the EU budget through redistribution to the poorer new members. Why then, did they assent to the accession of the CEECs, which required a unanimous decision of all member states? While the case of economic cost/benefit calculations of these countries is the most striking challenge for rationalist explanations, other member state governments feared that the political costs might not outweigh the benefits. The French government was concerned about a loss of influence (especially vis-à-vis Germany) in an enlarged EU and in particular the Benelux countries feared negative consequences for a further 'deepening' of integration. Why did none of them openly oppose or veto the decision to enlarge? Why did they allow the process to evolve so far, rather than blocking it at an earlier stage? Thus, a fundamental puzzle is why the EU committed itself to enlargement, despite the costs that arise for certain member governments which all have veto power.

A rationalist counter-argument is that the reluctant members can use the threat to veto enlargement to extract concessions and side-payments from those member states whose preference for enlargement is much more intensive. Yet there is no evidence of side-payments that offset the risks enlargement entails for them. A related possibility is that the reluctant member states considered enlargement inevitable, given the strong preference of some key members states (primarily Germany). It was then strategically opportune to try shaping the enlargement process, rather than losing their voice opportunities through outright opposition. Koch (1995: 8), for example, suggests that this view explains the behaviour of the Dutch government.

The strongest rationalist argument is that the incumbents could obtain enlargement on their terms, which would resolve redistributive issues at the expense of the new members (see also Moravcsik and Vachudova 2003: 51). It might then still seem at least surprising that they de facto agreed to enlargement well before the terms of accession were fixed; but it could be argued that they were secure in the knowledge that they could still veto enlargement at the last minute if it did not happen on their terms. However, while the incumbents can impose the terms of accession on candidates, once they are on the inside, their voice opportunities allow them to redress these terms, as in the cases of the UK or Spain. Thus, although the EU phased in the CEECs' receipts from the Common Agricultural Policy (CAP), capped the transfers from the structural funds, and allowed for a generous phasing out of current beneficiaries, these arrangements might be short-lived.

In sum, rationalist approaches provide a convincing explanation for the main sources of *opposition to enlargement*, for the strong initial reluctance among the member states to consider enlargement, and the incremental nature of the enlargement process. However, it remains a puzzle for rationalist, materialist approaches that these governments did not *stop* the enlargement process at an early stage.

Rationalist explanation of substantive policy outcomes

Most rationalist approaches would suggest that the content of EU policy towards the CEECs in specific policy areas depends crucially on the configuration of EU interest groups in a policy area. For liberal intergovernmentalism, in particular, the preferences that governments promote in inter-state bargaining at the EU level are a function of societal pressures. Liberal intergovernmentalism largely shares its view of domestic politics with pluralist or public choice approaches. The key political actors are bureaucrats and party politicians. They are self-interested utility-maximisers, either with regard to the budget of their bureau, their income, power, prestige, an easy life, or with regard to votes. Hence they have strong incentives to comply with the pressure of the dominant societal interest groups. Among the societal groups, producer groups are in a better position to organise and exercise pressure on the government than consumers, since they are smaller and have greater incentives for lobbying. As Moravcsik (1993: 487) puts it,

> the distribution of expected net societal costs provides a means of predicting the nature of political conflict and co-operation in the EC, both internationally and domestically. [...] To understand and predict the likelihood of international co-operation in any given instance, therefore, requires a more precise specification of domestic societal interests in particular issue-areas and the ways in which those interests constrain governments. [...] The prospect of international agreement will depend almost entirely on the configuration of societal preferences.

A liberal intergovernmentalist approach thus conceives of substantive policies of the EU towards the CEECs as a 'two level game' (Putnam 1988; see also Evans et al. 1993). More precisely, like other cases of the EU's external relations and international negotiations, they can be understood as a number of parallel three level games (see e.g. Paarlberg 1997; Patterson 1997). For each issue area, the policy outcome is determined in a vertical bargaining process that takes place simultaneously at three analytically distinct levels: between the EU and the CEECs, between the member state governments, and between their respective 'chief negotiators' and domestic groups. EU policy thus reflects the relative bargaining power of each group of actors, and the interaction between levels. Indeed, at least implicitly, most theoretically informed analyses of particular policies within the enlargement policy, in particular of the association agreements (or 'Europe Agreements'), follow this approach. In general, these studies demonstrate convincingly the constraints that domestic interest groups imposed on the accommodation of the CEECs' interests (see Friis 1997; Guggenbuhl 1995; Haggard et al. 1993; Niblett 1995; Nicolaïdis 1993; Shaffer 1995).

However, such an approach to substantive policies of eastern enlargement has two main weaknesses. First, while interest group pressure predicts well much of the general pattern of accommodation, there are significant exceptions. For example, despite strong countervailing interest group pressure, the EU accommodated the CEECs' preferences for free and unconditional access to the EU steel market. Likewise, although EU producer associations pressed hard for the EU to insist that CEEC firms align themselves early and strictly with EU environmental standards in the pre-accession period, the EU granted the CEECs some exceptionally long post-accession transition periods in this area. Conversely, the EU insisted on early alignment with EU social policy even in the absence of societal pressure for doing so.

Second, the policy process on these substantive policies was not generally characterised by inter-state bargaining. A number of empirical analyses of the EU's association policy contradict the assumption of a cleavage along national lines. While these studies often do not place these findings in a broader conceptual framework, they observe a conflict that cuts across member states according to whether policy-makers follow a broader political rationale or a narrower sectoral economic rationale (Sedelmeier 1994); a clash between the foreign policy-oriented framework of European Political Cooperation (EPC) and the EC framework in which sectoral concerns dominate (Niblett 1995); or a 'policy gap' between high-level 'ambitions' and actual policy as formulated at lower levels of the decision-making hierarchy (Torreblanca 1997). In sum, liberal intergovernmentalist predictions do not match the policy outcomes in particular policy areas, nor some central characteristics of the policy process.

The book's argument

While materialist rationalist approaches thus explain large parts of the EU's enlargement policy, they have shortcomings. Drawing on the current 'grand debate' in IR theory between rationalism and constructivism (see e.g. Katzenstein, Keohane and Krasner 1998), this book explores to what extent a focus on ideational and social factors can provide an explanation to these apparent puzzles. I argue that social factors, as well as material interests and bargaining power, drive the EU's eastern enlargement. A number of primarily descriptive studies have asserted that social factors rather than just material factors play an important role in the EU's eastern enlargement. For example, Grabbe and Hughes (1998: 1) claim that eastern enlargement 'is not motivated just by the logic of political, economic and security interests on both sides; but has an emotional and moral dimension in reuniting Europe and making up for the painful divisions of Yalta'.

While such studies thus suggest that this focus is indeed promising, they usually make no effort to situate and substantiate this claim in an explicit conceptual framework. A number of more recent studies have started to analyse the role of social factors in the EU's eastern enlargement (see Fierke and Wiener 1999; Friis 1998; Schimmelfennig 2001, 2003; Sedelmeier 2000a;

Sjursen 2002; Torreblanca 2001; and for an overview, Schimmelfennig and Sedelmeier 2002: 519–22). However, only few of these studies attempt to substantiate their claims in a causal analytical framework and none of them link their analysis of the evolving decision to enlarge with an analysis of substantive policies (for a similar observation, see Jileva 2004, and for an exception, see Sedelmeier 2001, 2002). This book sketches a framework to analyse the impact of social factors on the EU's eastern enlargement policy and seeks to demonstrate the impact of these factors empirically.

I argue that a key factor in the EU's eastern enlargement policy is the EU's collective identity vis-à-vis the CEECs. From the origins of the EC to the responses to the changes in the CEECs in the late 1980s, EU policy-makers have discursively constructed a particular role of the EU in its relations with the CEECs. This role ascribes to the EU a 'special responsibility' towards the CEECs – to support their systemic transformations and their integration into the EU. This role-specific collective identity of the EU has constitutive and regulative effects.

The social norms that characterise it are diffuse, but they entail behavioural obligations for policy-makers acting on behalf of the EU. In its strongest (constitutive) form, EU identity towards the CEECs prescribes to actively support the transformations in the CEECs and their integration into the EU. In a more minimalist (regulative) version, it silences opposition to taking account of the CEECs' preferences by de-legitimising opposition that is purely motivated by the incumbents' narrow self-interests. Identification and resonance with this aspect of EU identity is particularly strong among officials in the Commission responsible for relations with the CEECs. These policy-makers appear to have largely internalised the norms entailed in the EU's identity towards the CEECs, and thus formed a group of principled policy advocates who actively promoted eastern enlargement and the preferences of the CEECs in EU policy. This aspect of EU identity thus affected EU policy through the advocacy of a particular group of policy-makers inside the EU.

Both the evolution of the EU's decision to enlarge and the outcomes of substantive sectoral policies thus depended on the ability of these policy advocates to influence policy. In order to understand the policy advocates' influence on these two dimensions of the EU's enlargement policy, we have to consider that the impact of EU identity towards the CEECs varies across different groups of EU policy-makers, depending on how central this particular aspect of EU identity is to their multiple social identities. While my argument is thus clearly inspired by constructivism, I argue that the impact of the EU's identity, or more precisely, of this particular aspect of EU identity, is uneven across different groups of EU policy-makers.

The uneven impact is particularly relevant because of the specific characteristic of the EU's enlargement policy as a *composite policy*: it is a broad policy framework which is composed of a number of substantive policy areas and in which different groups of policy-makers, or policy communities, have primary competence for specific aspects of policy. Officials dealing with external relations in the member governments and in the Commission have a strong influence on the general direction and general parameters of the enlargement policy. But they have to coordinate, negotiate, or delegate, concrete decisions on specific aspects of policy substance in the particular issue areas included in this policy with the respective groups of sectoral policy-makers. The policy impact of the advocates of the CEECs' preferences thus depended on the extent to which this element of EU identity affected these respective groups of policy-makers. In general, identification with EU policy towards the CEECs, and hence the resonance of EU identity towards the CEECs, is much weaker among sectoral policy-makers. The weaker the resonance of identity with a particular group of policy-makers, the more important is the role of additional mediating factors.

With regard to the decision to enlarge, the resonance of the EU's identity towards the CEECs with high-level policy-makers in the member states and the Commission created the necessary scope for the policy advocates to obtain approval for successive policy initiatives that set the EU on an incremental, but increasingly irreversible path to eastern enlargement. The policy advocates could directly appeal to the EU's identity towards the CEECs in order to influence these policy-makers, as they are sensitive to the behavioural obligations that the EU's identity towards the CEECs entails for policy-makers acting on behalf of the EU. EU identity limited the range of arguments that they could legitimately make against the principle of eastern enlargement by proscribing opposition purely motivated by the incumbents' narrow self-interests. Although the EU's self-proclaimed role did not extend to forging a positive consensus on a proactive enlargement policy and on a consistent accommodation of the CEECs' preferences in substantive policies, it made it difficult for these policy-makers to oppose initiatives by the policy advocates. In this way, the EU's identity towards the CEECs empowered the policy advocates by creating an opportunity structure that enabled them to obtain approval for their policy initiatives.

In contrast, the influence of the policy advocates on substantive sectoral policies is much less direct. Appeals to the EU's identity towards the CEECs have much less effect, since the resonance of this aspect of identity is only minimal among the various sectoral policy-makers, both in the Commission and the member state governments. The accommodation of the CEECs' preferences therefore depended on additional factors that mediate the policy advocates' influence. Crucially, their policy impact is not simply determined by the pressure of sectoral interest groups in the EU.

Their influence is mediated by two main factors that respectively affect their access to decisions on particular sectoral policies and their ability to build 'winning coalitions' among the sectoral policy-makers involved in such decisions. First, the access of the policy advocates to policy decisions depends on the *structure of the policy coordination process* between the macro-policy-makers and the respective groups of meso-policy-makers. Essentially, the access of the policy advocates varies according to the degree of centralisation and fragmentation of the policy process. A centrally coordinated policy process facilitates access, while fragmentation of the policy process insulates the policy process at the sectoral level. Secondly, the ability to build 'winning coalitions' with sectoral policy-makers does not merely depend on the strength of interest group pressure on sectoral policy-makers, as rationalist pluralist approaches suggest. I argue that these preferences of sectoral policy-makers are significantly influenced by sectoral *policy paradigms*, i.e. the set of ideas that underpin EU policy in particular issue areas. Thus, the more compatible sectoral policy paradigms are with the preferences of the CEECs, the more likely is it that the policy advocates can build alliances with sectoral policy-makers, even in the face of strong interest group opposition.

In sum, the argument is inspired by two distinctive sources. It draws on constructivist insights to endogenise preference formation, which is shaped by the discursively constructed EU identity towards the CEECs. It draws on historical institutionalism to emphasise that this aspect of collective identity does not evenly determine behaviour across distinctive groups of actors in the EU, but that it might rather limit behavioural options through social control or internalised constraints. Thus, social factors – EU collective identity and sectoral policy paradigms – can induce path-dependence and incrementalism just as formal institutions can (see e.g. Pierson 1996).

Case selection

The two main dimensions of eastern enlargement – the decision to enlarge and substantive policy outcomes – require different choices for case selection. With regard to the decision to enlarge, the book sketches the overall evolution of the enlargement policy. I identify the key stages of policy development and examine the impact of EU identity at these various stages. I engage in process-tracing in order to analyse the relative importance of ideational and material factors that led the EU to embark, and remain, on a path to enlargement.

Variation in interest group pressure
With regard to the substantive policies that are part of the EU's enlargement policy, the book has to be more selective. As the main alternative rationalist explanation focuses on interest group pressure as the key independent variable, the case selection is according to variation in this variable. Liberal intergovernmentalism distinguishes between three categories of EU policy areas that 'engender characteristic distributions of costs and benefits for societal groups, from which follow variations in patterns of domestic mobilization' (Moravcsik 1993: 488). The three sectoral case studies in this

book fall each into one of these categories – 'trade liberalisation', the 'provision of socio-economic public goods' (e.g. environmental, social, and other regulatory policy), and 'political, institutional, or redistributional policies' (e.g. Common Foreign and Security Policy (CFSP), EU institutions, and regional funds). The strength of interest group opposition against an accommodation of the CEECs' preferences varies across the case studies. They thus differ in their predicted likelihood of an accommodation, which allows establishing a rationalist materialist, or liberal intergovernmentalist, 'null hypothesis' and testing it empirically.

In the case of steel trade liberalisation (Chapter 6), producer interests are strong and unified against the CEECs' interest to gain access to the EU market. Steel consumers do not significantly counterbalance producer interests. If, as liberal intergovernmentalism assumes, sectoral policy-makers primarily defended the interest of the strongest societal groups, the ability of the policy advocates to build a winning coalition in favour of an accommodation of the CEECs' preferences, should be highly constrained. It is thus a 'hard case' for accommodation; the likelihood is lowest among the case studies. In the case of the CEECs' regulatory alignment with the internal market (Chapter 7), the preferences of producers, trade unions and broader publics converge in opposition against the CEECs' demands for transitional arrangements for alignment, e.g. with EU social and environmental standards. From a liberal intergovernmentalist perspective, the constraints on accommodation in this case are thus also high, and the likelihood of accommodation low. However, this case needs to be disaggregated into separate observations: during the initial phase of policy development, interest groups did not assert their preferences, suggesting a higher likelihood of accommodation than in the subsequent phase.

By contrast, in the EU's Political Dialogue with the CEECs on foreign policy (Chapter 8), policy-makers are not constrained by societal groups. As there is a significant convergence between the preferences of the CEECs and EU foreign policy-makers, liberal intergovernmentalist approaches would consider that in this case an accommodation of the CEECs' preferences is much more likely than in the other two. It thus serves as a control case in which interest group opposition to an accommodation of the CEECs' preferences was absent. Table 1.1 summarises the predictions about the likelihood of accommodation across the cases that result from these different constellations of this variable.

Variation in policy paradigm compatibility and policy process

In the first place, the case studies were selected according to variation in the variable 'interest group pressure'. However, in order to avoid indeterminate research design, it is also necessary to establish to what extent the case studies vary on the other two explanatory variables, namely the structure of the policy process and policy paradigms. To gauge variation in the explanatory variables across the case studies, the analysis has to proceed in a first cut inductively. I identify the policy paradigm underpinning a particular policy area and determine the extent to which it is compatible with the preferences of the CEECs. The analysis can then proceed deductively and predict the likelihood of accommodation.

The predictions resulting from an analysis of policy paradigms in the different policy areas contradict in almost all instances those resulting from a focus on interest groups; which allows an assessment of their relative explanatory power. The paradigm on which the EU's Political Dialogue is based is incompatible with the preferences of the CEECs, making accommodation unlikely. In the case of steel trade liberalisation, the policy paradigm underpinning EU steel policy shifted towards a paradigm that is much more compatible with the CEECs' preferences, making accommodation more likely. The case of regulatory alignment is somewhat more complex. Although the EU's internal market paradigm forms an obstacle to accommodation, the prevalent view in Directorate General (DG) Internal Market, in charge of the drafting of the EU's regulatory alignment policy, was more compatible with a (temporary) accommodation. The constellation with regard to this variable and interest group pressure results thus in a degree of indeterminacy, which needs to be resolved through process-tracing analysis. Table 1.1 summarises the predictions according to variation on the variable 'policy paradigms'.

The third variable, 'structure of the policy process' does not only vary across the three policy areas, but also within cases, at different stages of policy development. These variations lead to a further disaggregation of the case study chapters into additional observations (see Table 1.1).

The column 'outcomes' in Table 1.1 allows us to contrast the various predictions with the results of the empirical analysis of the policy areas. At first glance, this pattern favours explanations based on policy paradigms and the structure of the policy process over explanations based on interest groups. The explanatory power of interest group pressure appears generally low, while a focus on policy paradigms, especially if complemented with an analysis of the structure of the policy process, corresponds well with observed outcomes. A remaining puzzle is the different outcomes with regard to regulatory alignment with social and environmental policy, on which the concluding chapter will elaborate.

One implication of my research design is that the theoretical propositions underpinning the book's analytical framework were partly derived from the empirical material to which it is applied.[4] Thus, while the case studies illustrate and seek to establish the plausibility of my argument, they do not constitute a crucial test of its validity. However, I do establish a generalisable explanatory framework that allows future research to use my arguments deductively and to design rigorous critical case studies to (in)validate them.

Table 1.1 Research design and case selection

Cases		Test variables			Policy outcomes
		Interest groups	Policy process	Policy paradigms	
Steel trade liberalisation	EA negotiations	Accommodation unlikely	Accommodation possible	Accommodation possible	Accommodation
	Implementation of the EAs	Accommodation unlikely	Accommodation unlikely	Accommodation likely	Accommodation
Regulatory alignment	Environmental policy (White Paper)	Accommodation possible	Accommodation possible	Accommodation unlikely	Accommodation
	Environmental policy (accession negotiations)	Accommodation unlikely	Accommodation unlikely	Accommodation unlikely	Accommodation
	Social policy (White Paper)	Accommodation possible	Accommodation possible	Accommodation unlikely	No accommodation
	Social policy (accession negotiations)	Accommodation unlikely	Accommodation unlikely	Accommodation unlikely	No accommodation
Foreign policy consultations		Accommodation possible/likely	Accommodation possible	Accommodation unlikely	No accommodation

Structure of the book

The structure of this book is as follows. Chapter 2 situates the theoretical argument within the debate between rationalism and constructivism and explores different elements of EU identity that could be salient for its eastern enlargement policy. The chapter identifies the discourse by EU policy-makers about their collective role in relations with the CEECs as a key aspect of their collective identity that affects the behaviour of EU policy-makers. Chapter 3 examines how this element of EU identity has a causal impact on EU policy and sketches the analytical framework, including the additional factors that mediate the policy impact on sectoral policies.

Chapters 4 and 5 analyse the overall development of the EU's enlargement policy. They examine the impact of EU identity primarily on the enlargement decision and trace how the policy advocates were able to gain approval for successive policy initiatives that set the EU on an incremental path to enlargement. At the same time, the chapters sketch how the broader patterns of the policy process affected substantive policy in various issue areas that are not covered in the sectoral case study chapters. Chapter 4 analyses the shift from the EU's initial reluctance to even discuss the question of an eventual accession of the CEECs to the endorsement of their membership perspective at the Copenhagen European Council in 1993. Chapter 5 traces how the general principle of enlargement was placed on a working footing through the agreement on a pre-accession strategy and the setting of an indicative date for accession negotiations at the Madrid European Council in December 1995, after which enlargement was firmly on track.

Chapters 6, 7, and 8 present the sectoral case studies of particular substantive policies: the EU's liberalisation of trade in steel products; its policy for the regulatory alignment of the CEECs with the internal market; and the Political Dialogue with the CEECs on foreign policy. The chapters follow a common template. Each chapter first examines the extent to which the preferences of EU interest groups are in opposition to those of the CEECs. The chapters then identify the policy paradigms underpinning the policy area in question and establish the extent of their compatibility with the CEECs' preferences. Subsequently, an empirical analysis of the evolution of policy within the policy areas establishes to what extent the three alternative mediating factors – interest group pressure, paradigms, and policy process – affected whether the EU accommodated the CEECs' preferences.

Notes

1　Cyprus and Malta joined on the same date. This book focuses on the CEECs only.
2　For similar counterfactual analyses, see Schimmelfennig 2001: 48–58, 2003: 55–62; Sedelmeier 1998: 1–3, 2000a: 165–6; Sjursen 2002: 497–9.

3   Especially in comparison to the status quo, the association agreements, which allowed
    the EU to enjoy already much of the potential economic benefits even without grant-
    ing the CEECs full membership (see also Schimmelfennig 2001: 56, 2003: 60).
4   I thank Jeff Checkel for alerting me to clarify this point.

2

Constructing the EU's collective identity vis-à-vis the CEECs

This chapter presents the first part of the analytical framework of the book. The following section situates the approach within the 'grand debate' between rationalism and constructivism. From a constructivist perspective, the EU is part of EU policy-makers' cultural and social environment. This normative structure constitutes (part of) their collective identity and provides the basis on which they form their interests and policy preferences. The key question is then which aspects of the EU's normative structure are relevant for the EU's enlargement policy. I therefore examine and trace the factors that are particularly salient for this policy. While some more general aspects of the EU's identity resonate in its policy towards the CEECs, the discursive construction of the EU's specific role vis-à-vis the CEECs is particularly important. A key component of this discourse is the assertion of a 'special responsibility' of EU towards the CEECs. Chapter 3 contains the second part of the analytical framework, which suggests how the policy impact of this identity can be conceptualised.

Rationalism, constructivism and European integration

The conceptual framework of this book is situated in the debate between rationalist and constructivist approaches in Political Science. This debate currently provides the main focal point of theorising in IR (see e.g. Katzenstein et al. 1998; Waever 1997), in EU Studies (see Aspinwall and Schneider 2001; Checkel and Moravcsik 2001; Pollack 2001; Risse-Kappen 1996), and in institutionalist debates in Comparative Politics (see Hall and Taylor 1996; Thelen and Steinmo 1992). Rationalism and constructivism are in fact social meta-theories that define a set of assumptions, on which a variety of substantive theories are based. For example, the main contenders in the 'third debate' in IR theory, neorealism and neoliberal institutionalism, share rationalist assumptions. The same goes for the traditional rival approaches in EU studies, liberal intergovernmentalism and neofunctionalism.

The main difference between rationalism and constructivism relates to their ontological assumptions, which in turn leads them to conceive of different logics of action (see e.g. Adler 2002; Checkel 1998; Jepperson et al. 1996; Risse 2004; Wendt 1999). Rationalism is based on methodological individualism, i.e. the basic units are actions by individual agents (including corporate actors), independent of the structures in which they operate. To the extent that structures matter, they are material, rather than social. Actors' interests are exogenous to the analysis; they are 'given' or treated by assumption as (usually material and narrow) self-interest, such as security or welfare. Actors are utility-maximers; their strategies follow a 'logic of consequences' (March and Olsen 1989: 160), i.e. they choose the course of action that is most likely to advance their self-interest, given the resources available to them. (Material) structures, such as formal institutions or the distribution of power in the international system, affect actors' behaviour by creating incentives for certain strategies, but they do not affect actors' underlying interests. Instrumental rationality might induce actors to change their strategies in response to changing circumstances, or in reaction to other actors' strategies. But it is only actors' behaviour or their operational goals that change, not their underlying interests.

By contrast, constructivism conceives of structures not only as material, but also social. Furthermore, these structures are not simply constraints on behaviour. Actors' environment has a constitutive effect on actors' identities, on the basis of which they conceive their interests. Depending on the social or cultural environment in which actors operate and the nature of their interaction with other agents, actors might form their identity and interests in ways that depart significantly from the preferences that rationalism assumes. In turn, structures are shaped by the interactions between actors. Agents and structures thus mutually constitute each other. This process of 'mutual constitution' leads constructivists to claim the middle ground in the agent/structure debate (Adler 1997). Actors' behaviour thus does not follow a 'logic of consequences', but a 'logic of appropriateness': they ask 'what the situation is, what role is being fulfilled, and what the obligations of that role in that situation are' (March and Olsen 1989: 160). In the case of European integration, constructivist approaches can thus conceive of the EU as a cultural and social environment that shapes actors' identities and interests (see e.g. Christiansen et al. 2001b; Jørgensen 1997; Katzenstein 1996a: 518; Risse 2000: 15; Risse-Kappen 1995b: 287; Wendt 1994: 392).

Apart from obvious misconceptions in the debate, such as a conflation of rationalism with materialism (even if most rationalist work is based on materialist assumptions), some key protagonists argue that the differences have been exaggerated (Fearon and Wendt 2002). Some authors have suggested a division of labour in which 'constructivists seek to understand how preferences are formed and knowledge is generated, prior to the exercise of instrumental rationality' (Katzenstein et al. 1998: 681), based on the view that 'once an actor knows what it is and what it wants, it will move instrumentally (even in the sociological model) to achieve its goals within the material and normative constraints it faces' (Kowert and Legro 1996: 457). The more recent trend is away from an either/or view of rationalism and constructivism as competing explanations. In particular 'moderate' or 'modernist' constructivists have fostered the view of the two approaches as partly competing, partly complementary (see e.g. Finnemore and Sikkink 1998). The main focus of the debate – not least in EU studies - has thus shifted towards the interface between construction and rational choice, and on the possibilities for synthesis, for example through specifying distinctive domains of application or a sequencing of approaches (Jupille et al. 2003).

In a similar vein, my analysis does not suggest that material factors do not matter for the EU's enlargement policy. Rather, I argue that an explanation purely based on material interests and bargaining power cannot explain important features of this policy, specifically the extent to which EU policy accommodates the preferences of the CEEC governments, both with regard to their membership aspiration and in specific sectoral policies. In the following section, I explore which aspects of EU identity could have a causal impact on its eastern enlargement policy.

Collective identify formation in the EU

What does a constructivist explanation of enlargement look like? What aspects or elements in the EU's collective identity would constructivists identify as consequential for its policy towards the CEECs? In general, constructivist approaches can conceive of two broad, analytically separate (yet complementary), ways in which identity might influence EU policy towards the CEECs. One way is to focus on *collective identity formation between the EU (member states) and the CEECs.* This approach essentially follows from the focus on state identities in Wendt's analysis (Wendt 1994, 1999). Wendt's primary concern is to what extent state identities might lead to cooperative, rather than competitive, patterns of interaction. The more actors' social identities include positive identification with the other, the more likely they are to lead to the definition of collective interests, rather than narrower self-interests. The formation of collective identities among states creates the basis for feelings of solidarity, community, and loyalty, opportunities for cooperation, and foundations for multilateral institutions (Wendt 1994).

The second broad approach is to focus specifically on the construction of *the EU's collective identity* and on the features of EU identity that might incline EU institutions and member states to accommodate the preferences of CEEC governments. Wendt's state centrism and his primary concern with broader patterns of cooperation and competition leads him to attach less importance to how specific normative elements of international institutions, which form part of the social environment of states, affect their collective identities, and shape their preferences on specific issues. Other authors have focused much more on specific types of norms and specific elements of actor identities to analyse empirically the effects of such norms and identities on specific policies (see e.g. Katzenstein 1996c; Risse-Kappen 1995a). These authors focus specifically on the causal impact of particular norms within the social environment (such as the international system or international institutions) that constitute actors' identities and shape their interests and behaviour.

From this perspective, the norms that have become embodied in the EU's institutional structure, and that create and reinforce collective identities of EU policy-makers, should have a significant impact on EU policy-making. If the EU forms part of the normative environment for the member states and policy-makers, or creates a collective EU identity as one aspect of their 'multiple social identities' (Risse 2001: 199; Wendt 1994: 385;), these norms should have a considerable effect on interest formulation and EU policy towards the CEECs. Indeed, a number of authors have suggested that the EU is a particularly salient case for constructivist analyses (Christiansen et al. 2001a: 2; Katzenstein 1996a: 518; Risse 2000: 15; Risse-Kappen 1995b: 287; Sandholtz 1996: 405; Wendt 1994:392). However, empirical studies that analyse how specific aspects of EU identity influence EU policy are still rather rare (Börzel 1997a: 130, Pollack 2001: 236) – even in a recent volume exclusively devoted to constructivist analyses of European integration (Christiansen et al. 2001b).

Among the most sophisticated empirical applications of the constructivist research programme to EU studies is the analysis of the impact of the EU on the evolution of nation-state identities among the members (Risse 2001). This research is primarily concerned with identities in a broad sense, i.e. identities concerning understandings of the state and political order. However, the distinction that Risse makes between such broader identities and specific identities, or specific components of identity with regard to specific policy areas, indicates a promising direction for the study of the impact of identity on EU enlargement. Identities and social roles are context-bound, which implies that different aspects of any given identity (or of multiple identities) are salient, depending on the policy area in question (Risse 2001: 201). The key question for the analysis of the impact of EU identity on its enlargement policy is thus to what extent particular aspects of EU identity or specific norms resonate with this policy. In other words, are particular aspects of EU identity in part defined through its relationship with the CEECs and thus at stake in EU policy towards these countries?

In the following sections, I first identify some broader aspects of the EU's collective identity that should be particularly salient in its relationship with the CEECs, and secondly, discursive statements of EU policy-makers on the EU's specific role in its relationship with the CEECs in particular.

General aspects of EU identity: pan-European vocation and liberal democratic norms

There are two main aspects of the EU's identity that are particularly salient for the question of enlargement and that bias the EU towards admitting new members. The first aspect concerns the EU's self-proclaimed pan-European vocation. The second aspect relates to the liberal democratic identities of the EU's member states.

The EU's self-image implies a broader European vocation of the EU. This pan-European vocation implies an obligation to remain open to new members beyond the founding member states. The openness of European integration is in contrast to the image of a club, which is designed to serve only the interests of its incumbents. Key expressions of this openness are references in the EEC treaty. In the preamble, the signatories state their determination 'to lay the foundations of an ever closer union among the peoples of Europe' – rather than just the founding states – and explicitly call for the other peoples of Europe who share their ideal to join their efforts. Article 237 of the EEC Treaty (Art. O TEU) stipulates that any (democratic) European state may apply to become a member of the EU. Along these lines, Preston (1997: 1) contends that 'enlargement has always been part of the EC/EU's "historic mission"'. Friis (1997: 90) suggests that as part of a 'self-styled logic' of the EU (Ginsberg 1989: 34–6), an important aspect in the EU's decision to enlarge is its 'own self-understanding'.

The pan-European vocation as part of the EU's self-image is also reflected in the notion that EU integration has broader responsibilities towards the rest of the continent. On the one hand, this notion engendered the EU's sensitivity to accusations of the emergence of a 'fortress Europe'. Part of the EU's policy towards the European Free Trade Association (EFTA) countries was an acknowledgement that the EU carries responsibilities to alleviate the negative externalities of EU internal integration for non-members. In the case of the CEECs, Friis (1998) points out that arguments about the role of the EU's role in pan-European geopolitical stabilisation were forcefully used by proponents of an inclusive approach to enlargement among the CEEC candidate countries.

The EU's pan-European vocation as such is not sufficient to trigger enlargement. Other more general aspects within the EU's identity construction stipulate that certain countries are more deserving of membership than others. This line of argument follows liberal theories that focus on identity-related factors within the constituent units of an international organisation.

From such a perspective, the constitutive values of the member states shape the identity of the international institutions that they form. A particularly prominent version of this argument emphasises the impact of the democratic identities of member states on cooperation within an international organisation that they form and on the behaviour of the organisation (see e.g. Risse-Kappen 1995a). In the case of the EU, in particular the *social* democratic identities of the member states might incline them to admit poorer and weaker states, such as the CEECs. Lumsdaine (1993) has argued that evolution of the international aid regime is the 'moral vision' of social democratic welfare states that induces a notion of solidarity with weaker and poorer states in international affairs. Certain aspects of the EU's policy towards the African, Caribbean and Pacific (ACP) countries could be explained along similar lines. For instance, Pedler (1994: 84, 88–9) suggests that some member state governments endorsed a restrictive Banana Trade Regime that favours ACP producers, despite their general free trade preferences, because of 'conviction politics' that presented the Caribbean, rather than the Central American producers, as the 'third world' growers.

In the case of eastern enlargement, Pedersen (1990: 87) suggests that the EU 'has always claimed to represent the whole of Europe and officially portrays itself as the catalyst of a wider European peace order. This in itself makes it difficult to reject democratic European states seeking membership.' Schimmelfennig (2001, 2003) has presented a most elaborate argument for the importance of the EU's democratic identity. As the EU is the institutionalisation of a liberal democratic international community, it enlarges to include those states that share these constitutive values. The EU's decision to enlarge thus reflects shared liberal democratic norms, rather than constellations of material interests and power. Indeed, the democratic identity of the EU has been institutionalised in the treaty's membership rules. Hayes-Renshaw and Wallace (1997: 267) also stress the normative dimension of the eligibility criteria:

> A key feature that distinguishes the EU from most other international organisations is that eligibility for membership is itself defined in terms of a list of criteria that have high normative content. [...] Often this line between 'us' and 'them' also involves more substantive and concrete reservations about other countries, but one should not underestimate the impact of choosing to express such reservations in normative language as a factor in hardening the definition of the norms for the insiders.

In sum, from a social constructivist perspective, the EU's pan-European vocation, its liberal-democratic identity and the notion of solidarity appear particularly salient factors that might incline the EU favourably towards the desire of the CEECs to join. Yet the history of EU enlargement shows that these broader identity-related factors are not always sufficient to trigger enlargement (see e.g. Preston 1997). Subsequent French governments had no inhibition in vetoing the UK's initial applications in 1963 and 1967. For a long time, EU institutions and member states have actively discouraged Cypriot and Maltese applications in view of the problems that the accession of these micro-states might cause for institutional representation and decision-making in the EU. In the Spanish case, member states were not reluctant to force long delays in the accession process. Nor do European vocation and democratic identity seem to lead as such to an accommodation of the preferences of the candidate countries in substantive policies, as e.g. the UK and Spain found out when they eventually obtained membership (see e.g. Dominguez 1988; Preston 1997; Ruano 1999).

Thus, these broader aspects of EU identity appear insufficient to trigger an EU commitment to enlarge, let alone an accommodation of the candidates' preferences in substantive policies. While they arguably contribute to, or reinforce, a notion of solidarity with the CEECs, they cannot fully explain why in the case of eastern enlargement, policy transcended the lowest common denominator of material self-interests.

However, apart from these more general aspects of EU identity, a constructivist perspective would attach particular significance to the specific role construction of the EU in its relationship with the CEECs. Thus the role that EU identity ascribes to the EU in its relationship with the CEECs might be different from its role towards other non-member states, apart from the differences in the particular security concerns, or of the longer term economic gains at stake.

The EU's specific role-identity in its relationship with the CEECs

The above elements of an EU identity have been constructed largely independently of the EU's perception of its specific relationship with the CEECs. While these general elements might also affect EU policy in the particular case of the CEECs, the crucial question is whether the EU's identity includes elements that are specific to this relationship with the CEECs. The EU's particular interactions with the CEECs, or the specific discursive construction of the EU's role towards the CEEC should be central for the perception of whether the CEECs are particularly deserving of accommodation, or whether non-accommodation is inappropriate with regard to the EU's identity.

In this section, I sketch the specific discourse about the role of the EU in its relationship to the CEECs. I identify the notion of an 'EU responsibility towards the CEECs' as a particularly prominent feature in this discourse. After the 1989 revolutions, this discourse provided the script on the basis of which EU policy-makers formulated their reactions and articulated the EU's role in post-Cold War Europe and towards the CEECs in particular. The discourse of 'responsibility' and of a 'historical opportunity' led to an EU commitment, which renders non-accommodation of the CEECs detrimental for the EU's self-image.

The discourse about the EU's role in its relationship with the CEECs dates back to the origins of the EU. In most respects, the EU's self-image was defined precisely in contrast to the command economies and authoritarian political systems of the CEECs. However, a central element in this depiction of communist CEECs as the EU's 'other' (see also Neumann and Welsh 1991), was the notion of the external imposition of this political system on the CEEC societies and their involuntary exclusion from the integration project.

A number of analysts suggest that the EU was always based on a 'broader definition of "European integration", aimed at overcoming the East–West division in Europe' (Sedelmeier and Wallace 1996: 354). Reinicke (1992) also identifies a broader notion of 'Europe' in the foundations of the EEC. He suggests that 'the principal purpose of the European Community was to address *European* problems' (1992: 4, original emphasis) and asserts that it 'has a historic responsibility to embrace the countries of Central and Eastern Europe' (1992: 79). Lippert and Schneider (1995: 25) suggest that the EU has to 'live up to a special responsibility for the neighbouring region'.

Among the early practitioners speaking on behalf of the EU, Jean Monnet stated: 'our Community is neither a small Europe, nor a restricted Community. Its limits are not fixed by us. They are fixed by those countries which, for the moment, do not join it. It depends only on them that our limits will be cast wider' (1955: 62).[1] Walter Hallstein affirmed that 'we share one wish above all others which is to overcome the division of Europe between East and West' (Reinicke 1992: 5). In 1963, Robert Schuman stated most clearly the EU's responsibility to remain open to the CEECs:

> We must build the united Europe not only in the interest of the free nations, but also in order to be able to admit the peoples of Eastern Europe into this community if, freed from the constraints under which they live, they want to join and seek our moral support. We owe them the example of a unified, fraternal Europe. Every step we take along this road will mean a new opportunity for them. They need our help with the transformation they have to achieve. It is our duty to be prepared. (Quoted in Fischer 2000: 3)

This discourse continued throughout the Cold War. For example, the Dooge Committee report (Council 1985: 11–12) of the representatives of the member states claimed that the EU had 'not lost sight of the fact that it represents only a part of Europe' and that 'any progress in building the Community is in keeping with the interests of Europe as a whole'. François Mitterrand stated in 1980:

> What we term Europe is a second-best option which alone cannot represent all European history, geography and culture. Looking at the Europe of the Nine, one cannot help asking: why Ireland and not Austria, why Denmark and not Poland.

> I know the response: war and again war, the victors, the vanquished, Yalta, the
> Wall, the two empires. (Quoted in Haywood 1993: 275)

The EU's discourse about its role towards the CEECs during the Cold War
stressed the involuntary exclusion of the CEEC societies from the integration
project. While the EU did not see it within its powers to change the status quo,
it stated its commitment to overcoming the division of Europe and to
supporting the integration of the CEEC.

When the 1989 revolutions made overcoming the division of Europe a
real possibility, the EU reaffirmed this commitment and pledged its support.
Rather than attempting to backtrack in the face of changed circumstances, the
declarations of EU policy-makers reflected a strong continuity of the
discourse. The Rhodes European Council in December 1988 'reaffirm[ed] its
determination to act with renewed hope to overcome the division of our
continent' (Council 1988: 19). After the fall of the Berlin Wall, the Strasbourg
European Council in December 1989 stated that 'the Community and its
Member States are fully conscious of the common responsibility which
devolves on them in this decisive phase in the history of Europe. ... The
Community is and must remain a point of reference and influence. It remains
the cornerstone of a new European architecture ... in its will to openness'
(Council 1989: 15–16). In a section entitled 'A Community of Responsibility
and Solidarity', it asserted:

> The Community's dynamism and influence make it the European entity to which
> the countries of Central and Eastern Europe now refer, seeking to establish close
> links. The Community has taken and will take the necessary decisions to
> strengthen its co-operation with peoples aspiring to freedom, democracy and
> progress ... The Community's readiness and its commitment to co-operation are
> central to the policy which it is pursuing and which is defined in the declaration
> adopted today; the objective remains, as stated in the Rhodes Declaration, that of
> overcoming the divisions of Europe. (1989: 9–10)

The continuity in the discourse, which was also validated by outsiders,[2]
suggests that EU policy-makers had indeed started to take for granted the
EU's self-ascribed role towards the CEECs and the commitment it entailed. At
the beginning of 1990, Irish Prime Minister Charles Haughey asserted on
behalf of the Council presidency that 'the EC can and must do more than
anyone else ... The dream of European unity is as old as Europe itself, we have
begun to see it realised ... The EC has an enormous load of responsibility
towards East Europe' (quoted in Torreblanca 1997: 114). The European
Council in Dublin in April 1990 expressed its 'deep satisfaction at developments in Central and Eastern Europe ... This process of change brings ever
closer a Europe which [has] overcome the unnatural divisions imposed on it
by ideology and confrontation' (Council 1990a: 7). The Rome European
Council in October (Council 1990b: 10) pronounced itself 'aware of the
Community's special responsibility towards [the CEECs]'.

In the Commission, its president, Jacques Delors (1990: 9), suggested that the EU 'was never conceived only for itself. The Schuman declaration … still reminds us of this. In keeping with the Community's destiny, it must today simultaneously deepen itself and respond to the wishes of the entire European continent.'[3] In 1994, he affirmed that 'it is even a historical duty to answer the requests from other countries, especially those of Eastern Europe (*Agence Europe*, 04.02.94: 7). External relations commissioner Hans van den Broek (1994: 11) expressed that 'some observers have suggested that Europe may have to chose between widening, which is needed to fulfil our responsibilities, and deepening, which is needed to save our souls. I believe that this is a false dichotomy and that both are needed.' An official in the DG for external relations claimed: 'The maintenance of an exclusive, 15–member Union and a refusal of further enlargement would not only be morally indefensible, it would also be a rejection of the overall goal [of EU integration]: durable peace, stability and individual well-being and freedom in Europe' (Mayhew 1997: 11).

Successive European Councils and individual policy-makers thus asserted a 'special responsibility' of the EU vis-à-vis the CEECs, which entailed an obligation to actively support the transformations in the CEECs and their integration with the EU. The continuity of the discourse further reinforced this aspect of the EU's collective identity. Karl Lamers (1995: 2), the foreign policy spokesman of the Christian Democrats (CDU/CSU) in the German parliament, expressed the importance of this role-identity for the EU's self-image most distinctly:

> The enlargement of the European Union is not just a question of our interest, let alone just a question of Germany's interest, but also a moral question, this is, of our understanding of ourselves. For decades we have promised the captive peoples of Europe that we will welcome them in our community and there cannot be any doubt that they have a historical, moral and cultural entitlement to this. If we do not keep this promise, both our moral position and our self-understanding would be irreparably damaged; and at the same time, our own interest, which lies precisely in having a stable environment, would be threatened.[4]

Council declarations and Commission documents also stated the long-term economic and security benefits from integrating the CEECs. For example, Jacques Santer as Commission president argued that 'EU enlargement is vital for the political stability of our continent, and will also have in the longer term, I am quite sure, a positive impact on the economic front for all' (*Euroeast*, August/September 1995: 2). Furthermore, presentations of the integration of the CEECs as a 'historic opportunity' to reunite the continent peacefully also can be read as references to the material utility of enlargement. However, the notion of an EU responsibility towards CEECs has become an independent, central feature of the discourse about EU policy towards the CEECs.

Crucially, not only policy-makers from countries that also have clear material interests in enlargement, engaged in this discourse. For example, Italy's Permanent Representative and eventual foreign minister, Renato Ruggiero, stated: 'the nascent European Union has the historic responsibility of making the unification process move forward. In doing so, it will complete its own union and gradually extend the process eastward' (*Europe Documents*, 19.03.92: 1). The Spanish Permanent Representative, Javier Elorza (1997: 10) claimed: 'As far as Spain is concerned ... the acceptance of enlargement is not just a legal question, but a political and *moral* one' (emphasis added). French foreign minister Alain Juppé (1994: 14) declared: 'Our wish in France is that this new round of enlargement should take place: it is in the nature of things and in line with the undertakings we made towards these countries when we said to them: "once you have shaken off the yoke of communism, you will one day be called upon to take your place among the European countries".' Prime Minister Eduard Balladur claimed 'we have no moral right, no political reason, and no interest not to welcome the nations that freed themselves from the former Soviet yoke' (*Le Monde*, 30.11.94). Jacques Chirac (1996: 9) stated 'Poland saw its European dream evaporate on the morrow of the Second World War, broken by the Iron Curtain. While the west of our continent was then able to embark on the path of union, France has always known – it expressed this forcefully through the voice of General de Gaulle – that Europe's construction could not be completed until all its nations were back in its fold.'

Furthermore, representatives from those member states that could have been suspected of ulterior motives continued the discourse after the key enlargement decisions were taken. For example, on the occasion of the opening of the accession negotiations, German foreign minister Klaus Kinkel referred to EU enlargement as a 'historical obligation and logical continuation of the European integration process'[5] (*Süddeutsche Zeitung*, 31.03.98) and UK foreign secretary Robin Cook declared: 'By enlarging the EU we are finally overcoming the cruel and unnatural division of our continent' (*Financial Times*, 31.03.98: 1). The Athens Declaration, adopted on the occasion of the signing of the accession treaties, reaffirmed: 'This Union represents our common determination to put an end to centuries of conflict and to transcend former divisions on our continent' (*Bulletin of the EU*, 4–2003: I-1).

In sum, from a social constructivist perspective, the EU can be seen as a normative structure and part of the cultural environment that affects EU policy-makers' preference formation with regard to policy towards the CEECs. This chapter identified certain components of a collective EU identity that are salient for this policy. Broader aspects of the EU's identity that resonate in its external relations more generally – the social democratic identities of the member states and the notion of the EU's pan-European vocation – might also favour an accommodation of the CEECs. However, historical precedents reflect that these factors alone are insufficient to result in a decision to enlarge or in an EU policy that accommodates outsiders' preferences. A crucial difference between these historical precedents and the case of the CEECs is that the EU's specific role-conception in its relationship with the CEECs is in important respects constituted by the notion of a 'special responsibility'. Through its prominence in the discourse of representatives of the EU and its member states, this notion can be considered a component of the EU's identity and (part of) the collective identities of policy-makers in EU institutions and member states.

However, while the notion of an EU responsibility might well have become embedded in the EU's collective identity, its implications for concrete policy are not immediately obvious. If we want to understand the impact of EU identity on its enlargement policy, it is not sufficient to merely identify and trace the components of EU identity that are at stake in EU policy towards the CEECs. The existence of an identity-based discourse, as such, does not yet tell much about its causal effect on EU policy. The following chapter presents a conceptual framework to analyse the policy impact of this role-identity.

Notes

1 'Je tiens à dire que notre Communauté n'est ni une petite Europe, ni une Communauté restreinte. Ses limites n'en sont pas fixées par nous. Elles sont fixées par les payes mêmes qui, pour le moment, ne s'y joignent pas. Il ne tient qu'à eux que nos limites en soient étendues.'

2 For example, US Secretary of State, James Baker (1989: 5), suggested it was the EU's 'national [*sic*] vocation' to build frameworks 'that can overcome the division of Europe'.

3 'La communauté n'a jamais été conçue seulement pour elle-même. La déclaration de Robert Schuman … est encore la pour nous le rappeler. Il est conforme à son destin qu'elle doive aujourd'hui simultanément s'approfondir et répondre aux attentes venues du continent Européen tout entier.'

4 'Die Erweiterung der Europäischen Union ist nicht nur eine Frage unseres Interesses, schon gar nicht nur eine Frage des deutschen Interesses, sondern auch eine Frage der Moral, das heißt unseres Selbstverständnisses. Haben wir doch jahrzehntelang den unfreien europäischen Völkern feierlich versprochen, sie in unsere Gemeinschaft aufzunehmen, und es kann doch auch gar keinen Zweifel daran geben, dass sie einen historisch, moralisch und kulturell begründeten Anspruch darauf haben. Wenn wir dieses Versprechen nicht einhalten, so würden Moral und Selbstverständnis einen nicht wieder gutzumachenden "Bruch" erfahren, und zugleich wäre unser Interesse, eben unser Interesse an einer stabilen Umwelt gefährdet.'

5 'Die Erweiterung der EU ist eine historische Verpflichtung und logische Fortsetzung des europäischen Einigungsprozesses.'

3

Conceptualising the impact of EU identity on the enlargement policy

This chapter provides the book's theoretical framework to analyse the impact of EU identity on its enlargement policy. From a constructivist perspective, the EU forms a normative structure and part of the cultural environment that affects EU policy-makers' preference formation with regard to policy towards the CEECs. The previous chapter has identified a self-ascribed 'special responsibility' of the EU towards the CEECs as a key component of its discursively constructed role-identity. How does this particular aspect of EU identity influence EU policy towards the CEECs? I argue that this identity creates a diffuse regulative norm: it prescribes to accommodate the CEECs' preferences to a certain extent and delegitimises opposition to such an accommodation on the basis of particularistic selfish interests. However, the effect of this component of EU identity is *uneven* across different groups of EU policy-makers. This uneven effect is particularly relevant in the case of the EU's enlargement policy that bears the characteristics of a *composite policy*. EU identity therefore influences the enlargement policy primarily through the principled advocacy of a particular group of EU policy-makers. In particular with regard to substantive policies, their influence is mediated by additional factors.

The policy impact of EU identity

EU identity as an evaluative standard

The EU's identity vis-à-vis the CEECs affects policy through the behavioural obligations that it entails. As identities are 'role-specific understanding and expectations about self' (Wendt 1992: 297), they specify evaluative standards for appropriate behaviour. EU policy-makers evaluate the compatibility of their policy with the role that they ascribed to the EU. Regulative norms specify the proper enactment of a given identity by prescribing appropriate ways of enacting it in varying circumstances (see e.g. Jepperson et al. 1996: 54). The extent to which the EU's role in its relationship towards the CEECs affects policy outcomes depends on its degree of *specificity* as an evaluative standard (see e.g. Legro 1997: 34). In the case of eastern enlargement, the specificity of the behavioural prescriptions is not unproblematic. The notion of 'EU responsibility' towards the CEECs is rather diffuse and the public statements of the EU's commitment to support the transformation and integration of the CEECs are rather general. However, although the EU's role does not define narrowly which concrete behaviour and policy are deemed appropriate, at least it rules out certain behaviour as inappropriate.

The notion of an EU responsibility proscribes indifference to the fate of the CEECs and requires the EU to demonstrate concern for the welfare of the CEECs in its policy. The EU has to play an active role in supporting integration and transformation of the CEECs. The EU can neither ignore the CEECs' desire to join, nor their preferences with regard to concrete policies. It cannot simply leave it completely to the CEECs to prepare for integration and membership, nor can it simply impose the adjustment burden exclusively on the CEECs. In this sense, EU identity prescribes a degree of accommodation of the CEECs' interests in EU policy. The extent of accommodation is an important (albeit somewhat loose) evaluative standard. However, it operates primarily as a 'negative' evaluative standard, by excluding inappropriate behaviour, which is more easily identified for the EU's role. The EU's role delegitimises behaviour which is exclusively oriented at EU actors' self-interest. EU policy that deviates significantly from the CEECs' preferences requires justification. Only those justifications can be considered legitimate that refer to countervailing community rules and principles, such as the future of the integration project, the functioning of the internal market, or solidarity among incumbent members.

In this way, EU identity affects policy by structuring the 'realm of possibilities' for available policy options (Price and Tannenwald 1996: 148–9; see also Klotz 1995: 461–2). It precludes certain options as inappropriate and it reinforces the legitimacy of others. The behavioural prescriptions are clearest with regard to the question of enlargement as such: the general principle of enlargement and the general eligibility of the CEECs for membership cannot be legitimately challenged. The prescriptions for substantive policies are more vague: they do not prescribe an absolute standard according to which the preferences of the CEECs have to be accommodated. At a minimum, the EU has to consider the impact of its policy on the CEECs' welfare and has to refrain from blatantly self-interested policies that are detrimental to the CEECs' preferences.

It is important to clarify that this argument does not imply (deliberate or conscious) altruism by the EU. Nor does it mean that EU policy which conforms to the notion of EU responsibility is indeed 'responsible' by any objective standard, or that an accommodating policy is necessarily in the CEECs' 'objective' interest. It simply means that the collective discourse of EU policy-makers has established a degree of accommodation of the CEECs' preferences as an evaluative standard that rules out behavioural options that do not meet this standard.

The uneven effect of EU identity vis-à-vis the CEECs across EU policy-makers

Yet the mere existence of behavioural prescriptions is not, as such, sufficient to generate accommodating policy outcomes. Indeed, a frequent criticism levelled against constructivist analyses is that their arguments are based often merely on establishing a correlation between identity or discourses and identity-conforming behaviour (Checkel 1998, 2004). This weakness stems from the frequent assumption that constitutive normative effects are uniform across the members of a group. In the case of enlargement, the assumption of such a uniform effect is untenable, in particular if we want to explain not only the EU's decision to enlarge, but also sectoral policy outcomes.

The effect of the EU's role-construction towards the CEECs is uneven across different groups of policy-makers that are involved in the enlargement policy. The uneven normative effect stems from the particular nature of EU identity in its relationship with the CEECs. This component of EU identity is a *collective* property of the EU, but it might not be equally *shared* by all policy-makers. This argument draws on the distinction by Jepperson et al. (1996: 54–5) between different properties of norms:

> Norms may be 'shared,' or commonly held, across some distribution of actors in the system. Alternatively, however, norms may *not* be widely held by actors but may nevertheless be *collective* features of a system – either by being institutionalized (in procedures, formal rules, or law) or by being prominent in public discourse of a system. ... A distinction between collectively 'prominent' or institutionalized norms and commonly 'internalized' ones, with various 'intersubjective' admixtures in between, is crucial for distinguishing between different types of norms and different types of normative effects. (Original emphasis)

In this sense, the prominence in the policy discourse of the notion of 'EU responsibility' for the CEECs has established this notion as a component of the EU's *collective* identity. The EU's role-identity vis-à-vis the CEECs has become a collective property of EU policy-makers through statements made on behalf of the EU, in particular in European Council declarations. However, the notion of the EU's role as a collective property of EU identity allows for an uneven normative effect of identity across different groups of policy-makers. We cannot assume that all policy-makers involved in EU policy towards the CEECs are equally receptive to its normative effects. The uneven effect results from the existence of 'multiple social identities' (Risse

2001: 199; Wendt 1994: 385). For some policy-makers, this element of EU identity is a more important part of their social identities than for others.

EU enlargement: a composite policy

The EU's enlargement policy has particular features that render such variations in the resonance of the EU's role-identity across different groups of policy-makers especially important. The distinctive structure of EU policy towards the CEECs characterises it as a *composite policy* (see also Sedelmeier and Wallace 2000: 429–31). A composite policy has two salient characteristics. First, it is composed of a 'macro-policy' and a range of sectoral 'meso-policies'. Enlargement and policy towards the CEECs is not a single policy issue, but rather the sum of a number of policies in distinctive areas. In other words, the EU's enlargement policy presents a broad policy framework. It is constituted by, or draws on, distinctive policy decisions across the range of sectoral policies that are part of the association policy, of accession conditionality, or of accession negotiations. These policy areas range from trade liberalisation across different sectors of industry, agriculture and services, over regulatory alignment with the single market, to political dialogue on foreign policy. Policies in these areas form policy subsystems within the EU's policy towards the CEECs. We can thus distinguish two dimensions of the enlargement policy: (1) decisions at the macro-level of policy, which determine the overall objectives and parameters of policy, including the decision to enlarge; and (2) decisions about the specific detail and substance of policy in particular sectors. These decisions determine to what extent concrete policy measures accommodate the preferences of the CEECs.

The second characteristic of a composite policy is that different groups of policy-makers, or distinctive policy communities, have primary responsibility for specific parts of this policy. The 'macro-policy-makers' have primarily responsibility for overall policy. In the case of the enlargement policy, this group includes the member states' foreign ministries and the Commission's DG for external relations (and its Commissioner's *cabinet*). Periodically, it also involves the heads of state or government and the Commission president. However, these macro-policy-makers cannot take decisions on policy substance within the various meso-policies autonomously. Such decisions have to be negotiated, in a process of horizontal policy coordination, with those sectoral policy-makers who have primary responsibility for the respective meso-policies.

Among these different groups of policy-makers, the extent to which the EU's role vis-à-vis the CEECs constitutes an important part of their self-understanding varies. In part, this variation relates to policy-makers' bureaucratic position. The EU's role should resonate most with those policy-makers who represent the EU externally and towards the CEECs in particular. Resonance should thus be high among the macro-policy-makers, but rather weak among the meso-policy-makers. Furthermore, among the macro-policy-makers, the normative effect of the EU's role towards the CEECs should be stronger among Commission officials than those from the member states, as the former identify more closely with the EU as such. The uneven effect of identity across policy-makers in a composite policy, such as the enlargement policy, means that the normative effects differ significantly for the macro-policy and the various meso-policies.

The impact of EU identity on the macro-policy

Constitutive and regulative effects of EU identity

The macro-policy-makers are thus collectively most receptive to the behavioural obligations entailed in the EU's role towards the CEECs. The normative effects of the EU's identity should be strongest among officials in the Commission's DG for external relations (DG I) and the Commissioners and their *cabinets* who are in charge of Commission proposals for EU policy towards the CEECs. These policy-makers are most likely to have internalised the behavioural obligations of the EU's role and to act according to a more far-reaching understanding of the EU's responsibility towards the CEECs. We could then conceive of these policy-makers as principled policy entrepreneurs and active advocates of the CEECs' preferences in the EU. They could be expected to actively promote enlargement and argue for an accommodation of the CEECs' preferences in concrete policy. Principled advocacy does not imply that these officials *only* promote enlargement and an accommodating policy because of normative prescriptions. They might well see these prescriptions as complementary to material (aggregate and long-term) benefits for the EU. However, they should believe that enlargement and an accommodation of the CEECs' preferences is not only the right policy because it is an effective means to promote selfish interests, but because the EU has an obligation to act in this way, apart from possible material incentives for doing so.

This normative effect is generally more limited among the macro-policy-makers from the member states. Depending on whether their particular identity constructions and material interests are compatible or competing with the normative role of the EU towards the CEECs, these policy-makers might either form a loose coalition that is broadly supportive of policy initiatives in favour of the CEECs or be rather reluctant about such initiatives. But even in the latter case, the normative effects of the EU's role are still significant. This group will still feel inhibited to oppose such initiatives, even if they create tensions with certain narrower interests, and to promote policy options that appear to serve merely their national or sectoral self-interests at the expense of the CEECs.

For example, at the origins of the EU's discourse about its relationship with the CEECs during the Cold War, the engagement of certain policy-makers in the EU's collective discourse might have been purely instrumental

rhetoric, designed to discredit the communist regimes. Indeed, from a rationalist perspective, such an identity-based discourse and references to the EU's
obligation towards the CEECs are mere 'hooks' to conceal 'real' interests (see
also Goldstein and Keohane 1993: 4). Yet even initially instrumental
discourse, albeit insincere, matters once it has become a collective feature of
EU self-image. For example, Snyder's argument about the instrumental use of
the 'myth of empire' (1991: 41) by political elites to manipulate mass publics
acknowledges in passing that 'the "blowback" of propaganda, the blurring of
the line between "fact and fiction … sincere beliefs and tactical argument",
entraps political leaders not only in their own confusion but in the political
context that they helped to create' (Katzenstein 1996b: 27). Similarly,
Keohane (1991: 232) suggests that

> for representative governments … it is difficult to separate 'real' from 'public'
> motivations. … Furthermore, even officials without strong moral principles have
> to defend their policies, and it is often convenient to do so in moral terms. This
> requirement may lead them, in order to avoid cognitive dissonance, to take on
> some of the beliefs that they profess. The act of piety may engender piety itself.

This perspective explains the continuity of the EU's discourse and its continued impact on behaviour, even if certain policy-makers only engaged in it
instrumentally during the Cold War, or paid insufficient attention to seman-
tics in the drafting of collective European Council statements. Although the
changed circumstances meant that acting in accordance with their discourse
could now contravene their self-interest, they had 'rhetorically entrapped'
themselves (see also Risse and Sikkink 1999: 28; Schimmelfennig 2001: 73) in
their collective statements and the expectations that they raised.

While such policy-makers are then unlikely to make a maximalist interpretation of the EU's role towards the CEECs, its normative effects should at
least define a bottom-line of appropriate behaviour. They might thus not
actively promote enlargement, but are still sensitive to what kind of behaviour
they should refrain from. With regard to substantive policies, we would
expect these policy-makers to avoid giving the impression that they
completely disregard the CEECs' preferences. They should be reluctant to use
their superior bargaining power to present purely self-regarding policies as
'take-it-or-leave-it' offers to the CEECs. Rather, collectively in the General
Affairs Council, as well as individually within their national decision-making
processes, we would expect them to argue in favour of a more far-reaching
accommodation and to defend it against sectoral policy-makers. With regard
to the broader question of enlargement, we would not expect them to challenge the general principle of enlargement and the eligibility of the CEECs in
principle; nor should they oppose accommodation in substantive policies on
purely self-regarding grounds. In this sense, their receptiveness to the EU's
role empowers the advocates of enlargement. They are susceptible to initiatives by the policy advocates that are presented as questions of principle and

as a test of the credibility of the EU's self-proclaimed image.

The regulative effect of the EU's role should constrain them from opposing initiatives designed to prepare the EU and the CEECs for enlargement. They might still raise specific concerns about enlargement, but only concerns that can be legitimised with references to countervailing values that are shared among the members. Such legitimate objections include, for example, concerns about the future of the integration project in a larger and more heterogeneous membership. Another set of concerns relate to the functioning of (market) integration if the future members were not adequately prepared for the obligations of membership. But the principle of enlargement as such and the obligation of the EU to solve internal obstacles to enlargement should not be open to debate.

As I will argue in the following chapter, in this way the EU's role created the scope for the policy advocates to incrementally set the EU on a path to enlargement that became increasingly difficult to reverse. The policy advocates fostered agreement on successive initiatives, each of which was hard to resist on principled grounds. Yet each of these initiatives further removed legitimate arguments that could be raised against further steps towards enlargement. In this way, they both narrowed the policy options available and strengthened the EU's discursive commitment to enlargement in such a way that deviating from this role became increasingly difficult to contemplate.

Rhetorical action and social influence

The uneven normative effect of the EU's role-identity towards the CEECs, which operates for some policy-makers primarily as a *constraint on opposition* to initiatives that can be legitimised with references to appropriateness, opens the possibility to use these normative arguments instrumentally. Indeed, Schimmelfennig (2001, 2003) presents a sophisticated, non-materialist, rationalist argument that explains the EU's decision to enlarge precisely with such a strategy of 'rhetorical action'. The argument presupposes 'weakly socialized actors … [that] belong to a community whose constitutive values and norms they share', but 'it is not expected that collective identity shapes concrete preferences' (Schimmelfennig 2001: 62). In such a context, actors can use normative arguments instrumentally in the pursuit of their self-interests. An institutional environment or a community's collective identity thus provides a resource for actors who can justify their selfish goals with references to institutional norms or identity. The legitimacy that these arguments bestow on their goals increases their bargaining power. Other actors acquiesce to such initiatives not because they are persuaded by the normative validity of such arguments, but in order to avoid the (social and reputational) costs of non-compliance with community norms. Compliance is thus neither the result of an internalisation of identity norms or of persuasion, but of a process of 'social influence' (Johnston 2001). From this perspective, the CEECs' governments (as well as those member state governments that expect material benefits from enlargement) successfully used references to the EU's constitutive liberal values and norms to shame the reluctant member states into accepting enlargement.

This argument shares two central points with my argument. First – in contrast to most rationalist and materialist approaches (e.g. Moravcsik and Vachudova 2003; Skalnes 2001) – social facts (the EU's role-identity or community norms), rather than only material factors, play a crucial role in the process, *at least* as a regulative constraint on behaviour. Second – in contrast to certain constructivist analyses (e.g. Fierke and Wiener 1999; Sjursen 2002) – not all policy-makers are assumed to have equally and fully internalised a 'maximalist' version of identity and to share it equally.

Apart from the question of which aspects of identity are salient in EU enlargement (see Chapter 2), one difference in the argument is whether EU identity might have more than a merely regulative effect on certain actors. This question concerns mainly whether the advocates of enlargement act purely instrumentally (to maximise their material utility) or whether such advocacy is principled (which does not preclude them to move strategically in order to achieve their goals). Another difference concerns how the regulative effect operates among those macro-policy-makers for whom identity constitutes primarily a constraint on opposition to enlargement and an accommodation of the CEECs' preferences.

Principled policy advocacy

What are the indications that the advocacy of enlargement was principled, rather than purely instrumental? An identification of the key policy advocates raises doubts that their advocacy can be explained purely on instrumental grounds. Empirical evidence shows that the main advocates of enlargement, who paved the way towards enlargement until 1995, were found in the Commission, rather than among those member states that can expect to benefit from enlargement. These member state governments, such as the German government, were broadly supportive of such Commission initiatives, but did not play a very active role and showed little urgency to push enlargement onto the agenda.

Empirical evidence also suggests that attempts by the CEECs themselves to increase their bargaining power with reference to the EU's obligations towards them had only rather limited success. These instances were often received rather badly inside the EU as unhelpful attempts at politicisation resulting from ulterior motives. The promotion of the CEECs' interests was most effective when undertaken not by the CEECs directly, but by insiders in the EU policy process. This observation fits well with Johnston's (2001: 497) argument that persuasion by the 'in-group' is more convincing than from the 'out-group'. In contrast to the CEECs or other actors obviously benefiting from enlargement, the Commission could not be suspected of ulterior self-interested motives.

Counterfactual arguments to explain the advocacy of enlargement of the Commission's policy-makers on purely self-interested grounds are difficult to make. One possible motive could be bureaucratic politics – turf and prestige. Once enlargement moved up on the EU's agenda, the public exposure and prestige of DG enlargement increased and it could eventually demand higher resource allocations. However, anecdotal evidence suggests otherwise, for example, in one key instance in which Jacques Delors, as Commission president, used policy towards the CEECs in order to increase the prestige of the Commission (and the EU more generally). His offer in July 1989 to coordinate the aid of the G24 came as a shock to the officials in DG external relations who had not been consulted and were terrified by the commitment which they knew would stretch their administrative resources to the limit.[1] Furthermore, by the time enlargement appeared on track, and hence when bureaucratic turf and prestige were set to grow, most of the officials in the Commission involved in making policy towards the CEECs had moved to positions elsewhere. Finally, bureaucratic self-interest in turf and prestige as well as in an 'easy life' does not fit well with the fact that the policy advocates in the Commission not only promoted enlargement as such. They worked equally hard to achieve an accommodation of the CEECs' preferences in sectoral policies and spent considerable time identifying strategies to prepare the CEECs for accession that were as far as possible compatible with their domestic priorities related to economic transformation.

Otherwise, evidence that the policy advocates in the Commission acted in a principled way is mainly anecdotal rather than systematic. In interviews, policy-makers in the Commission's unit responsible for policy towards the CEECs regularly referred to an obligation of the EU as a key reason to pursue enlargement. For some, personal background – such as family background or previous work experience in particular CEECs – inclined them to receptiveness to the CEECs' concerns.

The nature of regulative constraints

A second difference concerns how the regulative effect operates among those macro-policy-makers for whom identity constitutes primarily a constraint on opposition to enlargement. Some constructivists would argue that identity cannot be simply a regulative constraint (see e.g. Fierke and Wiener 1999; Sjursen 2002). But even if we accept the impact of identity as uneven, and its effect on certain groups as a merely regulatory constraint on behaviour, there is a further nuance: to what extent do they calculate at each stage of policy development the reputational costs of acting against the standards of appropriateness? Such a calculation implies that they consider open opposition to enlargement – at least in principle – a possible, albeit (too) costly, option. By contrast, anecdotal evidence suggests that even those policy-makers who are reluctant about enlargement have internalised the regulative constraints to the point that they cannot even conceive of acting against it; they take the limitation of their policy options for granted.

Either way, it is clear that even social influence 'hinges, of course, on an intersubjectively agreed upon notion of what socially valuable behaviour looks like. ... it could be considered a secondary socialization' (Johnston 2001: 501–2). But how deep is such socialisation, or the internalisation of role-specific constraints, in the case of eastern enlargement?

Some scholars address this question at the theoretical, rather than the empirical or methodological, level. Risse (2000: 8–9) presents a constructivist argument for why it is unnecessary to uncover actors' 'true motives'. Even in cases of an instrumental use of norm-based arguments, 'the "power" of ideas ... is linked to their consensuality. Ideas become consensual when actors start believing in their value and become convinced of their validity. ... Instrumental use of ideas works, because their value has been previously established in discursive processes of persuasion and deliberation' (Risse-Kappen 1996: 69–70). Schimmelfennig (2001: 66) agrees that agent motives are irrelevant, but his claim is based on the more limited (albeit non-material) rationalist argument that rhetorical action affects actors regardless of whether they have internalised norms or simply fear reputational costs. Other scholars insist that actors' motives not only matter, but that there are also methodological tools – process tracing, triangulation across sources and interviews – that make it possible for researchers to 'get between the earlobes' (Checkel 2004: 240; see also Checkel 2001; Johnston 2001).

However, in the case of eastern enlargement, it is particularly tricky to assess the depth of role-specific constraints. To the extent that normative arguments work through silencing opposition to enlargement, it is doubtful that those actors on whom it has this effect would admit – even in a private setting – their covert opposition. The absence of articulated opposition, and even a denial of opposition, are thus not necessarily an indication that constraints are internalised or taken for granted. It merely indicates that social constraints exist, but not whether they are internalised or the result of strategic calculation. The methodological difficulties involved in determining the motivation of the policy-advocates are even greater with regard to the other macro-policy-makers who acquiesced to their initiatives. Were they persuaded of the legitimacy of the initiatives? Could they simply not conceive of opposing them because their understanding of their role ruled this option out? Or did they calculate that the reputational costs of opposition were too high?

Nonetheless, there are empirical indications that at least some policy-makers from member states that were reluctant about enlargement have internalised the obligation to enlarge. Not only policy-makers from member states that have a material interest in enlargement referred to the EU's role-identity when talking about why the EU should enlarge. As Chapter 2 showed, this was equally the case for some representatives of countries that have to expect material disadvantages from enlargement. If they were concerned about the social costs of opposing enlargement, why perpetuate this discourse and further raise the potential costs, rather than simply remain silent or deny opposition? Such statements suggest that not simply conscious calculations of the reputational costs constrained the self-interested behaviour of such actors. Rather, the regulative constraints that limit behavioural options have acquired a degree of taken-for-grantedness, even if the EU's role-identity did not affect them in such a way that they positively promoted enlargement.

The impact of EU identity on sectoral policies

The uneven normative effect of the EU's role towards the CEECs across different groups of policy-makers involved in the EU's enlargement policy implies that its policy impact differs between macro-policy and on meso-policies. The effect is strongest, albeit to different degrees, among the macro-policy-makers. It is much weaker among the sectoral policy-makers. In contrast to the macro-policy-makers, who are receptive to the prescriptions embodied in the EU's role-identity, the resonance of arguments about the appropriateness of accommodating policies among the meso-policy-makers is weak. The weak resonance means that the meso-policy-makers do not feel inhibited from openly opposing policies that accommodate the CEECs' preferences to the detriment of their interests. The impact of the EU's role-identity on sectoral policies is thus rather indirect.

The policy impact of EU identity on sectoral policies, and by implication, the extent to which sectoral policies accommodate the CEECs' preferences, thus depends on the policy advocates among the macro-policy-makers. Policy impact depends on the ability of these advocates to identify policies that accommodate the CEECs' interests and to influence the EU policy process to promote them. The low salience of arguments relating to the EU's role towards the CEECs with meso-policy-makers means that for substantive sectoral policies, accommodation is the outcome of a political process, rather than a direct effect of identity. The question is then under which conditions these actors can successfully influence policy outcomes and which factors mediate their influence.

As the meso-policies within the EU's enlargement policy present sub-systems within the macro-policy, the key conditions for the policy advocates to influence particular meso-policies are not unlike those required for a successful policy impact of transnational policy entrepreneurs in world politics (see e.g. Risse-Kappen 1994, 1995b). To influence policy in 'target countries', transnational actors have to overcome two main hurdles: they need to obtain access to the political system and form 'winning coalitions' with domestic actors. Not dissimilarly, in a composite policy, the influence of these policy advocates depends on (1) their *access* to policy-making and decision-making on specific sectoral issues, and (2) their ability to form *alliances* with sectoral policy-makers that are sufficiently strong to overcome opposition to changing the status quo in this policy area. The following sections elaborate on the two factors that respectively affect access and alliance-building, namely the *structure of the policy process* and the *policy paradigms* that underpin EU policy in particular sectors.

Structure of the policy process

The literatures on bureaucratic politics and on intra-governmental coordination of public policy provide insights into the key factors that determine the access of the policy advocates to the meso-policies. The access of specific groups of policy-makers to the policy process in particular issue areas is determined by organisational rules. These rules and the organisational positions of actors stipulate the role that they can play in a given policy process. 'Positions [in an administration] define ... the advantages and handicaps with which each player can enter and play in various games' (Allison 1969: 709) and 'the organization of policy making affects the degree of power that any one set of actors has over policy outcomes' (Hall 1986: 19). If different groups of policy-makers have overlapping responsibilities for particular policy decisions, formal and informal rules, standard and ad hoc procedures, specify the mechanism through which these policy-makers coordinate their actions, take joint decisions, and solve conflicts that arise from diverging preferences. This policy coordination process regulates the access of the macro-policy-makers to decision-making in a specific meso-policy area. But how does the structure of the policy coordination process affect their access? How to operationalise variations in the characteristics of the process which obstruct or facilitate access?

Research in the areas of public administration and organisational theory on the intra-governmental coordination of public policy (see e.g. Benz et al. 1992; Mayntz and Scharpf 1975; Scharpf 1993) provides important insights into how the structure of the policy coordination process affects access and influence. Modern political systems are unable to formulate and implement policy in functionally differentiated, partly autonomous, subsystems hierarchically through central government or the core executive. In the absence of hierarchical coordination, the question is how horizontal self-coordination between officials, representing distinct organisational units with responsibility for particular issue areas, affects policy.

Scharpf (1997: 112–14) argues that under these conditions, policy outcomes generally result from 'negative coordination'. The policy options of the lead department, which is in charge of the overall policy, are constrained by the veto of other departments whose jurisdiction the policy might affect. Such negative coordination prevents adverse effects in related policy areas, but it creates a conservative bias by limiting the lead department's ability to maximise the effectiveness of the overall policy through a full utilisation of policy instruments that are controlled by other departments. In contrast, the objective of 'positive coordination' is to identify policy options that maximise the collective interest of the political system as whole, even if this requires compromising the interests of policy-makers in certain policy areas. The negotiation process that leads to negative coordination is characterised by 'bargaining', while positive coordination is characterised by (collective) 'problem solving' (Mayntz and Scharpf 1975; Scharpf 1993, 1997).

Two aspects of the coordination process can bias consultations towards positive coordination, and allow greater access to the policy-makers in the lead department. The first aspect relates to whether coordination between the units is bilateral or multilateral, and whether sectoral policy-makers have veto power. The more coordination relies on bilateral consultations between the lead department and other units, and if the latter can simply block any initiative they dislike, the greater the constraints on the lead department (Scharpf 1997: 112; see also Tsebelis 2002). Conversely, the more coordination between the units takes place in multilateral task forces, whose members have the authority to commit their units to compromises, the greater the scope for positive coordination and for the influence of the lead department (1997: 133).

Second, even if policy in complex governance systems results from horizontal coordination, rather than from hierarchical imposition, the likelihood that coordination takes account of broader preferences is higher, if the policy process is embedded in a hierarchical structure. This 'shadow of hierarchical authority' (Scharpf 1993: 71) means that if actors are unable to find mutually satisfactory solutions, a hierarchically higher level of the core executive will settle remaining disputes. Such settlements might favour the lead department's broader preferences over narrower sectoral interests. The shadow of hierarchy can therefore induce representatives of narrower interests to be more accommodating in anticipation of such settlements.

Applying these insights to EU enlargement policy suggests that the extent to which the policy process is *centralised* or *fragmented* is a key factor that affects the access of the policy advocates to decision-making in the various meso-policies. As these policy advocates are among the macro-policy-makers who have the lead in the enlargement policy, their access should improve with a higher centralisation of the policy process.

Centralisation is a matter of degree. In its strongest form, centralisation takes the form of hierarchical decision-making. The macro-policy-makers can take decisions on the meso-policies fairly autonomously. They do not only have privileged access, but can dispense entirely with the requirement to build coalitions with meso-policy-makers, whose concerns they can subordinate or circumvent.[2] In a weaker form, centralisation is characterised by positive coordination in multilateral consultation structures that are embedded in a strong shadow of hierarchy. It guarantees access for the policy advocates, but their influence depends on their ability to build coalitions with sectoral policy-makers. Policy change requires the agreement of sectoral policy-makers. But since none of them can unilaterally oppose changes in their policy area, there is an inherent pressure for compromise. At the other end of the spectrum, a fragmented policy process insulates policy-making among the various groups of meso-policy-makers and circumscribes the involvement of macro-policy-makers in decision-making. Policy is characterised by negative coordination; the meso-policy-makers can block any policy changes in their jurisdiction.

For the enlargement policy, the structure of the policy process matters both at the EU level and the national level. At the member state level, there are significant differences in the structures through which the national positions for EU-level negotiations are formulated (see e.g. Bulmer 1986; Hayes-Renshaw and Wallace 1997: 211–25; Kassim et al. 2000, 2001; Lequesne 1993; Spence 1995; Wright 1996). In some member states, policy formulation is generally more fragmented, giving greater autonomy to sectoral policy-makers in negotiations at the EU level. The key example of a strongly fragmented national process is Germany, in contrast to much higher levels of coordination in the UK or France.

At the EU level, coordination relates, first, to the formulation of policy initiatives and proposals in the Commission (see e.g. Spence 1994). Access of the policy advocates should increase, the more the unit in DG I and its Commissioner obtain formal authority towards sectoral DGs, and if the Commission established a special task force. Second, EU-level coordination concerns policy-making in the Council (Hayes-Renshaw and Wallace 1997: 29–32, 64–5, 286). The access of the macro-policy-makers should increase: (1) with the establishment of a special Council working group to take the lead on policy towards the CEECs; (2) the more such a working group is staffed with foreign ministry officials specialising in relations with the CEECs, rather than sectoral, or trade policy experts; (3) with the authority of this working group over sectoral Council formations; and (4) with the involvement of Council formations that can induce the shadow of hierarchical coordination, such as the General Affairs Council, the Committee of Permanent Representatives (COREPER), or the European Council.

In general, it is difficult to clearly identify a single (centralised or fragmented) structure for any particular meso-policy area. While structures of policy coordination are usually codified in institutional rules, the procedures might be ad hoc. Within a given policy area, the structure of the policy process might vary over time. Variations might relate to the stage of the policy-making cycle. Moreover, precisely because of its importance in granting access to decision-making, it is subject to actors' strategic manipulation. In order to predict the impact of the structure of the policy process on a given meso-policy, the analysis thus has to proceed inductively to establish variations in the structure of the policy process. If necessary, the observations within a particular meso-policy area need to be disaggregated according to such variations over time.

Sectoral policy paradigms

Access of the macro-policy-makers to decision-making in the meso-policy areas is only a necessary, not a sufficient condition for influence. Unless their access is exclusive, the macro-policy-makers need to build alliances among the meso-policy-makers that are sufficiently strong to lead to policy changes that accommodate the CEECs' preferences. For most rationalist approaches and liberal intergovernmentalism specifically, the configuration of societal interest groups in a particular sector determines the ability to build such alliances. The preferences of the meso-policy-makers reflect the balance of interest group pressure in a given policy area.

From a constructivist, or sociological institutionalist perspective, however, interest group preferences alone do not necessarily determine the policy impact of the macro-policy-makers. The preferences of the meso-policy-makers also depend on ideational factors. They might therefore clash in certain cases with societal interests, but policy-makers defend them nonetheless, despite strong countervailing interest group pressure (see e.g. Evans et al. 1985). Sociological institutionalism highlights the importance of institutions and organisational structures for preference formation (March and Olsen 1989; Powell and DiMaggio 1991; Thelen and Steinmo 1992). Crucially, institutions are not merely a formal constraint on strategic behaviour, but provide an ideational structure in which policy-makers operate. They include 'not just formal rules, procedures or norms, but the symbol systems, cognitive scripts, and moral templates that provide the "frames of meaning" guiding human action' (Hall and Taylor 1996: 947). Actors are (collectively) socialised into particular organisational roles and internalise standards of legitimacy that are attached to this role. Institutions provide 'cognitive scripts, categories and models that are indispensable for action … [and] influence behaviour not simply by specifying what one should do but also by specifying what one can imagine oneself doing in a given context' (Hall and Taylor 1996: 948).

In this sense, distinctive institutional factors affect the various meso-policies. These policy areas can be understood as 'intermediate-level institutions' (Thelen and Steinmo 1992: 6) that shape meso-policy-makers' preference formation. Indeed, this view of issue-specific policy-making systems as institutions in their own right allows us to capture the cleavage between the collective positions of macro- and various meso-policy-makers, and the tensions between macro- and meso-policy. The preference formation of the macro-policy-makers is more affected by components of the EU's identity vis-à-vis the CEECs than that of other EU policy-makers, who are in turn more receptive to the role-identities particular to their policy areas. Institutions thus structure not only actors' access to policy-making;

> organizational position also influences an actor's definition of his own interests, by establishing his institutional responsibilities and relationship to other actors.

> In this way, organizational factors affect both the degree of pressure an actor can bring to bear on policy and the likely direction of that pressure. (Hall 1986: 19)

But how can we capture the institutional factors that shape the preference formation of the meso-policy-makers? Peter Hall's concept of 'policy paradigms' (Hall 1993) allows one to operationalise the ideational factors that underpin policy-making in particular issue areas:

> policymakers customarily work within a framework of ideas and standards that specifies not only the goals of policy and the kind of instruments that can be used to attain them, but also the very nature of the problems that need to be addressed. Like a *Gestalt*, this framework is embedded in the very terminology through which policymakers communicate about their work, and it is influential precisely because so much of it is taken for granted and unamenable to scrutiny as a whole. [...] Policy paradigms can best be seen as one feature of the overall terms of political discourse. They suggest that the policymaking process can be structured by a particular set of ideas, just as it can be structured by a set of institutions. (1993: 279, 290).

Policy paradigms are specific to particular policy areas, as a distinctive feature within the normative institutional structure of these policy areas. Policy paradigms are not simply causal ideas about means–ends relations for an *effective* policy. They also incorporate principled ideas about what constitutes a *legitimate* policy, for example with regard to policy goals, appropriate policy tools, or about priorities between different groups that the policy affects. Policy paradigms become embedded in the normative institutional structure of a meso-policy area by acquiring a dominant position in the policy discourse that characterises the policy area. The more a policy paradigm is shared by the range of policy-makers and private actors within a certain meso-policy area, the more applicable are concepts from network analysis that focus on networks in which members share consensual knowledge, collective ideas, and specific belief systems (see e.g. Börzel 1997b; Peterson 1995), such as 'epistemic communities' (Haas 1992), or 'advocacy coalitions' (Sabatier 1988, 1997).

This view of the role of policy paradigms has strong affinities with the concept of 'policy frames' (Rein and Schön 1991; Schön and Rein 1994), which has found recently wider application in EU studies (see Dudley and Richardson 1999; Jachtenfuchs 1996; Kohler-Koch 2000; Lenschow and Zito 1998; Skogstad 1998). There are also certain parallels to an analysis of individual EU policy areas as distinctive 'governance regimes' (Armstrong and Bulmer 1998) or 'overlapping games' (Torreblanca 1998). In this book, I use the term policy paradigm to denote the set of ideas that underpin policy in a particular meso-area and that shape the preference formation of sectoral policy-makers, independently of the material structure of the interests in this sector.

The ability of policy advocates to build successful alliances in the meso-policy areas is thus not simply a function of the configuration of societal interest. The degree of compatibility between the preferences that they promote and sectoral policy paradigms is a key factor shaping the likelihood of successful alliance-building. A mismatch between the CEECs' preferences and sectoral paradigms might lead sectoral policy-makers to oppose an accommodation of these preferences, even independently of interest group pressure. Conversely, compatibility facilitates accommodation. Such compatibility increases the likelihood that the policy advocates might forge a strategic alliance with certain sectoral policy-makers that is sufficiently strong to bring about a policy change, even against countervailing interest group pressure.

However, the very concept of policy paradigms would lead us to expect that such cases of compatibility are rare. An accommodation of the CEECs' preferences would usually require a change in the status quo of a sector, since accommodation is otherwise highly unlikely to provoke opposition from sectoral interests. Yet the institutional bias in favour of the status quo is precisely so strong because it is usually underpinned by policy paradigms. In most cases, policy paradigms are therefore likely to form obstacles to an accommodation of the applicants' preferences, in addition to interest group pressure.

The most likely cases where paradigms favour accommodation despite strong opposition from interest groups are thus instances of paradigm shifts. These should be rather rare. The notion of policy paradigms denotes precisely a high degree of stability and taken-for-grantedness of the underlying ideas. Nonetheless, persistent policy failure might discredit the underlying ideas and the policy paradigm itself. In such cases, policy change towards accommodation might be possible, if such change is compatible with an *alternative* policy paradigm that challenges and successfully replaces the dominant policy paradigm. An important question is therefore whether the policy advocates can form a strategic alliance with those sectoral policy-makers who promote an alternative policy paradigm that is more compatible with their preferences. Chapter 6 argues that this is precisely what happened in the case of trade liberalisation in the steel sector.

A special case of paradigm compatibility, which is particularly relevant for enlargement, is the question of a *temporary* accommodation of the applicants' preferences. Applicants might ask for such temporary accommodation during the pre-accession period or in post-accession transition periods. Such accommodation might be possible as long as it does not challenge a dominant sectoral policy paradigm as such. Chapter 7 suggests that this applied to regulatory alignment with certain aspects of the internal market.

Methodologically, policy paradigms can be identified within the policy discourse of a particular meso-policy. Public statements and documents in which policy-makers justify their action with reference to certain problem definitions or normative ideas reflect such policy paradigms. Sometimes these might be more implicit. The identification of policy paradigms requires an inductive analysis of the history of policy development in a particular meso-policy. This analysis has to reveal whether the emergence of a particular policy regime is indeed based on coherent sets of ideas about cause/effect relations and legitimacy claims. An assessment of the political impact of policy paradigms requires an analysis of how consensual or contested these understandings are, and to what extent they are challenged by alternative ideas. A key methodological implication is thus that it is difficult to make predictions about the way in which policy paradigms affect a political process prior to the analysis.

Conditions for successful policy influence of the policy advocates

In sum, two key factors mediate the policy impact of the attempts of the policy advocates to achieve an accommodation of the CEECs' preferences in the meso-policies. Access to the relevant policy processes is institutionally structured by more or less formal rules that characterise the policy coordination process and assign particular roles to the macro- and meso-policy-makers respectively in particular policy decisions. The access of macro-policy-makers depends on the degree of centralisation or fragmentation of the policy process, which might vary not only across, but also within, meso-policies over time. The ability to build alliances with sectoral policy-makers that are sufficiently influential to change meso-policies depends not only on the configuration of societal interest in a policy area. Certainly, the more strongly societal groups are opposed to accommodating the CEECs' preferences, the more difficult is it to build a successful alliance. Yet alliance-building with meso-policy-makers might still be possible, if the advocated policies are compatible with the policy paradigm underpinning a particular meso-policy area.

Box 3.1 summarises the propositions that can be formulated on the basis of these factors that structure the policy advocates' access and alliance-building and thus mediate the influence that they can bring to bear on sectoral policies. If sectoral interest groups oppose an accommodation of the candidates' preferences, their advocacy is unlikely to be successful, if the policy process is fragmented and sectoral policy paradigms incompatible with their preferences (lower left cell). Conversely, the advocacy of accommodation might be successful, despite countervailing pressure from sectoral interest groups, if the conditions for both access and alliance-building are favourable, i.e. the policy process is centrally coordinated and policy paradigms are compatible with the CEECs' preferences (upper right cell). If policy paradigms are incompatible, then a centralised policy process might facilitate temporary accommodation, which is, however, unlikely to be sustainable in the longer term (lower right cell). Even if sectoral policy paradigms are compatible with the candidates' preferences, advocacy is likely to remain unsuccessful, as long as the policy process remains fragmented (upper left cell), but as soon as access is achieved, a sustainable accommodation is possible.

Box 3.1 Conditions for the influence of macro-policy-makers on meso-policies

		Policy process	
		Fragmented	Centralised
Policy paradigms	Compatible	mixed	favourable
	Incompatible	unfavourable	mixed

Summary: impact of EU identity on its enlargement policy

In sum, a collective EU identity towards the CEECs, which is built on the notion of an EU responsibility towards the CEECs, affects behaviour through the behavioural standards that it establishes. The proper enactment of this identity is evaluated against the extent to which EU policy accommodates the CEECs' preferences. It delegitimises opposition to such an accommodation on purely self-interested grounds. EU identity thus affects policy by delimiting the scope of 'appropriate' policy options.

The effect of the EU's role-identity is uneven across different groups of EU policy-makers. It is strongest on those policy-makers who are primarily in charge of EU policy towards the CEECs – the macro-policy-makers. Among those, it has constitutive effects on those who directly represent the EU; these policy-makers act as advocates of the CEECs in the EU policy process. On other macro-policy-makers EU identity might merely exercise a regulative effect. The effect is weakest among sectoral policy-makers. As a result of the uneven effect of identity, the key mechanism through which it becomes politically salient is through the advocacy of the group of policy-makers most receptive to this aspect of EU identity.

This argument does not imply that identity alone determines EU policy. Certainly material interests are an important part of the process. Proponents of enlargement frequently asserted that an accommodating policy towards the CEECs serves the EU's interests, both political and economic. Conversely, actors' negative costs/benefit calculations frequently created obstacles to accommodating the CEECs' preferences. What matters in this case is the effect on policy of the interaction between identity-based norms and material interests in bringing about the specific characteristics of the enlargement process, not an either/or causation. However, the EU's role-identity towards CEECs provided the necessary condition for enlargement and for an accommodation on substantive policies.

With regard to the general decision to enlarge, references to identity-conforming behaviour resonate with the macro-policy-makers and thus have a direct effect on bringing about agreement on accommodating policies. With regard to substantive policies, direct appeals to identity have more limited effect. Factors that mediate the policy advocates' influence are crucial. The fragmentation or centralisation of the policy process crucially affects their ability to obtain access to decision-making on meso-policies. Their ability to build winning alliances depends not simply on the configuration of interest group preferences, but on the compatibility of their advocacy with underlying sectoral policy paradigms. Contrary to liberal intergovernmentalist assumptions, accommodation is thus possible, despite an unfavourable constellation of societal interests, if these factors are favourable.

Notes

1   Interview, Commission DG I, 23.10.95.
2   Of course this is not to argue that such policy is more effective. The flipside of hierarchical decision-making is precisely that the resulting problems for legitimate interests in the meso-policy areas are insufficiently appreciated (see e.g. Jachtenfuchs 2001: 254–5; Scharpf 1997: 133).

Part II

The macro-policy

4

Setting the path to eastern enlargement: from initial reluctance to endorsement of the accession perspective

This chapter and Chapter 5 sketch the evolution of the EU's enlargement policy, as the 'macro-policy'. The chapters demonstrate that the parameters of EU policy were not set simply by the configuration of material interests and bargaining power. The resonance of the EU's role-identity vis-à-vis the CEECs allowed the policy advocates in the Commission to set the EU on an incremental path towards a decision to enlarge. Divergent enlargement preferences among the member states and within the Commission led to a strong aversion in the aftermath of the 1989 revolutions to confront their longer term implications for enlargement. However, such opposition to tackling the question of eventual enlargement was not presented with references to countervailing self-interests. Nor was it challenged in principle, but presented as a discussion that was premature. However, the proponents of enlargement in the Commission were able to foster agreement on successive policy initiatives that incrementally removed remaining legitimate justifications to oppose or postpone enlargement. Simultaneously, these initiatives reinforced the EU's rhetorical commitment to enlargement and thus made it increasingly difficult to contest enlargement at later stages in the process.

In addition to examining the key stage of the evolution of the macro-policy, these chapters also provide the context for the more detailed case studies of specific meso-policies. The overview of the broad lines of policy evolution also confirms that variations in the structure of the policy process affected the extent to which EU policies accommodated the preferences of the CEECs in substantive policies.

The division between Chapters 4 and 5 is chronological. This chapter sketches the change in the perspective of EU policy from a strong initial reluctance to even discuss the prospect of eastern enlargement to the formal endorsement of the CEECs' membership perspective at the Copenhagen

European Council in June 1993. It first analyses the initial reactions of the EU and the member states to the geopolitical changes in eastern Europe and the process leading to the decision that association agreements, or 'Europe Agreements' (EAs), should provide the main framework for EU policy towards the CEECs. The second section of this chapter analyses the formulation of the EAs' content. I examine first the intra-EU agreement on the Commission's negotiation directives, and then actual negotiations between the EU and the first three CEECs (Hungary, Poland and Czechoslovakia), which were concluded in December 1991. The chapter then traces the change in the overall perspective of EU policy towards the CEECs, announced at the Copenhagen European Council, which declared that the EU shared the objective of an eventual accession of the CEECs. Chapter 5 then analyses how EU policy followed the path on which the policy advocates in the Commissions had set it, putting the general principle of the CEECs' accession into practice.

The EU's first responses to the 1989 revolutions

EU policy in response to the political changes in the CEECs in the late 1980s was characterised by a broadly based consensus among the Commission, and the member states' foreign ministries and heads of state/government on the EU's central role in supporting the transformations in the CEECs. The main underlying disagreement was on how such a policy should affect the internal integration process. The resulting compromise was to conduct relations with the CEECs in the medium-term within the framework of association agreements.

Broad consensus on a prominent role for the EU

Before Gorbachev came to power in the Soviet Union, relations between the EU[1] and the Council for Mutual Economic Assistance (CMEA), or individual CEECs, were minimal (see e.g. Gautron 1991; Maresceau 1989; Pinder 1991: 8–23; Pinder and Pinder 1975). Systemic antagonism precluded formal relations between the EU and the CMEA. The low trade activity of the CEECs' planned economies also kept commercial exchanges at a low level. Trade relations were confined to limited sectoral agreements that regulated imports from the CEECs in those sectors in which the EU is particularly sensitive to external competition, namely agriculture, coal and steel, and textiles. Otherwise, trade policy loosely served the EU's political objective to encourage the CEECs to take independent positions from the Soviet Union. The EU thus rewarded Yugoslavia, and later Romania, with preferential trade agreements. Subsequently, the changes in the Soviet Union led to mutual recognition between the EU and the CMEA, reflected in the joint declaration of June 1988 (see e.g. Lippert 1990). The normalisation of the relationship enabled the establishment of direct, bilateral contacts between the EU and the CEECs.

The political changes in eastern Europe from 1988 brought into sharper focus some common interests among the member states, especially geopolitical stabilisation of the region, not least to prevent large-scale immigration, and the economic opportunities. Yet the intensity of these interests varied considerably, largely depending on geographical position. The German government became particularly active in re-establishing historical economic and political ties in the CEECs, especially with the German Democratic Republic (GDR). At the same time, the evolving political changes raised questions about the effect of the new geopolitical situation on the balance of power between the member states. The French government was keen to counterbalance German influence in the region and was particularly concerned about the prospect of German unification. The Thatcher government in the UK shared these concerns.

Unilateral policies of the bigger member states raised concerns inside the EU. The smaller member states and the Commission feared that such unilateralism could undermine a coordinated EU response and import tensions between the big members into the EU. They therefore called for common guidelines to coordinate national and EU level activities. The Belgian government especially advocated close coordination of EU policy towards the CEECs with the European Political Cooperation (EPC) framework (Nuttall 1992). The German government supported a coordinated EU approach in recognition of other member states' sensitivities about unilateral German initiatives in the CEECs. Furthermore, an active common EU policy would be much more effective in stabilising the CEECs than unilateral German policy. By contrast, the French and UK governments were more hesitant about procedures that might constrain their capacity for unilateral action, such as national export credit schemes, but nonetheless preferred a common EU policy over unilateral German initiatives.

The member states' preferences thus converged on a coordinating role of the EU. The emphasis on the geopolitical dimension of the 1989 revolutions led to an agreement on a close cooperation between the EPC and EC frameworks in formulating policy towards the CEECs. At the same time, the consensus on the EU's central role did not only reflect converging strategies. This consensus also reflected a continuity in EU policy-makers' rhetoric about the EU's self-ascribed role in the uniting of the continent. The Rhodes European Council in December 1988 'reaffirm[ed] its determination to act with renewed hope to overcome the division of our continent' (Council 1988: 19).

Two main uncertainties surrounding the changes in the CEECs affected attempts to devise a common EU approach and individual member states' strategies. The first relates to the pace and magnitude of the political changes. Starting from a more relaxed foreign policy in the Soviet Union and signs of gradual political change in Hungary and Poland in 1988 and 1989, developments accelerated dramatically at the end of 1989 with the opening of the

Berlin Wall and changes in the political leadership in virtually all CEECs. German unification became an increasing possibility. The second uncertainty, which directly affected concrete EU policies of aid and trade concerned the uniqueness of the transition from a planned economy to a market economy.

At this stage, the Commission took the lead with concrete initiatives for EU policy (Pelkmans and Murphy 1991). They initially focused only on Poland and Hungary, the frontrunners of political reforms, and were subsequently extended to other CEECs. Initial EU policy offered (rather limited) Trade and Cooperation Agreements (TCAs). After the G7 Summit in July 1989 asked the Commission to coordinate the assistance from the G24 (OECD members), the Commission also devised an 'Action Plan' specifically for EU assistance. The core of the Action Plan was the PHARE Programme (*Pologne et Hongrie: assistance à la restructuration économique*), designed to provide technical assistance for the transition to market economies. The Action Plan also included some far-reaching preferential trade concessions, such as GSP status (General System of Preferences) and the suspension of quantitative restrictions (QRs) for non-sensitive products, as well as financial assistance for macro-economic stabilisation (see e.g. Kramer 1993; de La Serre 1994; Lequesne 1991; Reinicke 1992; Sedelmeier and Wallace 1996: 355–62).

The changes in the CEECs accelerated dramatically with the fall of the Berlin Wall in November 1989. By early 1990, the majority of the CEECs had changed their political leadership and abandoned the command economy. Effective coordination at the EU level allowed the EU to react quickly. After the opening of the Berlin Wall, French president Mitterrand convened an informal European Council meeting ahead of the formal Strasbourg European Council to discuss the implications of the changes. The European Council agreed some concrete measures, such as the creation of the European Bank for Reconstruction and Development (see e.g. Dunnet 1991; Weber 1994). Furthermore, a debate started about the possibility of offering the more advanced CEECs some form of association agreements, and the European Council declared its willingness to develop relations with the CEECs beyond the more limited framework of the TCAs. As outlined in Chapter 2, these expressions of support were couched in strongly normative terms, which affirmed the EU's consciousness of its responsibility towards the CEECs (Council 1989).

Underlying divisions about medium-term policy

Despite the broad consensus to support the reform process, it emerged already during 1989 that the member governments differed considerably on the implications of policy towards CEECs for EU integration. All governments perceived membership of the CEECs as a very distant prospect. Nonetheless, differences existed over whether the EU should at this early stage pledge itself to their eventual accession. Such a pledge could give a clear encouragement to the CEECs, but under prevailing uncertainties, it might also get the EU into similar difficulties as the promise of membership in the 1963 association agreement with Turkey. In the medium term, the key question was whether the EU should slow down its internal agenda of 'deepening' integration to avoid raising further barriers for the eventual accession of the CEECs. The German and UK governments appeared to favour this option, while the majority of the other member states and the Commission leadership were strictly opposed to it.

The German government linked normative and utility-based arguments to argue that it was the EU's 'responsibility' to seize the opportunities offered by the changes in the CEECs. It thus advocated an EU pledge of eventual membership, as well as a 'new model of association' in the medium term. In April 1989, foreign minister Hans-Dietrich Genscher stated that

> the central question for the West is whether it regards the democratisation and reform of the socialist countries as a danger or as an opportunity that it is willing to make use of. The answer can only be: this is an historic opportunity. We must not let it slip by, nor idly look on from afar, but must seek to exercise creative influence. This is our responsibility. (Cited in Torreblanca 1997: 97)

In September, Genscher called on the EU to develop 'a new model of cooperation' which might 'later lead [the CEECs] to becoming Community members if they want to' (*Agence Europe*, 23.09.89: 4). At an informal EPC meeting in October, he suggested a 'new model of association falling short of, but with view to eventual membership' (Lippert 1990: 132). Chancellor Helmut Kohl stated as early as August 1989 that Hungarian EU membership was possible by 2000 (*Financial Times*, 14.08.89: 2) and his ten-point plan for a rapprochement with the GDR was underpinned by the idea of embedding closer relations between the two parts of Germany within a broader framework of association agreements between the EU and the CEECs.[2] At the same time, German policy-makers were concerned that intra-EU developments, especially plans for Economic and Monetary Union (EMU) and the inclusion of social policy, could raise barriers to an eventual integration of the GDR and other CEECs (*Financial Times*, 11.10.89: 2; 27.10.89: 2).

The UK government emphasised the need to live up to earlier rhetoric and appealed to the EU's self-image. In August 1990, Prime Minister Margaret Thatcher stated:

> I propose that the Community should declare unequivocally that it is ready to accept all of the [CEECs] as members if they want to join, and when democracy has taken root and their economies are capable of sustaining membership. We cannot say in one breath that they are part of Europe and in the next our EC club is so exclusive that we will not admit them. It will be some time before they are ready for membership, so we are offering them intermediate steps such as association agreements. But the option of eventual membership should be clearly, openly, and generously on the table. (*Financial Times*, 06.08.90: 3)

Similarly, her successor, John Major, called for an EU pledge for full membership for CEECs, as well as the Baltic States, 'as soon as they are ready politically and economically. [Although this will take] a long time, that possibility should be open to them too. And we should tell them so now' (*Financial Times*, 13.09.91: 13). The appeal to subordinate the internal integration agenda to openness towards the CEECs was more pronounced than in the German case, as Thatcher stated most distinctly in November 1990:

> The Community should be open to the [CEECs] ... if they want to join, once they are ready. It would be contrary to all we are trying to do politically to support democracy and to support those countries ... if the Community was to make itself an exclusive club which kept them outside. These are the standards – freedom and openness – against which I judge proposals put forward in the Community and why I am not convinced that the full Delors plan for EMU is either feasible or desirable. (*Financial Times*, 19.11.90: 17)

The French government agreed on the key role of the EU in policy towards the CEECs, but it differed markedly in its assessment of how this policy should affect the internal integration process. It insisted that an immediate strengthening of the integration process was in the interest of both the current and the future members. Mitterrand argued that 'it is the acceleration and strengthening of the Community construction of Europe which will make a major contribution to positive developments in the East' (*EPC Bulletin* 1989: 100–1). Internal deepening thus was not presented as an alternative to a policy that accommodated the CEECs' preferences, but rather as a strategy to support the CEECs. These considerations resulted in Mitterrand's (vague) proposal of a 'European Confederation' for the cooperation between the EU and the CEECs in areas of trans-European interest (see e.g. Vernet 1992), which would confirm the EU's role, while at the same time taking pressure off the integration process. While French discourse was thus lukewarm on the demands of the CEECs, it reinforced at the same time the perception of the legitimacy of their demands. After the informal European Council in November 1989, Mitterrand declared:

> The existence of a strong and structured Community is a factor for the stability and success for the whole of Europe. We should therefore affirm our identity as a Community, confirm our determination, strengthen our institutions and get the seal on our union. That in my view is the first lesson to be learned, because I can see no other alternative to the opening up of the East [than] the completion of the Community construction ... As events unfold in the East, the Europe of the Community, at the same pace, and indeed why not even a little more quickly to anticipate the result, must decide to strengthen itself more than it has yet done. (*EPC Bulletin* 1989: 100–1, 171)

The Commission's approach was more ambiguous. On the one hand, Commission policy-makers broadly accepted that the EU had to fulfil its historic mission to integrate the CEECs. The Commission leadership thus believed that the current member states should make substantive concessions to support the transformation processes.[3] On the other hand, there was an equally strong concern that policies towards the CEECs might distract from the internal integration process and eventually dilute integration. The position of Commission president, Jacques Delors, most distinctly reflected this ambiguity (see Ross 1995: 138–40). Close observers perceived a conflict between Delors's 'head and heart'.[4] He accepted that the EU should play an active role and generally supported generous economic concessions, frequently using the imagery of a family table, where places had to be made for new members.[5] Yet he was determined to limit the effect of policy towards the CEECs on the internal integration process and to prevent controversial debates about this policy from creating tensions among the member states. In response to Gorbachev's call for a 'common European home', he stressed: 'Our vision is of a European village ... I would see in it a house called the EC. We are its sole architects, we are the keepers of its keys; but we are prepared to open its doors and talk to our neighbours' (*Bulletin of the EC*, supplement 1/1989: 17–18). Delors therefore called for 'a qualitative leap in our conception of the Community [in order to respond to] the acceleration of history' (*Financial Times*, 18.10.89: 24).

The Strasbourg European Council's agreement to consider more far-reaching agreements with the CEECs reflected therefore an uneasy consensus to avoid, for the time being, a debate over the implications of the EU's policy towards the CEECs for the deepening process. The focus on concrete policy steps and general pledges of support were implying that primacy was accorded to the EU's internal agenda. Indeed, Mitterrand's motive for convening the informal European Council at the Elysée was to ensure that the agenda already agreed for Strasbourg, especially the decision to convene an Intergovernmental Conference (IGC) on EMU, would not become subordinated to discussions of relations with the CEECs (*Financial Times*, 14.11.89: 1).

The primacy of 'deepening' became more explicit after the rapid developments towards German unification in early 1990 shifted the German government's preferences firmly towards this position, leaving the UK government isolated. The disentanglement of German unification from EU policy towards the CEECs made it a less pressing concern for German policymakers. At the same time, they considered a commitment to deepening necessary to make unification acceptable to other member states. The Franco-German initiative for an IGC on Political Union expressed the support of the German government for the position promoted by the French government and Delors. The joint statement by Kohl and Mitterrand at the September 1990 Franco-German summit emphasised, however, the compatibility of this initiative with the EU's role towards the CEECs:

The process of European union has been a determining factor in favouring the upheavals in Central and Eastern Europe and German unification. This evolution will accelerate the union of Europe. Our objective is European Union as a solid basis for overall European unity.

The debate about the association agreements

At the beginning of 1990, the Irish Council presidency reaffirmed the importance of the CEECs on the EU agenda and the EU's responsibility towards them (Torreblanca 1997: 114). However, when the Commission submitted a first report on the possible shape of an association agreement to the Council (Commission 1990a), the preference of a majority of member states for separating policy towards the CEECs from the internal deepening and to avoid discussions of eventual CEEC membership became clear. The foreign ministers in the General Affairs Council, with the exception of the UK, insisted on separating the question of eventual membership from the association agreement (*Agence Europe*, 02.02.90: 5).

The Commission outlined the main elements of the proposed association agreements in a document for the Dublin European Council: political dialogue for regular exchanges with each CEEC on foreign policy; gradual establishment of free trade for industrial goods; moves towards the free movement of workers, services and capital; and financial and economic cooperation (Commission 1990b). Furthermore, it stressed the political conditionality attached to these agreements, relating to the rule of law, human rights, free election, multiparty systems, and market economies. Amidst reaffirmations of support for the CEECs and the goal of overcoming the division of the continent (Council 1990a: 7), the European Council adopted the general framework without detailed discussion. It affirmed that 'discussions will start forthwith in the Council ... on Association Agreements ... The Community will work to complete association negotiations as soon as possible on the understanding that the basic conditions with regard to democratic principles and transition towards a market economy are fulfilled' (Council 1990a: 9).

The decision to make the association agreements the main framework of EU policy towards the CEECs implied some changes to the policy process, which had significant effects on the further development of the substance of EU policy. First, the focus of policy changed. The key issues related no longer primarily to geopolitical concerns, or longer-term political and economic gains. Instead, sectoral economic interests moved to the centre stage. Fleshing out the general framework for association agreements shifted the focus to concrete trade concessions. At this stage, the EU had made some significant concessions through the granting of GSP status and the suspension of QRs. However, these measures had been considered as temporary and they had not touched the more sensitive sectors, which presented a considerable challenge for any ambitious plans to improve market access for the CEECs.

Second, the group of actors that had the lead over policy changed. Decision-making about the broader policy framework had been largely restricted to the foreign ministers and the heads of state and government, as well as the commissioners. Sectoral policy-makers, both in the Commission and the member states, were now to play a much more prominent role in the policy process. While this change was largely a corollary of the shifting focus of policy, a number of factors exacerbated the dominance of sectoral policy-makers.

The EPC framework disengaged from EU policy towards the CEECs. The stabilisation of the geopolitical situation shifted the discussions in EPC towards questions of the overall European security architecture within the framework of the Conference on Security and Cooperation in Europe (CSCE). The move towards association agreements settled the issue for EPC and there seemed little point in becoming involved in the complex economic detail of the agreements. Furthermore, the attention of EPC policy-makers (and the foreign ministers in the General Affairs Council) became increasingly occupied with pressing international issues, such as the Gulf crisis and political tensions in the Soviet Union and the Baltic states. The disengagement of EPC prompted an organisational change in the policy process. From 1988 (with the exception of the French presidency in the second half of 1989), Council debates on the CEECs were prepared in close cooperation between the Political Committee (presenting EPC input) and COREPER (presenting the EC side). After the informal General Affairs Council in April 1990, there was no longer any EPC input into the debate (Nuttall 1992: 281). The detachment of EPC eliminated one institutional factor that might have increased the scope for hierarchical coordination of the debates on policy substance.

In addition, the foreign ministers and the heads of state and government took a much more hands-off approach. After the European Council agreed that the Commission should draft negotiation directives for the association agreements, no in-depth debates took place among the foreign ministers about the broader strategy for EU relations with the CEECs, nor on the concrete detail of the agreements. During 1990, procedural issues about the launching of the IGCs and German unification dominated the agenda of the General Affairs Council. The disengagement of the foreign ministries characterised not only the policy process at the EU level, but also the approach of the German government, a key proponent of an active policy towards the CEECs. German policy-makers focused on the management of German unification. The continued presence of Soviet troops in East Germany seemed to temper the government's willingness to push for a more active strategy towards CEECs for fear of antagonising the Soviet leadership.

In sum, the agreement on the framework of association as the basis for relations with the CEECs reflected a broad consensus among the foreign ministers and heads of state and government on the need for a common EU policy and on its overall parameters. This consensus brushed over underlying tensions over the desirability of an eventual accession of the CEECs and how it should affect the EU's future development. However, this consensus appeared to reflect not only a far-sighted collective self-interest of the member states, but also the collective self-image of EU policy-makers, which made them accept a special role and responsibility of the EU.

The EU's response to the changes in the CEECs presents a continuation of the discourse about its role in overcoming the unnatural division of the continent. In part, rhetoric had to make up for lack of concrete measures and unwillingness to discuss the question of membership. In part, as in the case of the UK government, normative rhetoric might have covered an ulterior motive of diluting integration through early enlargement. But even those governments that were lukewarm on enlargement did not oppose the principle of enlargement as such. Their arguments did not refer to countervailing material interests, but countervailing norms – safeguarding integration. Moreover, the justification of deepening as a prerequisite for enlargement rhetorically reinforced the legitimacy of the CEECs' membership aspirations and the need for the EU to play an active role, rather than remaining indifferent. For example, Mitterrand reported to the European Parliament (EP) that the informal Elysée European Council was committed 'to back up and encourage democratic change' and that 'if we are to support the reform movement we cannot simply remain passive observers, counting the blows struck. We must enter into the movement, help to carry it further' (*EPC Bulletin* 1989: 172).

The Europe Agreements

Drafting the negotiation directives in the Commission
The central role of the Commission in the EU's initial responses established the commissioner for external relations, Frans Andriessen, and DG I (external relations), in particular the unit in charge of relations with the CEECs (DG I-E), as the key advocates of an active EU policy towards the CEECs.[6] Through numerous contacts with CEEC policy-makers, primarily in Hungary, Poland and Czechoslovakia, they believd that the most significant contribution that the EU could make to support the transformations in the CEECs was not only financial and technical assistance, but export-led growth through access to the EU market. After intensive consultations with the CEECs in the lead-up to the drafting of the negotiation directives, Andriessen and DG I were prepared to establish more far-reaching links between the association agreements and eventual membership than the majority in the Council and the commissioners' *college*, including Delors. They soon realised that there was insufficient support, but therefore fought to make the remainder of the agreements as advantageous to the CEECs as possible, through substantial improvements of market access, including the sensitive sectors.

To obtain the mandate to draft concrete negotiation directives, the Commission submitted an outline of the association agreements, to be called

'Europe Agreements' (EAs), in August 1990 (Commission 1990c). The deliberately general nature of the outline avoided entering at this stage into detailed consultations with sectoral DGs and national officials on specific parts of the framework. DG I was therefore able to draft the framework document with considerable autonomy.[7] The draft nonetheless anticipated opposition in the Council and in the other DGs, for example concerning the possibility of a reference to the CEECs' potential membership, or concessions on agriculture. However, its autonomy allowed DG I to put forward a rather ambitious draft, including the principle of an asymmetrical establishment of free trade in industrial goods, with the EU dismantling trade barriers much faster than the CEECs.[8]

The role of DG I in the policy process changed considerably during the drafting of the detailed negotiation directives. While DG I had the central coordination role inside the Commission, concrete proposals in the different areas of the agreement had to be drawn up in coordination with sectoral DGs and the relevant ministries of the member states. Formally, the negotiation directives required approval by the Commissioners' *college* and subsequently by the Council.[9] In practice, the Commission sought to anticipate possible opposition in the Council. The national Permanent Representations tried to influence sectoral DGs at the drafting stage (since it is politically more costly to amend the proposal in the Council) and sought support from the commissioners of their nationality and their *cabinets*.[10] Furthermore, interest groups, especially those active at the European level, tried to influence sectoral DGs and *cabinets*.

The drafting of the negotiation directives largely followed a process of 'negative coordination'. For the most part, DG I had to take account of the reservations of the sectoral DGs with specialised expertise and primary competence in specific areas. To an extent, some sectoral expertise within DG I-D (multilateral trade relations) made it possible for DG I to retain the lead entirely on some issues. At the same time, DG I-E encountered opposition to its ambitious approach even inside DG I. The officials dealing with trade defence instruments, for example, were guided by the continued perception of the CEECs as state-trading countries.[11]

An element of 'positive coordination' at the political level was introduced through consultations at the level of directors general. DG I was able to convince the sectoral DGs that substantial concessions in the sensitive sectors were politically important. As it proved difficult to obtain such concessions in the agricultural sector, the consultations led to a high-level agreement to make an effort to compensate limited agricultural concessions with more far-reaching concessions in the textile and steel sectors. But in the *college*, certain commissioners defended the sectoral interests of their respective DGs, including some commissioners without direct interest, who were lobbied by officials from the national Permanent Representations.[12] The Commission's final proposal for the negotiation directives (Commission 1990d) thus fell short of DG I's ambitions on a number of key points (see Box 4.1).[13]

Box 4.1 Commission proposal for the EAs' negotiation directives

Issue	Outcome
Membership perspective	Partial success for DG I: non-binding reference in preamble to 'the possibility for [the CEEC], as European state, to apply for membership in the Community'.
Free trade area	Proposal to eliminate QRs dropped.
Textiles, coal and steel	Removed from general framework into separate protocols.
Agriculture	Exclusion of processed agricultural goods and fisheries from quota increases.
Free movement of workers	DG I's proposal of generous increases in national quotas dropped.

Negotiation of the directives in the Council

The policy process in the Council for adopting the negotiation directives was the same as for the overview of the subsequent EA negotiations. At first glance, the procedural arrangements seemed to facilitate positive coordination. The EAs were based on article 310 (Ex-238) EEC Treaty, rather than on article 130 (Ex-113), as in the case of conventional trade agreements, allowing the Council working group on Eastern Europe (EEWG) to conduct the overview of the negotiations. The EEWG reported to COREPER; the foreign ministers in the General Affairs Council (GAC) took the final decision. In standard trade agreements, the Council's Article 113 Committee, consisting of national trade officials, conducts the overview and usually trade ministers, rather than foreign ministers, are in charge of settling disputes (see e.g. Hayes 1993: 122–33).

In practice, however, certain factors limited the scope for centralised positive coordination that might have facilitated the accommodation of the CEECs' preferences advocated by DG I-E and Andriessen. The delegates in the EEWG were predominantly officials from the national capitals in charge of trade policy, rather than relations with the CEECs.[14] The UK representative, a foreign office official from the Permanent Representation, was rather an exception. In the case of Germany, the foreign ministry lost an inter-ministerial conflict with the economics ministry to nominate a representative.[15] The representative acted on tight instructions from the sectoral departments and appeared to have little personal sympathy towards the CEECs.[16] A further constraint on hierarchical coordination was that much of the detailed negotiation was not conducted in the EEWG, but delegated to specialist Council working groups, such as the 113 ECSC (European Coal and Steel Community) working group, the Special Committee on Agriculture, and indeed the 113 Committee. The representatives in these working groups were from line ministries in the national capitals, or officials from the Permanent Representations under tight instructions from the capitals.

Despite fragmentation at the working group level, COREPER can often induce more centralised coordination. It generally takes a broader perspective on a dossier and frequently rises over the day-to-day political pressures prevailing in the capitals (Hayes-Renshaw and Wallace 1997). It is therefore often in a better position than the GAC to play a coordinating role across issues and to instil positive coordination into the policy process. However, a main strength of COREPER lies in overcoming internal differences and in finding agreements that accommodate minority positions among the members. Yet in negotiations with third countries, this procedure tends to produce mutual acceptance of the sectoral restrictions of different governments, rather than a burden-sharing of concessions for the benefit of external partners. This bias was pronounced in the case of the EAs. Costs from increased competition were unevenly distributed, both within particular sectors, in which often only a few member states had particular sensitivities, and across sectors, to the disadvantage of the southern member states that also appeared to gain relatively less in terms of political stability or economic opportunities.

The foreign ministers in the GAC take the final decision on the EAs and are in charge of solving disagreements within the EU that might arise during the negotiations. This feature might have embedded the negotiations at lower levels and in specific sectors in a 'shadow of hierarchy': sectoral policy-makers had to anticipate the stronger bias towards accommodating the CEECs' preferences in the GAC. However, the GAC hardly became involved in the detail of the agreements, as overloaded external relations agendas and internal deepening distracted the attention of foreign ministers. Even when the GAC got directly involved, often the foreign ministers were constrained by the outcome of national coordination processes, which privileged sectoral concerns. Only in the UK, Denmark and the Netherlands were the national positions across the different levels of negotiations fairly consistently in favour of concessions on market access. By contrast, notably in France, Spain, Portugal and Belgium, the restrictive positions at lower levels were mirrored in restrictive briefs at the political level. The representatives of Ireland, Italy, Greece, and Luxembourg generally kept a low profile in the GAC and supported the majority positions.

The case of Germany was more complex. Despite the general inclination of the government to accommodate the CEECs' preferences, the foreign ministry had to accept defensive positions on sectoral issues. In the interministerial coordination process, the ministry of economics prevailed over the foreign ministry. Within the ministry of economics, the sectoral departments won against the department with horizontal trade responsibilities, which had far less reservations about generous market access.[17] This outcome of the national coordination process resulted partly from the emphasis on the autonomy of sectoral departments (*Ressortprinzip*) in the federal bureaucracy. In addition, the main priority of the chancellor's office was to see the agreements as such concluded. Their concrete content appeared secondary, as long as it did not endanger the overall agreement.[18] In practice, German positions in the negotiations changed frequently when contested issues were referred to the political level in the GAC. In these instances, the foreign ministry generally obtained from the chancellor's office interventions that overruled sectoral positions.[19]

In the French case, differences in the positions of the foreign ministry and sectoral departments were less pronounced than in the German case. In such cases, the foreign ministry had similar difficulties in winning its arguments in the inter-ministerial coordination process. Furthermore, the efficiency of the central coordination mechanism in the *Sécretariat Général du Comité Interministériel pour les questions de coopération économique européenne* (SGCI), under the auspices of the Prime Minister, meant that the foreign ministry had little scope for reversing sectoral positions even in the GAC, in particular on agriculture.[20] In the Spanish case, policy-makers at the political level were generally positively inclined towards the overall preferences of the CEECs. However, the harsh treatment they had received during their own accession negotiations affected their positions on substantive issues. The foreign ministry and the prime minister's office had little sympathy for a more generous treatment of the CEECs on the detail of the agreements, but did not perceive this stance contradictory to their generally sympathetic position. In general, Spanish officials therefore showed little inclination to push for accommodating sectoral positions.[21]

In November 1990, after an initial discussion of the Commission's proposal in the EEWG, the GAC had the opportunity to discuss the economic substance of the agreements. Although the Commission representatives, Delors and Andriessen, deliberately stressed the political significance of the EAs and the importance of maintaining a political overview, the GAC routinely delegated most proposals to the lower levels for their technical examination (*Agence Europe*, 09.11.90: 5, 14.11.90: 8). Subsequently, the GAC only became involved if disagreements at the lower levels were irresolvable at other levels of the decision-making hierarchy. Such cases were rare during the negotiations on the directives, since on most issues, strong majorities for restrictive positions prevailed at the sectoral and lower decision-making levels.

DG I and Andriessen had hoped that the Rome European Council in December would inject some high-level backing into the Council negotiations. Yet while the European Council reaffirmed its 'special responsibility' towards the CEECs and declared that 'the Community hopes to conclude "European Agreements" as quickly as possible and that these will mark a new stage in the Community policy of developing increasingly close relations with those countries' (Council 1990c: 4–5), it did not discuss the negotiation directives in any detail and did not influence the on-going sectoral debates. The directives that the GAC endorsed on 19 December 1990 were thus significantly more restrictive than the Commission's proposal, which was already less accommodating of the CEECs' demands than DG I had intended (see Box 4.2).[22]

Box 4.2 The negotiation directives for the EAs

Issue	Outcome	Debate in the Council
Membership perspective	Deletion even of non-binding reference to Art. 237 EEC Treaty ('ability of [the particular CEEC], as European state, to apply for membership'); compromise: if unavoidable during the negotiation, the Commission might propose this non-binding reference.	Support for non-binding reference: UK, D, I, F; strong opposition: NL, B, E, P.
Financial cooperation	Strict opposition to financial protocol and multi-annual planning.	Insistence to ensure balance between assistance to CEECs and ACP/North Africa: great majority of member states, particularly E.
Free movement of workers	Limited to improvement of situation of workers already legally established in the EU.	Particularly D, UK, F, NL opposed to any opening of national quotas.
Free movement of services	Some further restrictions, e.g. road transport services will only be 'facilitated', not 'liberalised'.	Particular insistence by D.

Industrial free trade area	Reduction of asymmetry; More limited overall scope (maintenance of certain QRs); Liberalisation divided into two 5–year periods; transition to second stage conditional on EU decision, depending on progress with economic and political reforms.	Majority of member states, except UK; particular insistence of E, P (still facing restrictions on access the other member states' markets as result of their own accession negotiations) that concessions to the CEECs must not put them into a more favourable position.
Trade defence instruments	Insertion of a regional clause.	Particular pressure from E, P, F.
Textiles	Special, restrictive regime; connection with negotiations on MFA in the Uruguay Round.	Particular insistence from P, E, supported by F, I, Ire, Gr; support for more liberal regime only from D, UK, NL (interest in outward processing trade).
Coal and steel	Special, restrictive regime; Coal: only gradual phasing out of QRs; Steel: possibility to maintain or reintroduce VRAs.	Especially D, E on coal; E on steel, with very strong support of the majority of member states, except UK.
Agriculture	Further tightening of the already restrictive Commission proposal (e.g. maintenance of VRAs in the meat sector, further restrictions for processed agricultural products, strict reciprocity for concessions).	Overwhelming support for further restrictions.

Source: compiled from *Agence Europe*, 17–18.12.90: 6; 20.12.90: 5–6; interviews as above.

The Europe Agreement negotiations

On the basis of these negotiation directives, parallel bilateral negotiations with Poland, Hungary and Czechoslovakia started formally in December 1990. The officials of DG I-E, who conducted the negotiations on behalf of the EU, were in a difficult position. They were sympathetic to the CEECs' demands for more concessions, especially on trade in the sensitive sectors. At the same time, they had to negotiate in good faith on the basis of the Council's directives and had to communicate to the CEECs the limitations of the member states' position.[23]

In March 1991, the deep dissatisfaction of the CEECs with the EU's limited concessions became obvious. Their criticism focused in particular on the absence of a reference to the CEECs' accession objective and on the limited market access in the sensitive sectors – agriculture, textiles, and coal and steel (*Agence Europe*, 21.03.91: 9). The Polish chief negotiator Olechowski criticised the EU's 'technocratic approach in these negotiations which have a historical goal: to give Europe back to Poland and Poland back to Europe. Agriculture will determine Poland's fate' (*Agence Europe*, 21.03.91: 9). President Walesa publicly complained that the EU did 'replace the iron curtain with a silver curtain' (*Agence Europe*, 04.04.91: 5). Despite their sympathy for the CEECs' demands, even the negotiators of DG I-E perceived some of these claims as unrealistic and found in particularly the theatrical and strong moralistic rhetoric of the Polish delegation unhelpful. These criticisms nonetheless had an effect on the debate in the Council. In April 1991, the negotiating team of DG I-E convinced the EEWG that to conclude the negotiations successfully, it had to revise the negotiation directives. The revisions would need to address in particular the CEECs' accession objective, market access on textiles, agriculture and steel, and the movement of workers. However, any changes in the negotiation directives required re-opening negotiations in the Council.

The policy process for revising the negotiation directives largely mirrored the process through which they were initially established. The need to improve the concessions to the CEECs made untenable the internal equilibrium on a restrictive position, which had characterised the earlier negotiations. It strengthened the hand of the Commission and those member state governments favourable to more generous concessions; and gave foreign ministry officials a reason to challenge restrictive national bargaining positions at the highest political level domestically. Andriessen and DG I-E were therefore able to achieve more accommodating negotiation directives (see Box 4.3).

Box 4.3 Revised negotiation directives, April 1991

Membership perspective	In preamble: 'the final objective of [the CEEC] is to become a member of the Community *and … this association, in the view of the parties, will help to achieve this objective*' [emphasis added].
Free trade area	Reference date for standstill clause for CEECs is entry into force of the agreement, not 01.01.91; Agreement on principle of asymmetry; Industrial products in general: immediate elimination of QRs, consolidation of GSP, removal of tariffs within 5 years; Idea of two stages with conditional progression to second stage dropped.
Rules of origin	Cumulation between CEECs when necessary conditions fulfilled.
Movement of workers	Some flexibility (free movement of 'key personnel').
Coal and steel	Tariff reduction in 5 rather than 10 years.
Textiles	Elimination of tariffs after ten years, QRs on terms of Uruguay Round.
Agriculture	Consolidation of GSP and removal of QRs on entry into force (but exceptions).

Source: compiled from *Bull-EC* 4–91: 43; *Agence Europe*, 17.04.91: 7; 22.04.91: 7.

However, even these improvements did not satisfy the CEEC delegations, which demanded further concessions on agriculture and textiles, and criticised the lack of a financial protocol in the EAs. The Polish government subsequently refused to send any high-level delegations to the negotiations (*Agence Europe*, 13.07.91: 7; 12.09.91: 9). The Commission reported to the Council that it would be impossible to conclude the negotiations on the basis of the current negotiation directives and proposed greater flexibility on textiles and agriculture in particular (*Agence Europe*, 26.07.91: 5). However, the balance of opinion in the Council rather pointed in the opposite direction. Several delegations had requested restrictions on certain imports in the Agriculture Council (*Agence Europe*, 18.07.91: 9). Portugal, where the textiles industry was particularly sensitive to competition from the CEECs, announced its categorical opposition to any further concessions in this sector (*Agence Europe*, 26.07.1991: 5). On the other hand, the leaders of the big member states promised at the G7 meeting in London to 'undertake to continue improving access to our market for products and services from these countries, including sectors such as steel, textiles, and agricultural products' (*Agence Europe*, 26.07.91: 5). Andriessen also reminded the Council of the need to 'synchronise its political affirmations on support to reforms in Eastern Europe with the concrete concessions it is willing to make' (*Agence Europe*, 31.07.91: 7). However, negotiations in the Council remained blocked until September.

The attempted coup in Moscow in August 1991 induced in the Council a sense of urgency in concluding the negotiations. German foreign minister Genscher called for further concessions, stating that 'opening the borders would certainly have a negative effect on certain sectors in the EC – farming, steel and textiles – but it must be done to avoid far greater problems in the countries affected' (*Financial Times*, 29.08.91: 4). The Commission increased the pressure on the member states. Delors exposed the discrepancy between political declarations and policy behaviour: 'it's no good making fine speeches with a sob in your voice on Sunday and then on Monday opposing the trade concessions enabling those countries to sell their goods' (*Financial Times*, 21.08.91: 5).

In the Council, a breakthrough seemed possible. The Commission pledged a special regional policy initiative favouring Portuguese textiles regions to overcome Portuguese objections (*Agence Europe*, 05.09.91: 7; 09.09.91: 9). On agriculture, most member states signalled their preparedness for further product-specific concessions. However, the entire package became blocked through French opposition to an increase in CEEC quotas on beef (*Agence Europe*, 09.09.91: 9). Prior to the GAC, the French foreign minister Dumas had taken the unusual step of requesting two additional inter-ministerial coordination meetings in the SGCI in order to gain approval for the concessions (Niblett 1995: 251). In both cases, the foreign ministry lost the argument, as Prime Minister Edith Cresson succumbed to pressure from agricultural groups.

Most ministers avoided openly attributing the blame to the French delegation, but their irritation and concern about the damage to the EU's image was obvious in the bad-tempered atmosphere in which the Council meeting broke up. Council president van den Broek referred bitterly to 'the attitude of one delegation' (*Agence Europe*, 09.09.91: 9). Most outspoken was the Danish foreign minister Elleman-Jensen who called the outcome a 'disgrace' and criticised that 'certain countries make fine statements about Europe and democracy, but when it comes to small concessions and confronting their own vested interests, they behave as if they are living on another planet' (*Financial Times*, 10.09.91: 16). Leon Brittan, the competition Commissioner, stated his 'grave concern' for the EU's 'credibility' if it should not react in an 'adequate manner to the upheavals in eastern Europe' (*Agence Europe*, 11.09.91: 10). Delors reiterated: 'We cannot on Sunday make lofty declarations with voices choked with emotions and the following week not offer those countries the possibility of selling their goods and improving their standards of living' (*Agence Europe*, 21.09.91: 2–3).

Consultations between van den Broek and Dumas and a meeting between Delors and Cresson, in which he 'impress[ed] on her both Brussel's commitment to eastern Europe and the degree of hostility raised by France's stance' (*Financial Times*, 10.09.91: 16) produced a compromise on agriculture. The Commission proposed 'triangular operations', whereby the Community would finance CEEC foodstuff supplies to the USSR, as part of the EU's assistance to the country. In addition, the French government obtained guarantees on safeguards with regard to the volume and veterinary standards of beef imports from the CEECs (*Agence Europe*, 28.09.91: 8). The compromise allowed the Council to adopt the more flexible negotiation directives (*Bull-EC* 9/91: 45).

After the negotiations resumed, DG I-E was firmly in driving seat. The Dutch presidency's determination to conclude the negotiations before the end of its term provided the Commission with an important ally.[24] The Commission's position was further strengthened by the fact that foreign minister Genscher had obtained authorisation from the Chancellor's Office to instruct the German negotiators to back the Commission's positions during this final phase of negotiations.[25] In the final weeks of the negotiations, DG I negotiated directly for sectoral DGs on certain issues, such as for DG V on the movement of workers, or DG VII on transport. It negotiated compromises on issues that the sectoral experts had been unable to resolve, such as on intellectual property, competition, and rules of establishment. Andriessen and DG I made informally two further revisions of the negotiation directives,[26] in particular dropping a reference to the possibility of maintaining Voluntary Restraint Agreements (VRAs) on steel products (see also Chapter 6).

The EAs with the three CEECs, signed on 16 December 1991, were still considerably more restrictive than the CEECs' initial demands and Andriessen and DG I-E's proposal (see Box 4.4). This restrictiveness was most notable with regard to the free movement of workers; the absence of a financial protocol; the safeguard clauses and instruments for contingency protection available to the EU; the limited agricultural concessions; and specific national exemptions from the elimination of QRs, such as for Spain and Germany on coal. Key factors that allowed sectoral domestic interests in the member states to constrain a more generous accommodation of the CEECs' interests included the disengagement of the EPC framework from the association policy process, the lack of involvement of the foreign ministers and the European Council in the detail of the negotiations, and the failure of most member states' foreign ministries to influence the formulation of national negotiating positions.

Nonetheless, the final shape of the EAs came much closer to the demands of the CEECs and to DG I's proposals, than the Council's original negotiation position. This improved outcome is particularly striking given the weak bargaining position of the CEECs. To some extent, the strong commitment of DG I and the support from the Dutch presidency counterbalanced these obstacles. The structure of the policy process during the negotiations also played an important role. It allowed the Commission sporadically to involve the foreign ministers directly in the negotiations and thus to generate an element of hierarchical coordination that favoured the preferences of the CEECs.

Box 4.4 Content of the Europe Agreements

Political dialogue: regular bilateral meetings at highest political level and ministerial level to promote convergence on foreign policy.

Free movement of goods
Progressive establishment of free trade in industrial goods (transition
  period for EU 5 years, CEECs 10 years
- *elimination of tariffs*: immediate for some products, 1–5 years for most others (according to their sensitivity)
- *elimination of quantitative restrictions*: immediate; with *exceptions* for sensitive sectors:
  (1) ECSC products (coal: quotas after one year and tariffs after 4 years, with special derogations for Germany and Spain; steel: quotas immediately and tariffs gradually within 5 years);
  (2) Textile products (quotas within not less than 5 years and tariffs gradually within 6 years).
Agricultural products: consolidation of previous concessions and some
  reciprocal concessions;
Special provisions for rules of origin (requirement of at least 60% 'local
  content');
Safeguards: anti-dumping provisions; special and general safeguard
  clauses; unilateral measures possible;
Consolidation of GSP benefits;
Removal from the list of state-trading countries.

Other freedoms of movement
Workers: equal treatment for workers legally established in the EU;
Right of establishment: full national treatment for establishment and operation of new activities; transitional periods for application by the associates; freedom of movement limited to 'key personnel';
Services: progressive freedom of cross-border supply of services, special rules for transport;

> *Capital*: freedom of financial transfers for commercial transactions, provision of services and investment operations; repatriation of capital or investment benefits.
>
> **Approximation of legislation:** general commitment by CEECs to make legislation compatible with EU, long list of priority areas; most concrete for *competition policy*: (adaptation within 3 years; non-discriminatory public procurement; adaptation of protection of intellectual, industrial, and commercial property within 5 years).
>
> **Cooperation:** *economic cooperation* (covering 'all sectors of mutual interest); *cultural cooperation* (extending existing cultural cooperation programmes to associates, additional actions of mutual interest, priorities identified); *financial cooperaton* (eligibility for grants under PHARE and loans from European Investment Bank; possibility of macroeconomic assistance through G24; no financial protocol).
>
> **Institutions:** *Association Council* (ministerial level; to supervise implementation; possibility of binding decisions and dispute settlement); *Association Committee* (assists the Association Council); *Parliamentary Committee* (advisory role).

However, the impact of EU policy-makers' collective rhetoric about the EU's role was also an important factor in fostering compromises towards a more accommodating position. Crucially, those foreign ministers in the GAC who opposed concessions to the CEECs did not merely compromise for fear of being outvoted. They were ostensibly reluctant to defend positions that contradicted the collectively professed role of the EU. The Commission regularly appealed to the collective self-image of foreign ministers and warned of the possible damage to the credibility of the EU's commitments. Such appeals were a regular feature of the discourse and were most poignantly summarised by Andriessen (1991b: 11):

> We must not only affirm our commitment but also deliver, despite the short-term sacrifices which this may involve. This is the lesson of [the EA] negotiations, in which the Commission has had repeatedly to remind those most susceptible to sectoral interests that there exists also a wider European interest.

These appeals appeared to play a central role in generating compromises that accommodated the CEECs' preferences to a greater extent. Their importance was particularly apparent when behaviour in contradiction to this image was exposed. In the case of the temporary French veto against concessions on agriculture, the other delegations expressed their disappointment with their collective inability to make a more generous offer; and the French Foreign Minister Dumas, who had lost his argument in the national coordination process, came close to apologising publicly and revealing his own disappointment.

The context of negotiations induced an element of hierarchical coordination in the policy process, which changed, however, after the signing of the EAs. Sectoral policy-makers were in charge of the implementation of the EAs and the day-to-day application of the provisions in the various areas. This change was particularly salient, since in many areas more generous concessions to the CEECs were only achieved at the price of strong safeguards that could allow EU interest groups to reduce the benefits that the CEECs obtained during the negotiations. Chapter 6 examines how this affected the accommodation of the CEECs' interests in the case of trade liberalisation in the steel sector.

At the same time, the overall parameters of policy continued to develop. Both the substance and the overall policy objective were redefined under the strong advocacy of DG I and successive commissioners for external relations. These developments led notably to the EU's endorsement of the CEECs' membership objective at the Copenhagen European Council in June 1993, which fundamentally changed the perspective of EU policy towards the CEECs.

The EU's endorsement of the CEECs' membership objective

Almost immediately after the signing of the EAs, the advocates of the CEECs' preferences around DG I-E and the Andriessen *cabinet* started work on giving further impetus to policy towards the CEECs. Their main objective was to obtain the Council's formal endorsement of the eventual accession of the CEECs, which would change the perspective of EU policy. This change in perspective would make it easier to argue for the accommodation of the CEECs' demands in EU policy, since they could be treated no longer simply as 'third countries'. Moreover, it would allow pushing for a concrete strategy to prepare actively for the CEECs' accession, rather than leaving the adjustment burden entirely to the CEECs.[27] The policy advocates' second objective was further concessions on market access, particularly in the sensitive sectors. DG I considered such concessions both important in their own right, to support the recovery in the CEECs, and to enhance the credibility of the EU's commitment to the eventual accession of the CEECs. The third objective was to establish closer institutional links between the CEECs and the EU. This built on Andriessen's (1991a) still vague ideas of 'affiliate membership' for the CEECs in a 'European Political Area' (EPA).

All three objectives were highly controversial within both the Commission and the Council. The debate about the negotiation directives demonstrated the widespread reservations against even discussing the question of enlargement before the ratification of EMU and Political Union. Trade concessions seemed equally hard to obtain in the adverse economic climate of 1992/93. Finally, when Andriessen first floated the idea of affiliate membership and an EPA, he received severe criticism from within the Commission for courting the dangers of partial membership, which threatened the integrity of the EU's institutional framework.

Criticism of the EAs

The advocates of policy change in the Commission were empowered through the widespread criticism of the EAs. The academic community criticised the absence of an explicit EU commitment to eventual CEEC membership and of a constructive debate on the adaptation of its integration model, which denied the CEECs a long-term political perspective (see e.g. Kramer 1993; Reinicke 1992; Smith and Wallace 1994; Wallace 1991). Trade economists condemned the restrictiveness of the EAs' trade provisions (see e.g. Baldwin et al. 1992; Flemming and Rollo 1992; Hindley 1993; Messerlin 1993; Ostry 1993; Rollo and Smith 1993; Winters 1992). First, the restrictions on market access and the scope for further restrictions through the use of trade defence instruments severely limited the ability of CEECs to use their export potential. Second, the EAs' provisions for contingency protection and the absence of a clear membership perspective would deter much needed foreign direct investment. Third, the small share of CEEC exports hardly justified the EU's defensive attitude, even taking into account potential growth and effects on specific EU regions. Finally, the trade restrictions in the EAs were detrimental to aggregate welfare in the EU itself. Crucially, the academic debate criticised not simply the lack of *effectiveness* of EU policy, but also included a strong normative element, suggesting that more generous support for the CEECs was an objective in its own right and *appropriate* for EU policy.

A second source of pressure for policy change was continued criticism from CEEC policy-makers (see e.g. Saryusz-Wolski 1994; Suchocka 1992; Visegrád 1992, 1993). DG I actively encouraged the two Visegrád memoranda, which formulated their criticism in rather careful language and focused on concrete, pragmatic steps, making them less vulnerable to dismissal as theatrical and unrealistic demands. Issued before the Edinburgh and Copenhagen European Councils respectively, they were important both for their timing and as reflecting a coordinated response from the associated CEECs.

Developments in trade relations between the EU and the CEECs and in the economic and political situation in central and eastern Europe added further weight to the arguments of the policy advocates. After 1992, the scale and difficulties of the transformation processes were more fully appreciated, while indications of decreasing public support for reforms became manifest. Signs of rising tensions within and among the CEECs – e.g. the split of Czechoslovakia, the dispute between Slovakia and Hungary over the Danube dam project, or the war in Bosnia – raised concerns about political stability in the region. These developments contrasted sharply with a growing perception that the EAs benefited primarily the EU. The CEECs ran a trade deficit with the EU, which was not unexpected, as the transition economies needed to import investment goods, but the negative trade balance affected the sensitive sectors as well. Moreover, the first instances of the EU's use of trade defence instruments against the CEECs were widely interpreted as a sign of its unwillingness to implement the agreements in a generous spirit.[28]

The policy advocates' ability to influence policy was facilitated by changes in the constellation of key actors in the EU's policy towards the CEECs. The Council presidency rotated to governments that supported policy initiatives to boost eastern enlargement: the UK in the second half of 1992 and Denmark in the first half of 1993. Second, the policy advocates' access to the policy process at the level of the commissioners improved in the second Delors Commission. After Andriessen left the Commission at the end of 1992, the external relations portfolio was divided. DG I was now responsible for external economic relations and the newly created DG IA for external political relations and CFSP. Sir Leon Brittan, previously Commissioner for competition policy, obtained responsibility for DG I. He was a committed advocate of enlargement and market access for the CEECs; and was now in a position to influence policy much more directly. In addition, he carried greater political weight inside the Commission than his predecessor. Hans van den Broek, the former Dutch foreign minister, obtained charge of DG IA. Initially, the two commissioners were involved in turf disputes, but after these had been patched up, van den Broek's appointment strengthened the voices calling for an active enlargement policy among the commissioners.

Finally, changes in member state governments created a more favourable environment for the policy advocates. The French government perceived the need for a more positive approach to rectify the impression that France was a main obstacle to a more accommodating policy.[29] Similarly, the Spanish government felt that its tough stance on trade issues was misinterpreted as general hostility to an eventual eastern enlargement.[30] Prime Minister Felipe Gonzáles decided to give the foreign ministry more leeway to support the Commission's proposals, especially after a personal visit by the Polish Prime Minister Hanna Suchocka.

Strategy of the policy advocates

The first task for the policy advocates around DG I was to gain the Commission's support for their strategy. Notably Delors was deeply concerned that the endorsement of eventual CEEC membership, even if still a long time off, might start a deeply divisive debate among the member states that would undermine ongoing efforts at further integration. The Commission's report on enlargement for the Lisbon European Council in June 1992 reflected these differences inside the Commission. The report suggested that accession negotiations with the European Free Trade

Association (EFTA) applicants might start after the ratification of the Maastricht Treaty on European Union (TEU) and agreement on the Delors-2 budgetary package. It indicated that relations with the CEECs might develop beyond the EAs, but did not outline an agreed form of such a 'new partnership' (see also Michalski and Wallace 1992: 63). However, the report very explicitly articulated the EU's responsibility towards the CEECs and the need to act accordingly:

> The integration of [the] new democracies into the European family presents a historic opportunity. In the past, enlargement of the Community took place in a divided continent; in future, it can contribute to the unification of the whole of Europe. The Community has never been a closed club, and cannot now refuse the historic challenge to assume its continental responsibilities and contribute to the development of a political and economic order for the whole of Europe. (Commission 1992a: 158)

> Enlargement is a challenge which the Community cannot refuse. The other countries of Europe are looking to us for guarantees of stability, peace and prosperity, and for the opportunity to play their part with us in the integration of Europe. For the new democracies, Europe remains a powerful idea, signifying the fundamental values and aspirations which their peoples kept alive during long years of oppression. To consolidate their new-found liberty, and stabilise their development, is not only in their interests, but ours. (1992a: 167)

The UK presidency attempted to use the EPC framework, in the context of the political dialogue, to add momentum to the development of policy. In October 1992, it organised two high-level meetings, one between EU foreign ministers and their CEEC counterparts and one at the levels of the heads of state with the Commission and the presidency. The hope was that a joint document adopted in this high-level format could give impetus to the membership objective and further trade concessions.[31] The joint statement was drafted in DG I. The UK presidency fought hard in the Council to preserve its main thrust against the majority of member states that were concerned about further trade concessions and raising the issue of CEEC membership while uncertainty still surrounded the ratification of the TEU after its rejection in the Danish referendum. The UK presidency intended to include a statement that the Edinburgh European Council would consider the question of membership, but did not find sufficient support. In the end, the joint declaration of the ministerial meeting went some way towards both recognising the CEECs' eventual accession as a shared objective and towards agreement in the EU on the need for further trade concessions, but its language was much more cautious than the advocates of enlargement had hoped for.

> [The foreign ministers of the EU and of the Visegrád countries] recognise that this process serves their *common objective* of a gradual integration of the Visegrad countries into the Community. [...] It was accepted that the improvement of

> access to the Community's market is one of the most important means to
> strengthen the economic development and to reinforce the market economy in
> the Visegrad countries.[32] (Council 1992a: 1, 3; emphasis added)

However cautious, this commitment provided sufficient political backing for
the policy advocates to press inside the Commission for the adoption of a
document, on which they had been working since the signing of the EAs, to
be presented to the Edinburgh European Council (Commission 1992c). The
document contained embryonicly the proposals that were eventually adopted
at the Copenhagen European Council: the endorsement of the CEECs'
membership objective as *common* goal; initiatives for further trade liberalisation; financial assistance for infrastructure investment; and structured
institutional relations (the EPA). In view of the strong normative language of
the Commission's Lisbon report, it was difficult for the commissioners to
deny the legitimacy of the initiative. Still, only a vote in the *college*, in which
even Delors was outvoted, secured its approval. Delors insisted, however, on
the inclusion of additional qualitative criteria for CEEC membership: the
stability of the democratic institutions in the CEECs and the capacity of the
EU to absorb new members without endangering the momentum of
European integration.[33]

The Edinburgh European Council was too distracted with other business
to discuss the Commission report in detail, but stated that at its next meeting,
it would 'reach decisions on the various components of the Commission's
report *in order to prepare the associate countries for accession to the Union*'
(Council 1992b: 37, emphasis added). The agreement on the Delors-2 budgetary package and the solution of the problem caused by the 'no' to the TEU
in Denmark enabled the heads of state and foreign ministers to move
cautiously towards endorsing the CEECs' accession perspective. While this
agreement left open the question of trade concessions, or the possible shape
of an EPA, this statement, despite its vague nature, provided the necessary
authority – or 'shadow of hierarchy' – for the policy advocates to develop
more concrete proposals for the Copenhagen European Council.

Although Andriessen left the Commission at the end of 1992, there was
continuity and even a strengthening of the policy advocates in the second
Delors Commission of 1993. The member of the Andriessen *cabinet* in charge
of external relations entered the van den Broek *cabinet* and continued work
on the idea of an EPA. The Brittan *cabinet* worked closely with the CEEC unit
in DG I (now DG I-L) to secure trade concessions. The support of the Danish
presidency facilitated their influence in the Council. Foreign minister
Elleman-Jensen (1992: 9), as Council president, explicitly related their initiative to the EU's collective self-image and collective interest:

> [The CEECs'] fragile democracies may not be sufficiently firmly grounded to
> resist the threat of instability posed by the sudden unleashing of forces that were
> suppressed under Communist rule. ... We are faced with the opportunities of a

> lifetime that we simply cannot afford to miss, and responsibilities to the peoples
> of Europe and their future generations that oblige us to act and to do so now.

The Council's debate on a further Commission communication, which set out more concrete proposals (Commission 1993a), revealed that none of the governments would object to endorsing the eventual accession of the CEECs as a common objective. The most reluctant governments were not France or Spain, but primarily the Benelux countries.[34] A careful formulation of the qualitative criteria for membership provided the necessary safeguards for the more hesitant member governments. To deny the membership objective as such would have been incompatible with their professed image of the EU. As the qualitative membership criteria stated the legitimate potential objections to their eventual accession, it left no legitimate justifications to oppose the general principle of enlargement.

The agreement on the package of trade concessions resulted from a change of strategy by the Brittan *cabinet* and the Danish presidency.[35] It drew on the experience of the UK presidency's failed attempt to obtain product-specific concessions on a case-by-case basis, which had been blocked by sectoral concerns within the Commission or at least from one member state. Instead, the Brittan *cabinet* and the Danish presidency convinced the foreign ministers to put a 'high level group' of foreign ministry officials in charge of obtaining comprehensive concessions, horizontally across the range of sectors.

The Commission still had to scale down its proposals.[36] The acceleration of trade liberalisation remained more modest. The ambitious proposal of an EPA changed both in substance and name, to a 'structured relationship with the institutions of the EU', consisting of regular multilateral contacts between EU and CEEC officials in most areas of EU policy. These contacts would only serve for consultation, not joint decision-making; and would not allow CEEC representatives to participate directly in meetings of the various Council formations. Otherwise, the Council endorsed the vast majority of the Commission proposals (see Box 4.5). The Copenhagen European Council (Council 1993: 5) thus declared that

> the associated countries in Central and Eastern Europe that so desire shall
> become members of the European Union. Accession will take place as soon as an
> associated country is able to assume the obligations of membership by satisfying
> the economic and political conditions required. ... The Union's capacity to
> absorb new members, while maintaining the momentum of European integra-
> tion, is also an important consideration in the general interest of both the Union
> and the candidate countries.

Box 4.5 Decisions of the Copenhagen European Council

Endorsement of the CEECs' eventual membership

Conditions for the CEECs:

Stable institutions (guarantee of democracy, rule of law, human rights, minority rights);

Functioning market economy;

Capacity to cope with competitive pressures inside the EU;

Ability to adopt the *acquis*; acceptance of the aims of political, economic and monetary union.

Condition for the EU:

Capacity to absorb new members without endangering the momentum of EU integration.

Acceleration of market access

More rapid (than originally envisaged in the EAs) opening of EU markets across products, including (although to a more limited degree) the sensitive sectors.

Structured relationship with the EU

Reinforced multilateral Political Dialogue; extension of multilateral ministerial meetings to most EU policy areas.

Reorientation of PHARE assistance

Up to 15% of budget available for infrastructure projects.

In sum, the continued advocacy of the team inside the Commission was key in bringing about the acknowledgement of an eventual accession of the CEECs as a shared objective, as well as an improvement of the substance of the EAs. The policy change was facilitated by certain changes in the external environment, such as an increasing perception of political fragility in the CEECs, and some change in the constellation of actors in the member states. However, these factors alone seem insufficient to explain the policy change. The apparent vulnerability of EU policy-makers to the broadly based criticism of the EAs among academics, journalists and the CEECs allowed the policy advocates to shift the perspective of EU policy beyond the EAs towards an accession perspective. Rather than presenting the EAs as a take-it-or-leave-it offer, EU policy-makers responded to the criticism of their apparent failure to act in accordance with their collective self-image. Such sensitivity was particularly apparent in the case of Spanish and French foreign policy-makers, who were keen to rectify the negative perception of their attitudes towards the CEECs. The collective self-image limited the realm of acceptable policy options. Despite some underlying reservations, none of the commissioners, foreign ministers, or heads of state/government wanted to oppose the endorsement of the CEECs' eventual accession as a shared objective. The resulting agreement also allowed the policy advocates to achieve a greater accommodation of the CEECs' preferences in substantive policy. They obtained approval from the macro-policy-makers in the Council for a strategic move to circumvent sectoral policy-makers by putting a high-level group in charge of negotiating the economic package, although it was clear that this would imply substantive concessions.

Notes

1 For simplicity, this book refers throughout to the 'EU', although in certain instances the term 'EC' would be correct, either historically (i.e. prior to the entry into force of the Treaty on European Union in November 1993) or legally (i.e. activities carried out in the 'Community' pillar, such as trade policy).
2 Interview, German Chancellor's Office, 21.11.95.
3 Interviews, Commission DG I, Brussels, 24.10.95; Commission DG I, 23.10.95.
4 Interview, Commission DG I, Brussels, 24.10.95.
5 Interview, Commissioner's *cabinet*, Brussels, 15.12.95.
6 Interview, Commission DG I, 23.10.95.
7 Interview, Commission DG I, 23.10.95.
8 Interview, Commission DG I, 23.10.95.
9 The signing of the final agreements required unanimity in the Council and ratification by national parliaments, because the provisions on political dialogue and cultural cooperation concerned member state competences. Qualified Majority Voting (QMV) applies in principle to the trade-related decisions, but in practice the member states seek consensual decisions. In the EA negotiations, QMV was never used (Interviews, Commission DG I, 23.10.95; UK Permanent Representation, 09.07.93; German Ministry of Economics, 19.12.95).
10 Interview, Commission DG I, 27.10.95.
11 Interview, Commission DG I, 23.10.95.
12 Interview, Commission DG I, 27.10.95.
13 Interviews, Commission DG I, 27.10.95; Commission DG I, 23.10.95; Commission DG I, 26.10.95; UK Permanent Representation, 09.07.93.
14 Interview, Commission DG I, 27.10.95.
15 Interview, German Foreign Office, 15.12.95.
16 Interview, Commission DG I, 23.10.95.
17 Interviews, German Foreign Office, 15.12.95; German Ministry of Economics, 19.12.95.
18 Interview, German Chancellor's Office, 21.11.95.
19 Interviews, German Foreign Office, 15.12.95; Commission DG I, 26.10.95; Commission DG I, 23.10.95.
20 Interviews, French SGCI, 02.07.96; French Foreign Ministry, 03.07.96.
21 Interviews, Spanish Foreign Ministry, 18.06.96; Spanish Permanent Representation, 11.06.96; Spanish Foreign Ministry, 21.06.96.
22 Interviews, Commission DG I, 23.10.95; Commission DG I, 26.10.95; Commission DG I, 27.10.95; UK Permanent Representation, 09.07.93; German Ministry of Economics, 19.12.95.

23 Interview, Commission DG I, 26.10.95.

24 Interview, Dutch Permanent Representation, 31.01.95.

25 Interview, Commission DG I, 26.10.95.

26 Interview, Commission DG I, 26.10.95.

27 Interview, Commission DG I, 24.10.95.

28 After the entry into force of the Interim Agreements, the EU used trade defence instruments, e.g. against pig-iron and ferro-silicon imports from Poland; seamless steel and iron tubes from Poland, Czechoslovakia and Hungary; and urea ammonium nitrate from Bulgaria and Poland. Among the most publicised restrictions was the EU's temporary ban of live animal and dairy imports in April 1993 (*Euro-east*, 23.04.1993: 26).

29 Interviews, French Foreign Ministry, 10.07.96; French Foreign Ministry, 03.07.96.

30 Interviews, Spanish Foreign Ministry, 21.06.96; Spanish Foreign Ministry, 18.06.96.

31 Interview, UK Permanent Representation, 09.07.93.

32 'ont reconnu que ce processus sert leur objectif commun d'intégration progressive des pays de Visegrad dans la Communauté. ... Il a été reconnu que l'amélioration de l'accès aux marchés communautaires constituait l'un des moyens les plus importants pour accentuer le développement économique et renforcer le système d'économie de marché des pays de Visegrad.'

33 Interview, Commissioner's *cabinet*, 15.12.95.

34 Interview, UK Permanent Representation, 09.07.93.

35 Interview, UK Permanent Representation, 09.07.93.

36 Interviews, Commission DG I, 24.10.95; UK Permanent Representation, 09.07.93.

5

Following the path to eastern enlargement: from the general principle of membership to accession

This chapter examines how the endorsement of the CEECs' membership perspective at the Copenhagen European Council was put into practice. With the benefit of hindsight, the importance of the Copenhagen declaration cannot be overstated. While EU policy-makers' earlier discourse had merely implied that enlargement was appropriate, Copenhagen turned the discourse into a firmly articulated commitment to the CEECs' eventual accession. This commitment changed the perspective of policy; it moved EU policy on the path to eastern enlargement that proved irreversible. Indeed, most EU documents (and academic writing) at later stages of the enlargement policy identify Copenhagen as the starting point of the enlargement process and as a firm promise made to the CEECs.

Yet at the time, assessments were much more ambivalent. The Copenhagen declaration might have been merely cheap rhetoric. It did not involve any legally enforceable commitment. The qualitative formulation of the conditions – in particular that the EU itself had to be ready, which was entirely beyond the CEECs' control – could provide reluctant EU policy-makers with ample scope to stall the enlargement process. Several CEEC governments expressed scepticism along these lines. Conversely, many EU actors who were hesitant about enlargement did not perceive Copenhagen as a dramatic turning point in the process.[1] In part such assessments might stem from their reluctance to admit any opposition to enlargement. However, it also reflected the impression that the endorsement of the general principle of enlargement would satisfy its proponents for the foreseeable future and remove enlargement from the agenda.

This chapter shows that – just as the EU's role-identity enabled the agreement on the explicit commitment – the explicit commitment further narrowed the range of legitimate options. The formal endorsement of the CEECs' membership perspective, albeit legally non-binding, enabled the policy advocates to forge an agreement on a concrete strategy[3] to prepare the CEECs for accession, which put the general principle into practice and kept EU policy on the path to enlargement on which they had set it.

The first part of this chapter examines how this general objective was put on a concrete footing through the pre-accession strategy at the Essen European Council in December 1994 and the agreement on a rough road map for enlargement-related decisions at the Madrid European Council in December 1995. By the end of 1995, EU policy had shifted firmly onto an irreversible path to enlargement. In the second part of this chapter I sketch subsequent developments, including the EU's own enlargement preparation and the accession negotiations, culminating in the accession of the first eight CEECs in 2004.

From association to an enlargement policy

Some member states' governments had expected their endorsement of the accession perspective to close the debate for the foreseeable future. However, the development of EU policy did not stall after Copenhagen. The general principle of enlargement did not remain at the abstract level; it was translated into a concrete policy to prepare future members for accession – a 'pre-accession' policy. This section analyses the process leading to the adoption of the 'pre-accession strategy' at the Essen European Council in December 1994. A key factor in this process was the entrepreneurship of the policy advocates in the Commission and their very close cooperation with the German Council presidency.

The policy advocates in the Commission regarded the endorsement of the membership perspective an important success that would facilitate a more generous accommodation of the interests of the CEECs' in the implementation of the EAs. However, the team around the Brittan *cabinet* and DG I feared that if the European Council declaration was not followed up with some very concrete activities, the issue would lose momentum and drop from the immediate agenda. They therefore intended to build on the explicit commitment to CEEC membership to argue for a strategy that would map the way from the general principle to actual accession.[2] The challenge was both to devise the road map and to obtain the support of the Commission and the Council.

Devising a pre-accession strategy

The policy advocates believed that the core of a pre-accession strategy had to be economic, since this was the central part of membership.[3] To devise an adequate strategy, they cooperated closely with DG II (economic and financial affairs), academic trade economists and agricultural experts. One idea was to create a multilateral free trade area or a customs union to overcome the 'hub and spoke' mechanism created by the bilateral EAs (see e.g. Baldwin 1994: 208–15). A more ambitious proposal was a formal regime for regulatory alignment, along the lines of the European Economic Area (EEA) (see Baldwin 1994: 218–23; Peers 1995). However, the policy advocates feared that such formal regimes might create an institutionalised 'waiting room' that would delay full membership. Furthermore, the EEA would not allow the CEECs sufficient flexibility to take account of their specific economic context (see also Holmes and Smith 1997; Phinnemore 1999; Smith 1995; Smith et al. 1996). Nonetheless, as a result of the consultations, the policy advocates became convinced that the core of the CEECs' accession preparation should be their alignment with EU competition and state aids policy, and with the internal market more broadly, as long as the CEECs were able to set their own priorities.[4]

Alignment with EU competition and state aids policies could entail immediate benefits for the CEECs, irrespective of accession. It could contribute to the broader process of economic restructuring and simultane-ously reduce the threat of EU anti-dumping action. Moreover, DG I thought that regulatory alignment of the CEECs with the internal market was the most promising way to speed up the accession process. Doubts about the CEECs' ability to apply the EU's *acquis communautaire* presented the most serious obstacle on the CEEC side to membership. The CEECs should therefore start early with this part of their accession preparations. Furthermore, a focus on regulatory alignment as the core of a pre-accession strategy would minimise opposition inside the EU. Unilateral regulatory alignment of the CEECs entailed no costs to the EU and could distract from the more controversial issues of enlargement, such as the implications for the EU budget or the CAP. At the same time, a pre-accession strategy based on regulatory alignment could create an irreversible momentum for enlargement. As the internal market presented the economic core of EU membership, there would be no legitimate grounds for refusing full membership once the CEECs had created the conditions to apply the rules of the internal market.

Further consultations with DG XV (internal market) produced the idea to organise the alignment of the CEECs with the internal market around a Commission White Paper. This White Paper would identify and explain the key internal market legislation and suggest a logical sequencing for adopting these measures in the different areas. As economic flanking measures, the DG I team envisaged further concessions in agricultural trade and infrastructure projects in the framework of Trans-European Networks (TENs).[5] Brittan persuaded van den Broek to support this pre-accession strategy and the two commissioners agreed a division of labour. Brittan's *cabinet* and DG I devel-oped the economic part of the strategy. Van den Broek's *cabinet* and DG IA worked on proposals to make the institutionalised contacts between EU and CEEC policy-makers under the 'structured relationship' more operational.[6]

Forging support for the pre-accession strategy

The policy advocates anticipated opposition both from inside the Commission and in the Council. They therefore identified the German Council presidency in the second half of 1994 as a key ally. The German government was initially sceptical about a major policy initiative that would distract attention from domestic politics, as it faced in 1994 a total of 14 elections at the national, regional and local levels. However, it became increasingly enthusiastic about the idea of a pre-accession strategy. From spring 1994, the Commission team had almost weekly consultations with the German cabinet in Bonn to discuss their strategy.[7] This close cooperation allowed the initiative to gather momentum and eventually to find approval in the Council.

Inside the Commission, Delors and his *cabinet* were the main opponents of a pre-accession strategy. Delors felt that for the time being, the EU had done quite enough for the CEECs; the emphasis should be on consolidation, rather than further initiatives. He feared that if policy evolved too fast, it would divide the member states, especially while discussions on the next stages of integration, such as EMU or the EFTA enlargement, were still incomplete. Delors (1994: 5) warned:

> It is not sufficient ... to send out increasingly encouraging messages to the Visegrad countries. We have to know where we are going. The Commission will engage in a self-analysis, I would almost say a self-criticism, of its economic policies ... But we will also think about what this Greater Europe could be. [...] These considerations should lead us to a broader vision, or visions; scenarios that will allow us to place the next enlargement into a perspective. Because in fact this perspective is currently not clear. [...] What we are missing the most in Europe today is intellectual innovation and reflection, not action. In fact, there is plenty of action and it is often rampant.[8]

Delors intended this 'reflection meeting' in March 1994 (*Agence Europe*, 25.03.94: 5) to put further developments essentially on hold.[9] However, Brittan and van den Broek thwarted his plans, as their preparatory work had gained them the support of the majority of the commissioners. The policy advocates prompted the German government to press at the Corfu European Council in June 1994 for a statement in the presidency conclusions that asked 'the Presidency and the Commission to report to it for its next meeting ... on the strategy to be followed with a view to preparing for accession' (Council 1994b: 19). This explicit mandate gave the policy advocates an important advantage in the Commission's internal debate. Their preparatory work allowed them to table rapidly a broad outline for a pre-accession strategy and to gain approval at the level of the commissioners. The outline envisaged four main areas: an improvement of the 'structured relationship', regulatory alignment with the single market, enhanced trade opportunities, and a further shift of financial assistance towards investment projects (Commission 1994a).

However, the internal negotiations on a concrete, sector-specific follow-up document for the Council revealed persisting disagreement, in particular about the flanking measures. As a result, the Commission's final proposal (Commission 1994b) was much more cautious on the use of trade defence measures, elimination of subsidies for agricultural exports to CEECs, full cumulation of rules of origin, and financial transfers.

The Council further eroded the Commission's proposal. Notably the concessions on agricultural trade were further reduced, primarily upon insistence of the German Minister of Agriculture.[10] For the 'structured relationship', the Commission had to drop plans for contacts at the level of experts to prepare for ministerial meetings between EU and CEEC policy-makers in the different policy areas. The great majority of member state governments feared that this might undermine the integrity of the EU decision-making process and lead to some form of membership through the back door. However, particularly the idea of a White Paper (WP) remained intact and the Essen European Council formally endorsed the pre-accession strategy (Council 1994d).

The small amount of controversy around the WP proposal can be explained by the ambiguity of the regulatory alignment process, and its perception as a technical exercise with little political significance. Regulatory alignment of the CEECs did not involve any costs for the member states, but entailed advantages for EU companies exporting and investing in the CEECs. Furthermore, rather than creating momentum for enlargement, regulatory alignment could provide a safeguard against politically motivated early accessions, by making the regulatory accession requirements more explicit. The French government, for example, emphasised the need for a thorough preparation to merit membership.[11] The WP thus seemed to serve the interests of various actors on the EU side, who all claimed 'parenthood' of the idea, including the French SGCI and the German economics ministry.[12] The WP's technical nature aroused little suspicion and there was no debate about its specific content at this stage.

The close cooperation between the policy advocates in the Commission and the German presidency, and the presidency's mix of skill and heavy-handedness, eased the proposals through the Council. Already at the start of the German Presidency, the Council largely endorsed the Commission's general approach. However, on many details of policy, this support was fragile. Informal meetings in September began to move the debate forward, such as a Franco-German agreement to endorse the call for the Commission to draw up a WP on regulatory alignment (*Financial Times*, 21.09.94: 2). The presidency devised a tight timetable of Council sessions, each devoted to individual aspects of the proposed pre-accession strategy. The Commission team drafted informal presidency papers that formed the basis of discussion.[13] The presidency emphasised that these informal papers required no explicit decisions, but then announced shortly before the European Council meeting that they should be adopted as Council papers. This move cut out the experts in the Council working group and forced COREPER to discuss the details of the proposals.[14] A COREPER *restreint* meeting (only two persons per delegation), which further limited access to the policy process, adopted the Commission's proposals and the GAC endorsed them formally (see Box 5.1).

Despite the agreement on the Commission's pre-accession strategy, some resentment remained among several member states' representatives who felt that they had been 'steamrollered';[15] and in the Commission; Delors felt that the policy advocates' 'irresponsible activism' amounted to 'treachery'.[16] Nonetheless, from acknowledging the membership perspective of the CEECs as a shared goal, the European Council had now made a commitment to actively support the accession preparations of the CEECs. The European Council declared that 'this strategy reemphasises the commitment of the Union to the accession of the associated countries while recognising the scale of the effort required for the necessary adjustments to developing Union policies' (Council 1994d: 25).

Box 5.1 The pre-accession strategy

Structured relationship: extension of the multilateral contacts at the ministerial level to the first and third pillar, connected to corresponding Council, on annual basis (bi-annual for GAC and JHA Council); schedule for joint meetings agreed at the beginning of each year between the two presidencies, rather than previous *ad hoc* meetings.

Preparation of the CEECs for integration into the internal market:
EU action:
Identification of key *acquis* essential for the creation and maintenance of
    the internal market in each sector;
Suggestions for sequencing of legal approximation through identification
    of priority measures to be tackled first (but not priorities *between*
    sectors);
Specification of administrative and organisational structures for effective
    implementation and enforcement;
Adaptation of PHARE assistance to pre-accession alignment;
Establishment of TAEIX (Technical Assistance Information Exchange
    Office): database on alignment with internal market; clearing-house to
    match requests for assistance with expertise available in Commission,
    member states, and private bodies ('twinning');
Regular monitoring of implementation and recommendations for further
    progress.
CEEC action:
Phased adoption of EU legislation and regulatory systems, standards, and
    certification methods;

Establishment of national work programmes to identify priorities and timetables for alignment.

Supporting policies: e.g. development of infrastructure; cooperation in TENs; intra-regional cooperation; cooperation in culture, education, and training (PHARE funding).

Sketching the agenda for eastern enlargement

Chapter 7 elaborates in detail on the Commission's White Paper on the regulatory alignment of the CEECs (Commission 1995a, 1995b), which the Cannes European Council in June 1995 adopted without much discussion, due to its perceived technical nature. The subsequent developments in the EU's policy towards the CEECs reflect the fact that the European Council declarations at Copenhagen and Essen had indeed shifted policy irreversibly to an enlargement policy. The declaration of the Madrid European Council in December 1995 set out a timetable – albeit a rough and indicative one – for making enlargement a reality, both with regard to the start of accession negotiations and with sketching the tasks ahead with regard to the reforms required from the EU. The Madrid European Council thus declared:

> Enlargement is both a political necessity and a historic opportunity for Europe. [...] Following the conclusion of the Intergovernmental Conference and in the light of its outcome and of all the opinions and reports from the Commission ..., the Council will, at the earliest opportunity, take the necessary decisions for launching the accession negotiations. The European Council hopes that the preliminary stages of negotiations will coincide with the start of negotiations with Cyprus and Malta. (Council 1995d: 23)

In the evolution of policy from the endorsement of the WP to the Madrid European Council, the initiative shifted from the Commission to the member states. In 1995, the Commission's new president, Jacques Santer, reallocated the external relations portfolios along geographical lines. Van den Broek and DG IA obtained responsibility for policy towards the CEECs. Brittan's *cabinet* and DG I no longer had a direct role in the policy process. Some of these officials moved on to new jobs, partly because they thought that the new constellation would limit their ability to shape policy, and partly because they believed that the key decisions had been taken to put enlargement firmly on track.[17] The breaking up of the successful group of policy advocates changed both the style of Commission policy and its leadership ambitions in eastern enlargement.

At the same time, the member states, in particular the German government, played a much more active role. The German government lobbied among the other governments to declare at the Madrid European Council in December 1995 an indicative date for the start of accession negotiations, as well as a target date of 2000 for completing them.[18] Moreover, Chancellor Kohl favoured – in contrast to the foreign ministry – a clear commitment to open accession negotiations initially with Poland, Hungary, and the Czech Republic.[19] In the Council, none of the other governments objected to setting an indicative date, but the suggestion to identify already a particular group of candidates was highly controversial. The Spanish presidency brokered a compromise: the European Council would set an indicative date for accession negotiations to start, but it would leave the assessment on whether to differentiate among the CEEC candidates to the Commission's opinions.[20]

The European Council thus declared that it hoped to open accession negotiations with the CEECs alongside Cyprus and Malta, i.e. six months after the end of the IGC scheduled to start in July 1996. In addition, the Commission should present after the conclusion of the IGC certain key documents to take the enlargement process forward: its opinions (*avis*) on the candidates, which would recommend with whom to start negotiations, as well as a 'composite paper' on enlargement, containing an evaluation of the effects of enlargement on the EU's policies (particularly agriculture and the structural policies) and proposals for the EU budget's 'financial perspective' from 2000 to 2006.

The agreement on the indicative timetable for starting accession negotiations was facilitated by an earlier agreement, in April 1995, in response to the Greek government's insistence on a date for negotiations with Cyprus in return for endorsing the customs union with Turkey.[21] The indicative date for the Mediterranean states provided a focal point for those pressing for a date for the CEECs. Crucially, the agreement on this indicative date rested on the precondition that the impending IGC to start in 1996 would need to create the necessary institutional conditions to ensure the effective functioning of the EU after enlargement. This formula reassured the reluctant member states, but at the same time made it difficult for them to object to such a conditional date for accession negotiations. Insufficient institutional reform was a legitimate objection to taking enlargement further, but once accession was made conditional on successful reform, it was difficult to justify opposition.

Thus, by the end of 1995, the perspective of policy had shifted from association and pre-accession to an eastern enlargement policy, albeit conditional on successful institutional reform. However, although the 1996/97 IGC failed to agree on the key issues of institutional reform, the member states nonetheless agreed to conclude the IGC in June 1997, which enabled the Commission to publish the documents that the Madrid European Council had requested and thus for the enlargement process to go ahead. The continuation of the enlargement process, despite the failure to meet an agreed precondition, is a further indication that the EU's commitment in principle developed its own dynamism, as the EU's credibility to deliver on its commitment was on the line.

The conclusion of the 1996/97 IGC allowed the Commission to publish the collection of documents on enlargement, which it entitled 'Agenda 2000' (Commission 1997a, 1997b). Following Agenda 2000, the EU embarked on separate tracks with regard to the main issues of the enlargement process. The key decisions with regard to the CEECs concerned the selection of candidates for accession negotiations. Following the decision of the Luxembourg European Council in December 1997, the first five CEECs started accession negotiations in March 1998, joined by the others in 2000. Negotiations with eight CEECs concluded in December 2002. In parallel, the EU embarked on internal reforms to prepare itself for enlargement. The question of policy reforms was set in the context of an agreement on the financial perspective for 2000 to 2006. The first attempts at institutional reforms started during the 1996/97 IGC, preceding Agenda 2000, and continued at a specially convened IGC in 2000.

Crucially, to start accession negotiations prior to an agreement on internal reforms sent out a clear signal that the EU was committed to enlargement. This commitment obliged the EU to ensure that enlargement did not break down due to its failure to do its homework and by extension made it unacceptable for individual member states to cause such failure.

Preparing the EU for enlargement

Reform of institutions and decision-making

The initial reason for convening an IGC in 1996 was a commitment in the TEU to review the workings of the pillar structure. However, the link with institutional reforms to prepare the EU for enlargement was made early, given the repeated emphasis at successive European Councils on the need to strengthen the institutional capacity to handle enlargement. Both the 'Reflection Group' of member state representatives charged with preparing for the IGC, and the Commission presented enlargement as a main rationale for the IGC (see e.g. Sedelmeier 2000b). The key issues for institutional reform that the IGC identified with a view on enlargement centred on the representation of the member states in EU institutions, Council decision-making, and possible changes to the integration model (see also Phinnemore 2004).

The representation of member states in the Council of Ministers concerned the weighting of votes of individual member states in qualified majority voting (QMV) that accompanied calls for an extension of QMV. The original formula of the founding treaties was deliberately generous to the smaller member states and did not tie weighted votes directly to member states' population. Since this formula had been simply extended in subsequent enlargements, the larger member states had become increasingly critical of the apparent overrepresentation of small member states and pushed for a re-weighting, given the prospect of the accession of a further wave of small members (see e.g. Edwards 1998, Kerremans 1998). Questions of efficiency and representation also concerned the debate about limiting the number of Commissioners and MEPs (see e.g. Dinan 1998), which became caught up in the debate about a re-weighting of votes in the Council.

The debate about changes to the traditional integration model was based on an assumption that in a more heterogeneous EU, on an increasing number of issues not all member states would be engaged in the same degree of integration. The IGC tried to find a formula for such 'flexible integration', which would allow smaller groups of member states to cooperate more closely on some issues (see e.g. Stubb 1997; Wallace and Wallace 1995).

Both the 'Reflection Group' and the Commission emphasised the importance of a successful conclusion of the IGC. The Reflection Group referred to enlargement as 'both a moral imperative and a new opportunity for Europe' (Council 1995e: 3)[22] and the Commission called on the IGC to 'be the occasion ... to make clear that Europe, far from being an aggregate of selfinterest, is the sum of the wealth of this continent' (Commission 1996). Yet despite these attempts to use enlargement as a lever for reform, the Amsterdam Treaty failed to solve the crucial questions.

This failure is probably not all that surprising, given the timing of the IGC, which did not make it a credible deadline for agreeing institutional reforms and thus did not force the negotiators to make difficult compromises. More surprising might appear that despite the insufficient institutional reforms, the member states agreed to conclude the IGC nonetheless. The member states accepted that these issues would remain unresolved for the time being and agreed to revisit them at a further IGC. Despite failing to meet the Madrid European Council's precondition, they let the enlargement process go ahead by allowing the Commission to present its opinions on the candidates and to start accession negotiations with those CEECs deemed to be ready.

The Belgian, French, and Italian governments recorded in the minutes of the Amsterdam European Council their insistence that enlargement could not take place without prior settlement of institutional reform. At the same time, the conclusion of the IGC underlined that despite fears that some member states might abuse the fourth Copenhagen criterion in order to derail enlargement, all member states accepted that it was the EU's duty to keep its own homework in order to keep its side of the commitment.

The Cologne European Council in June 1999 agreed that the remaining issues would be solved at a short IGC during 2000. The negotiations at the 2000 IGC were no less difficult than at the 1996/97 IGC. If anything, they were complicated by the negotiation strategy of the French presidency. Rather than facilitating an overall compromise by making same concessions of its own, it unabashedly promoted its narrow self-interest. Increasingly bitter arguments brought the Nice European Council in December 2000 to the brink of failure, as some smaller member states – notably Belgium and

Portugal – considered walking out. Yet in the end, the IGC agreed on institutional reform (see Box 5.2 and for more detail, Phinnemore 2004). All member states were conscious that the credibility of their commitment to enlargement hinged on their ability to deliver an agreement and were determined to conclude the negotiations successfully. The CEECs welcomed the agreement with much relief, notwithstanding some criticism, especially from the Hungarian and Czech governments, of the inequitable allocation of seats in the EP (which they subsequently redressed in accession negotiations).

Box 5.2 Decisions in the Treaty of Nice on institutional reform

Re-weighting of votes	More favourable to big member states, but small members still receive more votes relative to population; parity between Germany and France (and other big states).
Double majority	Qualified majority requires 74.6% of weighted votes plus the backing of countries representing 62% of EU population.
Number of commissioners	Big states give up second commissioner from 2005; size of Commission may be capped at 20 from 2007.
Extension of QMV	Moderate, e.g. into trade in services.
'Flexible integration'	Eight countries or more required to pursue closer cooperation that does not include all EU members in certain areas.

Internal policy reform and the budget

The pressures that eastern enlargement created for the CAP, and regional and cohesion policy stemmed primarily from their budgetary implications. The negotiations of the financial perspective from 2000 to 2006, during which the first accession were expected to occur, had to address the question of internal policy reforms. The key decisions therefore coincided with the German Council presidency in the first half of 1999.

The Commission's proposals for policy reform in Agenda 2000 were cautious compared to previous enlargements. It did not recommend an increase in the EU budget to cope with the accession of significantly poorer countries with large agricultural sectors. The main contributors to the budget had made very clear that they were not prepared to increase their contributions, but rather sought to reduce them. The proposals in Agenda 2000 were thus important in framing the negotiations in a way that appeared acceptable to the incumbents. The Commission suggested that enlargement could be financed within the existing limits of the budget at 1.27 per cent of EU GNP and that additional expenditures could be financed through economic growth in the member states.

The Cardiff European Council in June 1998 had set the Berlin European Council in March 1999 as the deadline for concluding agreement on the budget. All member state governments were conscious that their ability to keep the deadline was crucial for the credibility of their professed commitment to enlargement, especially after the initial failure of institutional reform in the Amsterdam Treaty.

The foreign ministers (meeting in 'conclave' in February), rather than sectoral ministers, were put in charge to negotiate the budget deal and struck a preliminary agreement. The European Council still faced difficult negotiations, but reached an agreement (see e.g. Baun 2000: 156–64). French President Chirac insisted on more moderate reforms of the CAP (see e.g. Laffan and Shackleton 2000: 235). On the structural funds, most heads of state and government successfully pleaded for a generous phasing out of their beneficiary regions, while the cohesion countries obtained the preservation of the cohesion fund.

The agreement thus fell short of the Commission's – already cautious – proposals and was described as primarily a deal for the incumbents (see e.g. Allen 2000: 262; Mayhew 2000, 2002). For the candidate countries, the deal ring-fenced funds running from €6.45 billion in 2002 to €16.78 billion in 2006 to include both pre-accession aid and post-accession receipts. The allocations appeared relatively modest, compared to incumbent full members, but assessments were difficult, as it was not yet clear when individual countries would join; moreover, final decisions on the level of receipts from structural funds and the CAP would only be taken at the very final stage of accession negotiations. Yet the key importance of the deal was that agreement was reached at all; something that only a few months earlier only few observers would have predicted (see e.g. Laffan and Shackleton 2000: 232). The European Council declared that the agreement 'send[s] out a message of reassurance to the countries negotiating for accession. Enlargement remains a historic priority for the European Union' (Council 1999: 17). Chancellor Schröder declared after the summit:

> A good compromise hurts everyone. This is also the case for the compromise reached on Agenda 2000 in Berlin. ... The agreement that we have reached in Berlin is a clear signal ... to the accession candidates. A signal that in the end we all put our common responsibility before individual self-interests.[23] (*Süddeutsche Zeitung* 27.03.99)

Accession negotiations

Candidate selection

The Luxembourg European Council in December 1997, which followed the publication of the Commission's *avis* in Agenda 2000, had to decide with which candidates to start accession negotiations. In the run-up to Agenda 2000, considerable uncertainty surrounded the *avis*. It was unclear which particular candidates the Commission would recommend for accession negotiations, or whether it would make firm recommendations at all. This uncertainty stemmed largely from a novel feature of the *avis* on the CEECs. Unlike in previous cases, the Commission did not assess the applicants' current preparedness for membership, but their ability to meet the conditions for membership in the medium term. The Commission used 2002 as a rough reference date and recommended starting negations with the Czech Republic, Hungary, Poland, Estonia and Slovenia (as well as Cyprus). The first three CEECs had been widely expected. Slovakia was judged to meet the economic and *acquis* criteria, but was excluded for failing the political conditions. Estonia and Slovenia were selected as the most advanced of the remaining CEECs (Avery and Cameron 1998: 34–92).

The European Council endorsed the Commission's selection, but there was considerable debate about a more inclusive approach that a number of member states advocated (Baun 2000: 77–94). Some governments, such as the French government, were suspected of promoting a larger number of candidates for negotiations in order to delay the enlargement process by congesting it. The Nordic member states' argument that an inclusive approach was more in line with the EU's pan-European vocation and its mission to stabilise the continent on a larger scale, carried considerable weight (Friis 1998). While these arguments did not lead to changes from the Commission's candidate selection, the European Council agreed to soften the dividing line between the 'first wave' and remaining candidates. It underlined the importance of regular reviews of the accession preparations through the Commission, which could lead to the inclusion of the remaining CEECs in negotiations at a later stage.

Indeed, two years later, in December 1999, the European Council in Helsinki decided that negotiations would also start with the remaining candidates,[24] following a recommendation in the Commission's regular report from October 1999. Slovakia was included due to the changed political situation after the electoral defeat of the Mečiar government; Lithuania and Latvia due to progress with economic reform and accession preparations. While progress with accession preparations in Bulgaria and Romania had been more limited, they were rewarded for their support of the NATO campaign in Kosovo and compensated for the economic difficulties that the conflict had created for them.

Concluding accession negotiations

Negotiations with the first wave of candidates started officially in March 1998 during the UK presidency. After the conclusion of the screening process, negotiations proper started in October during the Austrian presidency. The 'Helsinki group' started negotiations in February 2000. In November 2000, the Commission recommended a 'roadmap' for completing the negotiations by the end of 2002, which the Council adopted. The roadmap considerably accelerated the negotiations by setting a timetable for the formulation of EU positions and committing successive presidencies to concluding the negotiations on particular issues. In the light of the progress of the various candidates with accession negotiations and parallel preparations for accession, a consensus started to emerge around a 'big bang' enlargement: the simultaneous accession of all candidates, except for Bulgaria and Romania. The Laeken European Council in December 2001 confirmed that negotiations with these ten countries could be concluded by the end of 2002, 'if the present rate of progress of the negotiations and reforms in the candidate States is maintained' (Council 2001: 3).

In the first half of 2001, the environmental chapter was closed (for details on the negotiations, see Avery 2004; Mayhew 2000, 2002). The CEECs obtained long transition periods of ten years or more for certain investment-intensive regulations that did not affect product standards, despite initial opposition from certain member states and parts of the Commission. The other most difficult issues were settled in the final phase of the negotiations. The CEECs had to accept transition periods of up to seven years until their workers would enjoy full freedom of movement. In return, the CEECs were allowed to maintain restrictions on the sale of land for up to twelve years.

The agreement on receipts from the CAP and structural funds deeply disappointed the CEEC negotiators, even if it was still more favourable than the initial position of some member states and parts of the Commission. These had, for example, opposed direct income support to CEEC farmers, which was originally designed to compensate EU farmers for reductions in previous price support. According to the final package agreed at Copenhagen in December 2002, direct payments from the CAP are initially only 25 per cent and rise to 100 per cent after a ten-year transition period. Receipts from the structural funds per capita are much lower than for the incumbents. Nonetheless, the agreement allowed the conclusion of negotiations and allowed the new members to join in May 2004, after a successful ratification of the accession treaties by the member states and the European Parliament, as well as by referenda in all CEEC candidate counties.

Conclusions

Relevance and limits of rationalist approaches

Rationalist approaches highlight key factors that shaped the development of the enlargement policy. Especially during the period of relative uncertainty about the depth, scale and reversibility of the changes from 1988 to early 1990, common long-term interests of the member states in political stability and the economic opportunities arising from the transition of the CEECs to market economies were important factors in forging support for a common EU policy to support these changes.

Material interests were also crucial factors that constrained the extent to which such a common policy towards the CEECs accommodated their preferences. The bargaining power of the CEECs vis-à-vis the EU and the member states was weak. Responses to the CEECs' demands for a membership perspective were constrained by the member states' perceptions of long-term risks for their relative influence in the EU, their material benefits from membership, and their preferences regarding the future development of the EU integration process. Concerning trade liberalisation, domestic sectoral interests and their defence in inter-state bargaining restricted concessions to the CEECs.

Rationalist approaches correctly identify the primary supporters of an active EU policy towards the CEECs and their eventual accession. Germany, Italy, and the new member states, Austria, Sweden and Finland, stand to gain most from political stability and economic opportunities in the CEECs. The UK and Denmark are least concerned about a potential negative impact of enlargement on further EU integration. The Commission's key role in the initial EU policy allowed it to increase its status in the EU and international affairs more generally.

However, while material self-interest played an important role in the evolution of EU policy, the explanatory power of material rationalist approaches is more limited with regard to some key aspects of the enlargement policy. They cannot fully explain why substantive policy accommodated the preferences of the CEEC governments to a greater extent than the lowest common denominator of sectoral interests suggests. The overriding political interests of some powerful member states in enlargement are not an entirely convincing explanation, since German officials, for example, were more often than not responsible for restrictive policy outcomes.

Crucially, materialist rationalist approaches have difficulty explaining fully why EU policy continued to evolve after the signing of the EAs to the point that it firmly set the EU on a path to enlargement. Although there was no dramatic change in the security environment, policy shifted towards a better accommodation of the CEECs' demands, both on market access and the membership perspective. Why did the member states agree to eventual CEEC membership, despite the threats to their material interests?

Policy impact of the EU's collective identity vis-à-vis the CEECs

The analysis in these two chapters suggests that the apparent puzzles for material rationalist approaches can be solved with a focus on the EU's collective identity. Numerous statements about the EU's role in overcoming the division of the continent and its 'responsibility' towards the CEECs discursively constructed this identity, which implied a principled obligation to support the transformations in the CEECs and their integration into the EU.

This role-identity contributed to the emergence of a group of policy advocates, who promoted the accommodation of the CEECs' interests in EU policy. This group of policy advocates was based primarily within the Commission, including the commissioners responsible for external relations, and DG I, in particular the unit dealing with policy towards the CEECs. For these policy-makers, this aspect of EU identity is particularly salient as they represent the EU directly towards the CEECs and identify most directly with the EU. These policy advocates supported an accommodation of the CEECs' interests not merely because of far-sighted self-interest, but for its own sake. Their advocacy did not necessarily imply altruism, but appropriate behaviour for the role prescribed by EU identity. Among the rest of the macro-policy-makers – the member states' foreign ministers and heads of state or government – EU identity created an environment receptive to their arguments.

One strategy of the policy advocates to influence policy were arguments relating to the EU's and the member states' far-sighted self-interest, as they perceived complementarities between identity-conform behaviour and a maximisation of long-term self-interests. Many of the policy advocates had an economic background, which made them perceive long-term benefits and opportunities, rather than risks, from sectoral competition induced by the integration of the CEECs.

An initially unintended, but highly effective way in which the policy advocates achieved influence on policy was through affecting the structure of the discourse about EU policy towards the CEECs. The reinforcement of a discourse of collective responsibility limited the legitimacy of arguments based on defensive material interests of the incumbents. The explicit acknowledgement of the CEECs' membership perspective presented a significant reinforcement of arguments based on the EU's collective identity, which was a key incentive for the policy advocates to pursue such an explicit acknowledgement as an objective in its own right.

The normative discourse did not determine outcomes, but limited the realm of acceptable policy options. The diffuse nature of the role prescribed by EU identity meant, however, that these limitations were not very narrowly cast. It was more obvious to identify what appropriate behaviour would consist of with regard to the membership perspective, than with regard to economic concessions. Still, the macro-policy-makers in general perceived of a need to accommodate the preferences of the CEECs to a certain extent and were reluctant to use their superior bargaining power to present policies purely oriented at their material self-interest as 'take-it-or-leave-it' options. The importance of EU identity and of the terms of policy discourse was reflected in the apparent sensitivity and vulnerability of policy-makers to criticism of a lack of accommodation. Albeit not linked to material resources, the criticism both of the CEECs as well as from academic circles created pressures for policy change.

Importance of the structure of the policy process

These two chapters also suggest that variation in the structure of the process of policy coordination in a composite policy – both at the national and the EU level – had important implications for substantive policy outcomes.

The fragmentation of the policy process from the start of the drafting of the negotiation directives for the EAs, limited the access of the macro-policy-makers and the policy advocates to substantive decisions on sectoral policies. The hands-off approach of the foreign ministers in the GAC reduced their influence on policy and strengthened the role of sectoral policy-makers.

The framework of EA negotiations embedded the policy process in a shadow of hierarchical coordination and facilitated its occasional centralisation. In turn, during the implementation of the EAs, the fragmentation of the policy process and the autonomy of sectoral policy-makers increased; it became more difficult to attract the attention of the highest political level to induce a degree of hierarchical coordination. The few instances in which the macro-policy-makers were able to centralise coordination and circumvent sectoral policy-makers facilitated an accommodation of the CEECs' preferences. Such instances included the instruction of the high-level group of foreign ministry officials to negotiate the economic package for the Copenhagen European Council and in the strong reliance on COREPER for agreement on the pre-accession strategy before the Essen European Council.

The impact of the degree of centralisation or fragmentation of the national policy coordination processes is harder to assess. In the case of France, the very effectiveness of the central policy coordination mechanism constrained the foreign ministry in pursuing more accommodating positions during the EA negotiations, especially with a prime minister vulnerable to domestic pressures before the RPR/UDF election victory in 1993. By contrast, in the German case, the fragmentation of the national coordination process limited the foreign ministry's influence on national sectoral positions by enhancing the autonomy of sectoral officials during the EA negotiations and particularly in their implementation. On the other hand, fragmentation of the presentation of German positions at the EU level enabled the foreign ministry to reassert its authority in those instances when policy issues had to be deferred to the GAC.

The focus of these two chapters on the broad patterns of policy is necessarily sketchy and the focus on the macro-level of policy has a cost. First, it neglects the implementation stage in the various meso-areas, which is obviously a crucial part of the policy process, and policy outcomes might contrast with those at the decision stage. Second, my overview of the developments in substantive policies has not elaborated on the nature of opposition to an accommodation of the CEECs' preferences. It appears to suggest that sectoral policy-makers generally act according to interest group pressures and that those are the main sources of opposition to more accommodating substantive policies. Differences in the structure of the policy process then appear to determine to what extent these pressures affect policy outcomes and concessions result primarily from hierarchical coordination that limits the influence of sectoral policy-makers.

However, a more detailed analysis of individual meso-policies shows that the behaviour of sectoral policy-makers is not as easily predictable as a function of protectionist pressures from interest groups as certain rationalist approaches suggest. There are thus also other ways to achieve an accommodation of CEEC preferences than hierarchical coordination that strategically excludes sectoral concerns, but potentially also deeper obstacles than interest group pressure alone. The following chapters present in-depth analyses of selected meso-policies in order to better understand the relative importance of interest group pressure, policy fragmentation and issue-specific ideational factors.

Notes

1   Interview, French Permanent Representation, 08.07.93.

2   Interviews, Commission DG I, 24.10.95; Commissioner's *cabinet*, 02.02.95.

3   Interview, Commission DG I, 24.10.95.

4   Interviews, Commission DG I, 24.10.95; Commissioner's *cabinet*, 02.02.95.

5   Interview, Commission DG I, 24.10.95.

6   Interview, UK Foreign Office, 20.03.96.

7   Interviews, Commission DG I, 24.10.95; Commissioner's *cabinet*, 02.02.95.

8   'Il ne suffit pas ... d'avoir des propos de plus en plus encourageants pour les pays de Visegrad. Il faut savoir où nous allons. La Commission va se livrer a une auto analyse, je dirais presque à une autocritique de ce qu'elle a fait sur le plan économique ... Mais elle va aussi réfléchir sur quelle pourrait être cette Grande Europe [...] [Cette réflexion] devrait nous amener ... à avoir une vision d'ensemble ou à des visions d'ensemble, des scénarios qui permettraient de replacer le prochain élargissement dans une perspective. Car il est vrai que la perspective actuellement n'est pas claire. [...] Ce qui manque le plus aujourd'hui à l'Europe, c'est l'innovation intellectuelle, la réflexion et non pas l'action. Car l'action, elle existe, elle est parfois débridée.'

9   Interview, Commissioner's *cabinet*, 02.02.95.

10   Interview, Commission DG I, 24.10.95.

11   Interview, French Foreign Ministry, 03.07.96.

12   Interviews, French Foreign Ministry, 10.07.96; German Ministry of Economics, 15.12.95.

13   Interview, Commission DG I, 24.10.95.

14   Interview, Dutch Permanent Representation; 31.01.95.

15   Interview, Dutch Permanent Representation; 31.01.95.
16   Interview, Commission DG I, 24.10.95.
17   Interview, Commission DG I, 24.10.95.
18   Interview, German Foreign Ministry, 13.12.95.
19   Interview, German Foreign Ministry, 15.12.95.
20   Interviews, Spanish Permanent Representation, 11.06.96; Spanish Foreign Ministry, 18.06.96.
21   The understanding also applied to Malta, until the incoming Labour government suspended the membership application.
22   The final version replaced 'moral imperative' with 'political imperative' (Council 1995f).
23   'Ein guter Kompromiss tut allen weh. Das gilt auch für den in Berlin erzielten zur Agenda 2000. … Die Einigung die wir in Berlin erzielt haben, ist ein klares Signal an … die Beitrittskandidaten. Ein Signal, dass wir alle am Ende unsere gemeinsame Verantwortung vor die jeweiligen Einzelinteressen gestellt haben.'
24   Malta was included, after change in government led to a reactivation of the membership application.

Part III

Meso-policies

6

Liberalisation of steel trade

EU trade policy in the steel sector is a meso-policy that was most salient during the earlier stages of EU policy towards the CEECs. This policy area presents a hard case for approaches that focus on material interests and interest group pressure. The balance of interest group preferences in the EU steel sector suggests that an accommodation of the preferences of the CEECs is highly unlikely. The CEECs have a strong interest in free and unconditional access to the EU steel market. In particular Poland, the Czech Republic and Slovakia have large steel sectors, both in terms of industrial activity and share in employment. Sales on the EU market are a key source of foreign currency earnings and of funds for the necessary industrial restructuring in the sector. However, in the EU there is firm opposition to a liberalisation of steel trade. The sector is generally considered as one of the most import-sensitive sectors in the EU (see e.g. Hindley 1993; Messerlin 1993; Rollo and Smith 1993). Despite overwhelming interest group pressure against trade liberalisation, EU policy significantly accommodated the preferences of the CEECs. This finding clearly contradicts the predictions of interest-based approaches. I argue that a crucial factor facilitating the accommodation of the CEECs' preferences was a shift in the dominant policy paradigm underpinning EU steel policy. The shift towards a paradigm more compatible with liberalisation of market access allowed the policy advocates in the Commission to build successful alliances with sectoral policy-makers in favour of a change in EU steel policy.

The first part of this chapter outlines the configuration of societal interests in the EU steel sector. This overview suggests that if public policy-makers simply reacted to interest group pressures, we could not expect any significant liberalisation in the EU's steel trade policy. The next section identifies the key ideas that underpin EU policy in the steel sector and examine its implication for trade policy. A liberalisation of market access for the CEECs is incompatible with the policy paradigm that dominated EU steel policy since the establishment of the ECSC, as the main function of trade policy within the policy paradigm is to provide a stable external environment for the EU steel market. However, in the early 1990s an alternative paradigm much more favourable to trade liberalisation had started to emerge and by the mid-1990s largely replaced the previous paradigm.

The final part of this chapter examines the influence of the main factors of this analysis – interest group pressure, policy paradigm, and structure of the policy process – on EU policy at different stages of the development of steel trade policy towards the CEECs. These stages are (1) policy from 1989 to the EAs; (2) the provisions of the EAs; and (3) their implementation, in particular in the context of the restructuring plan for the EC steel industry in 1993/94. I conclude that the influence of societal interests on EU steel trade policy is far more limited than materialist rationalist accounts and a liberal intergovernmentalist approach would predict. Changes in the structure of the policy process account for some variation in the outcomes, but the crucial factor accounting for the accommodation of the CEECs' preferences despite interest group opposition is the paradigm shift in EU steel policy.

Configuration of interest group preferences in the EU steel sector

Interests of steel producers
Certain differences in the steel industries of the member states notwithstanding, their main characteristics and the effects of competition from CEEC exports are fairly similar (see e.g. Klepper 1991; Woolcock 1982). Major changes in production technology have transformed the steel industry into a modern, high productivity and high technology sector (Ferner et al. 1997: 58; Hudson 1994: 102–3). Nonetheless, overcapacities, which have been the industry's main structural problem since the 1970s, still afflict EU producers. The distinctive features of the steel sector – such as the dominance of large production plants with high fixed costs – make it extremely difficult for producers to respond to changes in the demand with capacity reductions (see e.g. Cockerill 1993; Glais 1995). As specialisation between the different national markets is low and the cross-elasticity of demand between different producers is high, competition is mainly driven by prices. During cyclical downturns in demand, firms thus try to maintain production and market shares by lowering prices, even if these fall below unit costs, inducing a downwards convergence of prices across national markets.

The price sensitivity of the steel market caused strong and unified opposition from EU producers against liberalising market access for CEEC producers, who primarily compete through low prices. Even considerations of the CEECs as an export market or investment location do not change this fairly homogeneous producer interest in protection from CEEC imports.[1] The strong common preferences of producers for trade protection is reflected in the absence of controversial debates surrounding the adoption of position papers in EUROFER, the European Steel Producer Association.[2]

Producer interests are well represented in the policy process. At the national level, steel producers have traditionally enjoyed particularly close relations with policy-makers (see e.g. Dudley and Richardson 1990; Esser and Fach 1989; Goldberg 1986; Jones 1986; Rhodes 1989; Woolcock 1982). At the EU level, EUROFER has obtained privileged access to the Commission (Grunert 1986).

Interests of steel consumers

As the main consumers of steel products are themselves industries, such as automobiles or construction, we might expect a significant mobilisation for liberalisation and against protectionist producer pressures. However, the consuming industries did either not have sufficient incentives, or were not powerful enough to press successfully for a more liberal steel trade policy towards the CEECs.[3] For example, powerful end-users, like the automobile industry, can refuse price increases or demand price drops from their suppliers in the secondary processing sector, such as small or medium-sized engineering companies or foundries, which are, in turn, not vocal enough to influence policy (*Financial Times*, 04.05.93: 9; *Agence Europe*, 21.07.94). Discussions in the ECSC Consultative Committee did not pitch steel producers against consumers. Its resolutions largely converge with the preferences expressed by EUROFER and have been adopted with large majorities (ECSC Consultative Committee 1991, 1993).

In sum, the configuration of societal interests in the EU steel sector generates strong pressures on policy-makers to provide continued protection, especially from CEEC exports. Materialist rationalist approaches emphasising the balance of societal pressures would thus lead us to expect strong constraints on the ability of the policy advocates in the Commission to obtain a significant accommodation of the CEECs' preferences and that trade liberalisation in this sector is highly unlikely.

Competing policy paradigms for EU steel policy

The managed restructuring paradigm

From the establishment of the ECSC in 1952, EU steel policy has been based on a specific understanding and interpretation of the economics of the steel sector, which could be described as a 'managed restructuring' paradigm. Within this paradigm, the main policy objective is the modernisation of the EU steel industry to ensure its survival in a competitive international environment. The policy instruments designed to achieve this objective reflect the belief that the nature of competition in the steel sector is different from other sectors of the economy. As the production structure induces price competition, market forces alone fail to produce rationalisation. Market forces will either lead to uncompetitive practices through producer cartels, or lead to cutthroat competition that may even force long-term competitive producers out of the market. Especially in times of crisis, industry will only engage in cutting overcapacities as part of a collective endeavour. Public policy has to establish guidelines for a burden-sharing in capacity reductions and provide a stable environment in which the process can take place. Trade policy is a crucial instrument that creates such a stable environment by guaranteeing protection from external competition.

The ideas underpinning this policy paradigm became institutionalised in the legal framework of the ECSC. The ECSC Treaty of 1951 emphasises modernisation, based on the principles of increased competition on the one hand, and the possibility of public intervention under adverse economic circumstances on the other. Tsoukalis and Strauss (1986: 189) conclude that while

> the underlying economic philosophy of the Paris Treaty is fundamentally liberal [...] faith in market forces was tempered by some economic realism which was in turn based on historical experiences. The economic system set up by the Paris Treaty was aptly described by Walter Hallstein as one of 'regulated competition', with provisions made for central crisis management.

The interventionist element of the paradigm became embedded through the experience of EU policy during the steel crisis from the mid-1970s to the mid-1980s (see e.g. Mény and Wright 1986). The Commission's Davignon plan (1977 to 1986) created a highly regulated environment for the EU steel market. The Commission declared a 'manifest crisis', which allowed it to use its full powers under Article 58 ECSC. The measures included temporary compulsory production and delivery quotas, as well as price regulations (Grunert 1986). The consensus among EU institutions, national governments and the industry about the Davignon plan validated the managed restructuring paradigm and the important role of intervention at the EU level. Dudley and Richardson (1999: 236) confirm that

> for a period, Davignon had succeeded in creating a genuine policy community ... in European steel, with consensus achieved through a process of mutual adjustment and accommodation between the Commission, EUROFER and the Council of Ministers. [...] Underlying this community was a policy 'frame' specifying the relationship between the state and steel, and steel as a special case.

The Davignon plan also established a specific function for trade policy within the paradigm. While the ECSC treaty does not include provisions for a common commercial policy, the Davignon plan used EU trade policy as the 'external element' of the restructuring plan. The EU induced its major trading partners to either respect a system of minimum prices, or to enter into Voluntary Restraint Agreements (VRAs), both on quantities and prices (Jones

1986: 128–31; Wang and Winters 1993: 9–11). Crucially, even after the end of the Davignon plan, the trade policy regime largely remained in place.

Davignon emphasised that trade policy was not simply a protectionist measure that allowed the industry to delay or avoid modernisation. Rather, by providing temporary stabilisation, it was a precondition for modernisation:

> Having been personally involved in the formulation of the Community trade policy during those difficult years, it is my firm belief that protection can never be a proper substitute for adjustment in a world economy characterized by rapid shifts in comparative advantages. However, it is equally true that, in the face of these radical changes, a number of industries need 'breathing space' in order to reorganize themselves at an acceptable social cost. By making transition smoother, the judicious use of the instruments authorized and controlled by GATT can usefully contribute to adjustment. (Quoted in Hayes 1993: 51).

Furthermore, within this paradigm, steel trade policy is based on arguments about 'fairness' rather than 'efficiency': it has to ensure that external price competition does not exploit and undermine an orderly restructuring effort of the EU steel industry. The assumptions of the specific nature of trade competition in the steel sector and of the importance of the fairness argument are also reflected in the principles underpinning the EU's trade defence measures, notably its anti-dumping policy. Most trade economists who focus on efficiency arguments only consider the case of 'predatory dumping' problematic. EU anti-dumping legislation considers any case in which companies sell at lower prices on the EU market than their home market as 'unfair' competition even if there is no intention to drive competitors out of the market in order to abuse the subsequently acquired dominant position by raising prices (see e.g. Holmes and Kempton 1997). The Commission's anti-dumping report reflects the particular salience of these fairness arguments with regard to the understanding of the steel industry (Commission 1993b: 9):

> 'Cyclical' dumping occurs in industries subject to periodic excess supply and capacity in which there is an incentive to export during the period of shrinking domestic demand to dump the excess production at prices below full costs, thus exporting unemployment. Cyclical dumping can be expected in industries with high investment and consequent high fixed costs, like the steel or chemical industry and has the effect of exacerbating the difficulties facing an industrial sector in the importing country which is already affected by economic recession.

Furthermore, the fairness argument is also particularly salient with regard to competition from the CEECs, in view of their legacies as state trading countries. The Commission's anti-dumping report considers 'state trade dumping from economies whose main aim may not be cost efficiency but to earn hard currency at any price' as 'particularly damaging' (Commission 1993b: 9). Although the EU formally eliminated the CEECs from the list of state-trading countries since the conclusion of the EAs, many policy-makers and industry representatives still openly doubt that the economic practices had fundamentally changed at this stage of economic transition. In their view, current practice still resembles state trading, in which 'the margins by which the prices of the Community producers are undercut may be unusually high. Because the exporters in question often do not follow normal business behaviour, this type of dumping is unpredictable in view of its occurrence, volume, price and duration' (1993b: 9).

In sum, the managed restructuring paradigm is not simply protectionist, but it considers trade policy an important and legitimate instrument to facilitate the restructuring of the EU steel sector. It induces strong reluctance among policy-makers towards unconditional market opening, in particular towards the CEECs.

The non-intervention paradigm

In the late 1980s, a competing policy paradigm for EU steel policy started to emerge. This paradigm, which I label 'non-intervention' paradigm, is much more compatible with liberalising market access for the CEECs. The new paradigm challenges the assumption that the steel sector is a 'special case' and thus the very basis for intervention.

A range of factors contributed to establish this paradigm as a serious alternative to the 'managed restructuring' paradigm. In addition to broader changes in economic ideas, specific changes in the steel sector have challenged the viability of the managed restructuring paradigm. First, the experience with the Davignon plan shed doubt on the effectiveness of interventionist policies (Rhodes 1989: 74–6). Cyclical upswings of the steel market revealed the limits to a collective restructuring process and of a close cooperation between public policy-makers and producers. The more competitive producers were unwilling to deliver further capacity reductions through works closures and to adhere to price and production constraints.

Second, the nature of the steel industry changed 'from a high-volume, standardised, price-competitive production pattern towards a high-volume, customised, quality-competitive production pattern' (Bacon and Blyton 1996: 780). Technological developments, such as the emergence of minimills, made it easier for producers to adjust flexibly to changes in demand patterns. Changes in the industry structure, such as the increasing trend towards privatisation, mergers and an internationalisation of firms, facilitated rationalisation and increased competitiveness (Bacon and Blyton, 1996; Hudson 1994). The painful transformation of the EU included a drastic reduction of the workforce from 870,000 in 1975 to 280,000 in 1999, and capacity reductions of more than 63 million tonnes since 1980 (*Financial Times*, 14.05.99). Mergers and alliances included Germany's Thyssen and Krupp, Luxembourg's Arbed with Spain's Aceralia, Stahlwerke of Bremen and Sidstahl of Belgium, and Belgium's Cockerill Sambre (which already owned Ekostahl in Germany) with France's Usinor.

The resulting changes in market behaviour challenged some of the economic assumptions underpinning the managed restructuring paradigm. Finally, the impending expiry of the ECSC Treaty in 2002 became the focal point of the debate on whether the EU should continue to treat the steel sector as a special case.

Crucially, a new advocacy coalition started to emerge that promoted the spread of free market ideas in the steel sector, consisting of policy-makers in the Commission and in the member states, and actors from within the industry, in particular the newly privatised producers such as British Steel and Usinor-Sacilor of France (see Dudley and Richardson 1999). The changed views in the Commission's DG Industry were expressed in its 1990 report on the longer term objectives in the steel sector, which claimed that steel was a sector like any other and that market forces were the way forward (Commission 1990e). The EU's 1993/94 restructuring plan, triggered by the renewed steel crisis in the 1990s, presented a last, and ultimately failed, attempt to resurrect the managed restructuring paradigm. The termination of the restructuring plan indicated the dominance of the new paradigm.

With regard to trade policy, the non-intervention paradigm is much more favourable to trade liberalisation. Within this paradigm, the main function of trade policy is to open new markets abroad and to expose domestic producers to market forces, considered an effective instrument to induce restructuring and greater competitiveness. In the Commission, the ascendance of the new paradigm was reflected in a more general scepticism towards sectoral intervention. Martin Bangemann, commissioner for industry and the internal market, expressed this changing mood, even if he remained open to pragmatic exceptions to assist the EU steel industry:

> Sectoral approaches to industrial policy can work during a period but they entail inevitably the risk of delaying structural adjustments and thereby creating job losses in the future. Openness to international trade and respect of rules governing such trade deliver the right signals to the economy and preclude the recourse by the Community to the various types of defensive measures commonly used to protect domestic producers in the furtherance of such policies. (Commission 1990f: 5)

In the early 1990s, the new emphasis on the creation of a liberal international trading environment was reflected in the EU's support for a Multilateral Steel Agreement (MSA) that would eliminate all tariff and non-tariff barriers – thus, crucially, also VRAs – and impose strict international discipline on state aids. However, despite the growing support for the new policy paradigm, EU producers remained opposed to the application of its trade element, especially towards the CEECs, on the basis of the 'fairness' argument. The most vocal criticism of the EU's restrictive practices came from trade economists (see e.g. Hindley 1993; Messerlin 1993; Winters 1995a) and parts of the press that advocated market access for the CEECs both as an end in itself and as an effective means to achieve restructuring of the EU steel industry, as expressed in the following *Financial Times* editorial:

> It is doubtless true that, at the margin, imports from CEECs are disruptive. If obsolete plants are run for cash with no thought of replacement, a business run as a going concern cannot hope to compete on price. Thus to allow free access to eastern steel risks adding to the ranks of jobless EC steelworkers. The snag is that the alternative might be playing host to jobless Polish and Czech steelworkers instead. In the face of small-scale, flexible methods of steel production, the EC's integrated steel-mills might be industrial dinosaurs anyway. The longer they're propped up, the more the EC risks ending up without a steel industry in the long run. In terms of competitive advantage, this might not necessarily be negative. But in social as well as economic terms, it points an obvious moral. Rather than keep workers unproductively employed, the trick is to find them something better to do. (23.02.93)

The emergence of this alternative paradigm for EU steel policy, albeit far from being widely shared, or firmly embedded, provided potential allies for the policy advocates in DG I seeking an accommodation of the CEECs' preferences. The more influence the non-interventionist paradigm exercised on internal EU steel policy, the more scope for granting the CEECs market access, despite sustained opposition from interest groups. The following section analyses to what extent the policy entrepreneurs were able to influence the EU's evolving steel trade policy towards the CEECs. It examines in particular the respective impact of interest group pressures, structure of the policy process and the policy paradigm on policy outcomes at different phases of policy development.

The new regime for steel trade with the CEECs

After the changes in 1989 prompted a reorientation of EU policy towards the CEECs, the EU's steel trade policy evolved in four main stages: (1) annual renewals of the VRAs from 1990 to 1991; (2) the negotiations of the ECSC protocol of the EAs in 1991; (3) the use of trade defence instruments in the steel sector during the implementation of the EAs; and (4) the negotiations of the 'external element' of the 1993/94 restructuring plan for the EU steel industry.

Steel trade policy before the Europe Agreements
The policy framework for steel trade between the EU and the CEECs before the EA negotiations was essentially based on arrangements which had been put in place in 1978 and reflected the role of trade policy within the managed restructuring paradigm. As the 'external element' of the Davignon plan, agreements with the main trading partners provided the internal restructur-

ing process with comprehensive protection from disruptive imports. The EU's main trading partners were given a choice: either they adhered to a system of basic prices and faced automatic anti-dumping measures in case of non-compliance, or they entered into VRAs (Jones 1986: 128–31; Wang and Winters 1993: 9–11). Most partners, including the CEECs, found the latter preferable. Under these VRAs, the CEECs had to observe minimum prices as well as quantitative restrictions. A so-called triple clause stipulated that exports had to be spread evenly across the year, national markets, and product groups. At the same time, the VRAs guaranteed the CEECs a certain market share, since the level of the minimum prices allowed them to undercut EU producers by a certain margin, while the EU renounced the application of anti-dumping measures against these exports.

These arrangements were subject to annual renewal by a unanimous decision of the Council's 113 ECSC working group, which usually happened routinely, without significant debate. These arrangements remained in place even when the internal measures of the Davignon plan were gradually relaxed and finally totally abandoned in 1986. The VRAs thus provided the framework for EU steel trade policy towards the CEECs until the entry into force of the trade-related measures of the EAs, including its ECSC protocol, through the interim agreements in March 1992.

As part of the reorientation of EU policy towards the CEECs after 1989, the Commission's DG I pressed for improved market access for the CEECs within this policy framework. For 1990, DG I-E originally proposed a preferential thirty per cent increase in the quotas for Hungary and Poland – then the only CEECs included in PHARE – in comparison to other countries covered by the VRAs (*Agence Europe*, 16.12.89: 15; 19.01.90: 7). Andriessen argued that a central finding from visits to eastern Europe was that steel was a key sector where better access to the EU market could promote the Commission's 'most pressing desire' to help the CEECs (*Financial Times*, 17.01.90: 3).

Other parts of the Commission, where the non-intervention paradigm had gained ground, supported a significant opening of the EU steel market within the arrangements, in particular parts of DG I-D (trade policy), DGs II (economy and finance), III (industry), and IV (competition). Their support for the argument that the steel sector should no longer be given special treatment was triggered by a number of factors, including the expiry of the last internal measures of the Davignon plan, the impending completion of the single market and expiry of the ECSC treaty in 2002, as well as the start of talks about the MSA in the framework of the Uruguay round. The improvement on the steel market around 1989/1990 also appeared to make the changes less contentious.

Despite these indications of broader support for changes in EU steel trade policy, differences remained within the Commission. With a worsening of the steel market in 1991, differences also emerged between the commissioners

Andriessen (external relations) and Brittan (competition) on the one hand, and Bangemann (industry) on the other. The latter pragmatically favoured protection for the EU industry. The differences were particularly pronounced among the member states. While most member states opposed an improved market access, the Commission proposals were supported by the general free trade supporters, the UK, Denmark and the Netherlands, as well as the German government. Although in Germany the steel sector is traditionally one of the exceptions from the general free trade philosophy, German policy-makers did not want to endanger the prospects for the MSA and better access to the US steel market.[4] Table 6.1 below outlines the main positions in the internal negotiations.

Table 6.1 Intra-EU negotiations for the renewal of the VRAs in 1990 and 1991

	1990	1991
Commission proposal	+18%	**maintain 1990 level**
Negotiation positions:		
Andriessen, Brittan	'generous increase'	maintain 1990 level
Bangemann	support for Andriessen	−5%
Council decision	+15%	**maintain 1990 level**
Negotiation positions:		
France, Belgium, Italy,		
Luxembourg, Spain	+5% to +10%	−5%
UK, Denmark	support for Commission	further quota increase
Netherlands, Germany	support for Commission	support for Commission

Source: compiled from *Agence Europe*, 19.01.90: 7; 05.02.90: 8; 17.02.90: 9; 02.03.90; 09.01.91: 7; 16.01.91: 10; 15.02.91: 8.

The renewal of the VRAs for 1990 and 1991 was thus the result of prolonged and highly controversial debates. In both years, the Commission proposal was only agreed at the level of the *college*. In the Council, the 113 ECSC working group had to refer the decision to COREPER, which in 1991 still required five sessions to reach a compromise. The outcome of the negotiations entailed tangible improvements for the CEECs. For 1990, the quotas were increased by fifteen per cent. For 1991, quotas stayed at the same level, but this implied a relative increase in the CEECs' market share, given the contraction on the EU steel market. However, despite these improvements, the principle of the VRAs as such was not put into question. The minimum prices, which are the primary concern of the steel trade, thus remained unaffected.

The EU steel industry strongly opposed an opening to imports from the CEECs. Significantly, the industry did not simply call for protection from increased competition. The arguments focused on the incompatibility of greater market access with key assumptions of the managed restructuring paradigm, in particularly the distinction between 'free trade' and 'fair trade'. EU producers insisted that it was not a competitive advantage that allowed CEEC companies to undercut EU prices, but public subsidies and the state-trading tradition in the CEECs, which meant that companies were not used to recovering their production costs. For example, François Mer, chairman of EUROFER and president of Usinor-Sacilor, asserted that CEEC producers had 'no clear notion of their real prices' (*Agence Europe*, 08.01.90: 9). The ECSC Consultative Committee claimed that their imports took place 'in non-economic conditions and at unrealistic prices' (*Agence Europe*, 22.02.90: 13) and that the Commission's 'minimalist outlook' on external protection would 'encourage [the CEECs] to increase their production capacities with the help of unfair subsidies' (*Agence Europe*, 02.04.90: 11). EUROFER suggested that 'certain increases [of CEEC imports in 1990] can only occur by means of systematic, large-scale dumping' (*Agence Europe*, 11.02.91: 8). Ruprecht Vondran, chairman of the German Steel Federation, concluded that the Commission had adopted a policy of 'complete liberalisation in favour of low prices from subsidised producers' (*Agence Europe*, 08.03.91: 13).

In addition, EU producers argued that the EU did not have to make a choice between protecting the interests of EU producers and helping the CEECs. While endorsing the notion of partnership and cooperation with the CEECs, they disputed that trade policy was an appropriate instrument. François Mer argued that trade liberalisation would not benefit the CEECs' producers, but steel traders, as the intermediaries, who were 'Westerners from elsewhere' (*Agence Europe*, 08.01.90: 8). These traders exploited the CEEC producers' inexperience with pricing to buy at such low costs that even considerable profit margins would still allow them to sell in the EU significantly below market level. Trade liberalisation would encourage such practices not only to the detriment of EU producers, but also entailed few benefits for the CEECs.

EUROFER suggested that EU support should therefore concentrate on ECSC instruments, such as investment credits for technical aid and transfer of knowledge, helping the CEECs to upgrade their products and improve their management and marketing skills (*Agence Europe*, 08.01.90: 9). The ECSC Consultative Committee also favoured EU assistance for technological and environmental improvements of existing installations, which enabled productivity gains, rather than capacity increases (*Agence Europe*, 22.02.90: 13). Assistance should be made conditional on the CEECs abiding by 'the rules of fair competition on export markets' (*Agence Europe*, 22.02.90: 13). The German Steel Federation suggested further conditions, such as capacity reductions through concentrating production on more profitable installations, the privatisation of steel companies or corresponding management of public firms, and the reduction of state aids according to a fixed timetable and the subsequent application of a state aids code compatible with the ECSC (*Agence Europe,* 08.03.91: 13).

In sum, even before the EA negotiations, EU steel trade policy towards the CEECs had become more open. The lack of influence of the steel producers on the Commission's position reflects a change from the close cooperation that had previously characterised EU steel policy. The emergence of the non-intervention paradigm for EU steel policy explains the ability of the advocates of the CEECs' preferences in DG I to find significant support in important parts of the Commission, and partly among the member states.

The compatibility of improved market access for the CEECs with the new policy paradigm provided the promoters of this paradigm within the Commission with a focal point to press for policy change. Still, support for the non-intervention paradigm inside the Commission was fragile, and it remained strongly contested by a majority of member states. EU producers comprehensively rejected the validity of extending the non-intervention paradigm to trade policy towards the CEECs. Nonetheless, the notion of a preferential policy for the CEECs had entered the EU discourse on steel trade policy.

The structure of the policy process also provided the necessary conditions both for the improvement of market access and the maintenance of the VRAs. In the Commission's policy process, the prominent role of DG I and the involvement of commissioners from other DGs reduced the influence of DG III and Bangemann. In addition, the decision rules in the Council for renewing the VRAs favoured those member states pressing for greater market access. Since a renewal required a unanimous decision, a failure to reach an agreement would have meant the expiration of the VRAs and thus led to a complete liberalisation of steel imports. At the same time, as the negotiations were locked in the framework of the VRAs, the scope for policy-makers from outside the sector to press for abolition of the system was limited. Despite the quota increase, the minimum price arrangements therefore remained unaffected.

The ECSC protocol of the Europe Agreements

The ECSC protocol of the EAs considerably improved market access for the CEECs over the previous regime. The EAs abolished the VRAs and thus eliminated the price constraints. All quantitative restrictions (QRs) were completely eliminated with the entry into force of the Interim Agreements (March 1992), in stark contrast to other sectors, such as agriculture, textiles, or coal. The only trade barriers that remained in place were tariffs, and these only temporarily. Tariffs, in turn, are not a major trade barrier in steel trade. EU tariffs on steel are fairly moderate (3.5 per cent for unworked products, 5.6 per cent for semi-manufactures, and 5.4 per cent for manufactures; GATT 91: 196). The negotiation directives stipulated that the EU would phase out the tariffs over a ten-year period, but in the negotiations the CEECs obtained a reduction to six years (*Agence Europe*, 17.04.91: 6), subsequently reduced to five years by the Copenhagen European Council in 1993.

The crucial, and most controversial, issue in the negotiations on the ECSC protocols was whether the agreements would allow the reintroduction of VRAs after the entry into force of the EAs. If development of CEEC exports could trigger a reintroduction of VRAs, an initial elimination of QRs appeared tolerable to EU producers, and preferable over the political cost of entering into a major conflict on this issue. Contingent use of VRAs provided a more flexible, and more effective, means of protection than QRs fixed in the agreements: the uncertainty surrounding the development of the CEECs' steel industries made it difficult to predict in which areas protection was most needed. According to Wang and Winters (1993), the price arrangements under the VRAs had had a more restraining effect on the level of CEEC exports than the quantitative restrictions.

The resolution of the ECSC Consultative Committee on the EA negotiations thus identified as the key concerns of the EU industry, first, the application of a strict discipline on state aids by the CEECs, and second, the availability of instruments for the defence against 'unfair' competition that allowed the Commission to intervene 'rapidly and effectively' if distortions should be maintained or introduced (ECSC Consultative Committee 1991). Such defence instruments concerned the provisions on anti-dumping, countervailing duties, and the general safeguard provisions of the EAs, but referred also to the possibility of reintroducing VRAs.

The question of whether the EAs would retain the possibility of concluding VRAs after the entry into force of the agreements became the main issue in the intra-EU negotiations on the ECSC protocols. One possibility was a statement in the ECSC protocols that the agreements did not exclude a reintroduction. An alternative was a more specific statement of the conditions under which the CEECs would agree to enter into VRAs. Such a provision would function as a special safeguard clause for the steel sector, triggering VRAs, in addition to the general safeguard clause of the EAs, which allowed the use of anti-dumping or anti-subsidy instruments.

During the drafting of the negotiation directives inside the Commission, horizontal coordination successfully established parameters for sectoral negotiations. DG I-E (relations with the CEECs) argued strongly that as a political signal, the EU should make some substantial concessions in the 'sensitive' sectors, where the CEECs had export potential. After consultations revealed that concessions would be extremely hard to obtain in the agricultural sector, the steel and textiles sectors became the focus of liberalisation efforts.[5]

While DG I-E conducted the overall EA negotiations and coordinated the drafting of the negotiation directives, the ECSC protocols were drafted in DG I-D, in coordination with DG III. These services were broadly sympathetic to ending VRAs, both as a generous deal for the CEECs and a signal for longer term policy in the steel sector. Yet consultations in the 113 ECSC working group indicated that only the UK delegation was in favour of completely abandoning the VRAs, while in particular the Spanish delegation insisted on an explicit reference in the ECSC protocols. As a compromise, the Commission's draft negotiation directives foresaw a review of such a decision after five years, but the opposition from the majority of governments led the Commission to drop it. The negotiation directives therefore stipulated for the ECSC protocols that 'the above provisions will not affect current voluntary restraint arrangements and those which could possibly succeed them'.[6]

At the later stages of the negotiations, this agreement within the working group became contested. Although the ECSC chapter was thought closed after the concessions on phasing out the tariffs, the Polish delegation challenged the inclusion of a reference to VRAs in the ECSC protocols.[7] The negotiators in DG I-E and Andriessen were sympathetic to the demands of the CEECs. However, although the former were sceptical about obtaining agreement from the Council, Andriessen assured the CEECs that he would attempt to avoid the inclusion of a reference to VRAs.[8] Andriessen's support for the CEECs' demand led to a politicisation of the issue, which had two main effects. On the one hand, COREPER and the General Affairs Council now dealt with the issue almost exclusively. It subsequently became clear that these actors were extremely reluctant to jeopardise the conclusion of the EAs on this issue. However, the politicisation also alerted higher-level political actors with industry portfolios, particularly in the case of Spain, who were more sensitive to lobbying from national steel producers.

An important factor in the debate was that the Council adopted in April 1991, in the context of the Uruguay Round, a mandate for the Commission to negotiate the suppression of all VRAs by March 1992. The Council's decision mobilised additional groups of actors to oppose the possibility of reintroducing the VRAs in the EAs. Policy-makers with horizontal responsibility for trade policy in the member states, notably in the German economics ministry, but also DG I-D within the Commission, feared that such a provision might jeopardise the implementation of a more open international steel trade policy, in particular the chances of concluding the MSA in the General Agreement on Tariffs and Trade (GATT).

The apparent contradiction between the Commission's mandate for the Uruguay Round and the EA negotiation directives resulted in different interpretations of these directives by the opposing camps in the Council.[9] The Spanish, French, Italian and Portuguese governments strongly advocated the possibility of reintroducomg VRAs. They argued that the Commission had to act according to the original negotiation directives, which in their view compelled it to negotiate an explicit reference to such a possibility. The British, Dutch and Danish governments were strongly opposed to the possibility of reintroducing VRAs and claimed that the mandate of April 1991 excluded this possibility. A third group, including Germany, Greece, Belgium, Luxembourg and Ireland, was more ambivalent. Although these governments were keen to preserve the possibility of concluding VRAs at a later stage, they did not press for an explicit reference in the agreements. In their interpretation, such a possibility existed as long as the agreements did not explicitly exclude it.

Internal consultation in the Commission led the DG I-E negotiators to propose that COREPER accept the CEECs' demands. COREPER rejected this proposal, because of strong opposition from the Spanish delegation, supported by the French, Italian and Portuguese representatives. In the General Affairs Council, Andriessen nevertheless firmly refused to change the Commission's proposal, emphasising the negative repercussions for the negotiations of an MSA (*Agence Europe*, 08.11.91: 9). The Dutch presidency had to conclude the issue without reaching a result.

In the following COREPER meeting, the Spanish and French representatives, backed by the Portuguese and Italians, demanded the inclusion of a 'joint statement' in the agreements, to specify that if the CEECs should fail to 'respect the constraints set out in the agreements', notably concerning state aids, the conclusion of VRAs to limit their exports could be envisaged (*Agence Europe*, 08.11.91: 9). However, it became clear that there was no majority for the inclusion of such a statement into the ECSC protocols and except for Spain, none of the delegations were prepared to block the entire agreement on this issue. The French delegation settled for entering a unilateral statement into the COREPER minutes, stating its interpretation that under the terms of the negotiation directives, the EU still had the option of concluding VRAs with the CEECs, even if the agreements themselves did not contain an explicit reference to this possibility.[10] The Spanish, Italian, Portuguese, Luxembourg and Belgian delegations associated themselves to this statement, while the UK and Dutch delegations recorded their differing interpretations.[11] Most delegations considered that this ambiguous compromise had settled the issue, but the Spanish Representative put a formal reservation on the steel protocol. Nonetheless, at the following General Affairs Council, the last meeting before the scheduled initialling of the agreements, the Dutch Presidency stated that it regarded the ECSC protocol settled with the outcome of the COREPER meeting and did not put it on the agenda.[12] The Commission thus formally concluded the EA negotiations and initialled the agreements without an explicit agreement in the Council on this issue.

The Spanish government protested heavily against this procedure (*Agence Europe*, 21.11.91: 7). It accused the Commission of acting in bad faith and denounced the presidency's approach as a major contradiction to internal rules. At the same time, differences within the Spanish government became apparent. While the ministry of industry appeared prepared to block the entire agreement over the ECSC protocol, the foreign ministry and the Permanent Representation did not want to jeopardise the EAs (see also Torreblanca 2001: 260–7).

As the negotiations were formally concluded, the Commission and the Council presidency attempted to draft a declaration that would satisfy Spanish demands. The Spanish government insisted on a declaration in the final act of the EAs, or at least an exchange of letters with the CEECs, which explicitly stipulated that VRAs should be triggered if CEEC exports affected EU regions where the restructuring process had not yet been completed. It therefore rejected as insufficient both a unilateral Commission declaration that 'the possibility of quantitative solutions could be considered, consistent with the Community's international obligations' and the presidency's proposal that the Commission would inform the CEECs of 'the importance certain member states attached to the respect of competition rules under the EAs in the steel sector'. Finally COREPER reached an agreement on a joint declaration of the Council and the Commission, which in addition to the above-mentioned declarations, committed the Commission to take precautionary measures, including a system of import licences to monitor prices and quantities of CEEC exports and a close monitoring of the restructuring of the CEEC industries.

However, at the General Affairs Council meeting on 16 December 1991, just prior to the signing ceremony, the Spanish delegation – led by the minister of industry, rather than the foreign ministry – dramatically rejected the agreement previously endorsed by the Spanish representative in COREPER and insisted that the joint declaration should be included as an annex to the final act of the agreements.[13] After a frantic and increasingly ill-tempered last-minute search for a solution between the Spanish delegation, the Commission and the Council presidency, and consultations with the CEEC negotiators and Prime Ministers, who had already arrived in the Council building for the signing ceremony, the Spanish delegation backed down from blocking the EAs. Following assurances from Andriessen that future EAs would contain a reference to the possibility of quantitative restrictions, the delegation accepted Andriessen's compromise proposal of a verbal reference to the existence of the Council/Commission declaration that was entered into the minutes of the signing ceremony.[14]

In sum, the ECSC protocols of the EAs accommodate the CEECs' preferences to a strikingly large extent. The elimination of the VRAs and of the possibility of reintroducing them in the future presents a significant liberalisation of market access. The internal Commission-Council declaration and the statement in the minutes of the signing ceremony served primarily for the Spanish government to save face in domestic politics. A key factor that made this far-reaching policy change possible, despite strong opposition from some member states and EU producers, was the appeal of arguments embedded in the non-intervention paradigm about the importance of liberalising international steel. These arguments mobilised support for abolishing the VRAs, especially from the Commission's DG I-D and they minimised opposition within some member states, such as Germany, which had previously supported more restrictive trade policies in the sector.

Still, the broader appeal of the new policy paradigm alone cannot explain the extent of the policy change in comparison to the earlier stage of trade policy towards the CEECs. A key difference during this stage concerns the structure of the policy process. The context of the EA negotiations allowed the advocates of an accommodation of the CEECs' preferences to employ strategies that minimised the influence of opposition from sectoral policy-makers. The EU's trade negotiations are often fragmented according to sectoral issues and this was also the case for many aspects of the EAs. However, in the case of steel, the initial drafting was characterised by a high degree of horizontal coordination and at the final stages of the negotiations decision-making was strongly centralised.

Horizontal coordination within the Commission during the establishment of the negotiation directives forged an agreement on substantive concessions in the sensitive sectors, which made it difficult for policy in the steel sector to remain insulated. The negotiators' ability to force more centralisation of the policy process that reduced the autonomy of sectoral policy-makers played a crucial role in the late stages of the negotiations. Politicisation of the debate during the negotiations, which forced policy-makers at higher levels of the Council hierarchy to negotiate the issue, did not as such restrict the access of sectoral policy-makers, as the case of Spain demonstrates. However, with the more direct involvement of the macro-policy-makers in the member states, it became clear that none of the delegations – except for Spain – wanted their opposition to endanger the conclusion of the EAs. These constraints enabled the presidency and the Commission to employ the rather heavy-handed strategy of creating *faits accompli* through initialling the agreements despite remaining Spanish opposition.

The start of the paradigm shift in combination with a more centralised policy process during the EA negotiations thus provided the necessary conditions for a significant accommodation of the CEECs' preferences, despite strong interest group opposition. At the same time, the acrimonious process of forcing agreement in the EAs also reflects the fragility of the deal. First, Andriessen was forced to give assurances for a more restrictive policy in future EAs. Furthermore, the steel industry and the member states that felt that their concerns had not been sufficiently taken into account were prone to use the trade defence instruments in the general provisions of the EAs to regain some of the concessions obtained by the CEECs. Much hinged therefore on the extent to which the CEECs would come under pressure to constrain their exports during the implementation of the agreements. Crucially, during the implementation of the agreements the policy process was bound to change, giving a much stronger role to sectoral policy-makers.

Implementation of the Europe Agreements

The key question for the implementation of the ECSC protocols was whether
the CEEC producers would come under pressure to restrain their exports,
especially with regard to prices. Such pressure is difficult to analyse, since it
need not be reflected in formal policy changes. EU producers might exercise
such pressure informally, using the threat of the use of trade defence instruments, such as anti-dumping and safeguard measures. Indeed, Rollo and
Smith (1993: 173) suggest that EUROFER had entered informal discussions
with CEEC producers in an attempt to cartelise the steel trade.

A useful indicator of such informal pressures is the development of prices
on the EU market (Messerlin 1992: 90). In the absence of constraints on
CEEC exports, prices should fall. Indeed, price data in 1997 indicates a down-
ward convergence of prices on 520 DM/tonne for hot rolled coil. EU prices
fell from a temporary peak of 700 DM/tonne at the end of 1995, while prices
in Poland and the Czech Republic rose from around 450 DM/tonne in early
1995 (*Financial Times*, 29.04.97: 24).

Another indicator is the use of trade defence measures against CEEC
producers. Apart from the direct consequences of individual measures on
trade, the actual use of such measures increases the credibility of threats from
EU producers towards CEEC firms. The EU indeed used safeguard and anti-
dumping action against CEEC producers in a number of cases. Yet the
incidence of cases alone does not necessarily reveal much about their
economic merit, nor does it say anything about cases in which the
Commission or the member states resisted pressures from the industry. I
therefore focus on two particular cases in which the CEECs were threatened
with trade restrictions, to analyse how and to what extent EU producers were
able to influence the Commission and member states. The first is the use of
safeguards against certain Czech and Slovak steel products in August 1992,
the first occasion on which the EU took action against CEEC producers after
the entry into force of the interim agreements. The second case is the 'external element' of the EU's restructuring plan for the steel industry from 1993 to
1994, which threatened to reintroduce a restrictive trade regime for all
CEECs.

Safeguard measures against certain CSFR products
The EU industry strongly condemned the EAs' ECSC protocols. Soon after
the signing of the EAs, criticism of the steel regime was voiced by the ECSC
Consultative Committee (*Agence Europe*, 19.12.91: 16; 30.01.92: 11),
EUROFER (*Agence Europe*, 11.02.92: 8), individual firm's representatives,
such as the chairman of Ilva (*Agence Europe*, 30.01.92: 12), and national
producer associations, e.g. the German Steel Federation (*Agence Europe*,
16.05.92: 16). The industry denounced the application procedures of the
trade defence mechanism as ineffective. It alleged a lack of political will in the

Commission to apply them, which CEEC producers would interpret 'as an invitation to increase their exports ... by adopting abnormally low prices, favoured by considerable public subsidies' (*Agence Europe*, 11.02.92: 8).

The producers presented their criticism in the terms of the managed restructuring paradigm, claiming that it was 'absolutely unacceptable that the socially painful restructuring measures should be made redundant by an indulgent attitude of the Commission which allowed dumped and subsidised products to disturb the situation on the EC market' (*Agence Europe*, 30.01.91: 11). Rather than simply exercising political pressure, industry representatives defended the role of trade policy within the policy paradigm and argued that the advocates of free trade insufficiently understood the functioning of competition on the steel market. François Mer argued:

> In their minds, the European market is like a glass of oil, in which one could add a drop of vinegar, ... Eastern European steel at dumping prices. ... But our markets are more like a glass of water in which one would suddenly add a drop of wine. The whole glass would then be discoloured. A few percentage points of steel consumption sold at low prices disrupt the whole market. (Quoted in Cadot and Melo 1995: 146)

In parallel to this general criticism of the EAs' steel trade regime, producers voiced their concerns about the rates of increase and low prices of specific CEEC steel exports. EUROFER complained in November 1991 about imports of cold-processed stainless steel bars, alloy bars and reversing mill plate (*Agence Europe*, 15.11.91: 12), in January 1992 about steel beams from Poland (*Agence Europe*, 11.02.92: 8) and in June about steel imports from Czechoslovakia in general (*Financial Times*, 02.06.92: 6).

The Commission initially resisted these pressures, but soon divisions became apparent. Andriessen and DG I-E wanted to avert the use of trade defence measures against the CEECs, but Bangemann, parts of DG III, and officials in DG I-D in charge of the EU's trade defence policy, were much more sympathetic to the industry's arguments. Faced with these pressures, Andriessen appeared to prefer that officials in DG III and DG I-D used informal pressure on the CEECs, to keep volumes and prices at a level acceptable to EU producers (*Agence Europe*, 16.01.92: 12), over the initiation of trade defence measures that might be more damaging to relations with the CEECs. By contrast, Leon Brittan, the competition Commissioner, and his *cabinet*, strongly objected to trade defence measures. Their concern was both about trade policy in general and the welfare of the CEECs, who – in their view – did not engage in predatory dumping but 'simply try to make a living'.[15]

Commission representatives assured the ECSC Consultative Committee in December 1991 that the Commission did 'everything possible to make its eastern European partners aware that it is in their own interest to avoid an export policy which in time would be detrimental to both parties' (*Agence Europe*, 19.12.91: 16). In January 1992, they reported to the committee that they had asked the Polish authorities to explain prices and that similar contacts would be made with the Czechoslovak authorities (*Agence Europe*, 30.01.92: 11). In May 1992, the EU–CFSR Contact Group on ECSC matters, established under the EA, met to discuss these issues. Commission and member state officials expressed concern about the rates of increase and the low prices of imports (*Together in Europe*, 14.05.92: 14). In a joint communiqué both sides agreed to evaluate 'means that would minimise the necessity for having recourse to the application of anti-dumping and safeguard measures'. The CSFR authorities would consider a partial reorientation of certain steel exports 'with the aim of ensuring better equilibrium in the geographical and commodity structure of deliveries' (*Agence Europe*, 01.06.92: 9). The Czechoslovak representatives stated that they would attempt to persuade their producers to maintain their prices to achieve higher profit margins, rather than to increase volumes and market shares at lower prices (*Financial Times*, 02.06.92: 6).

However, after the CSFR authorities did not deliver such a commitment from their producers, EU producers who initially preferred informal arrangements to restrict CEEC exports, pressed for formal measures. Such formal measures would also have a signalling effect on other CEEC exporters; evidence of their ability to obtain such measures increased the credibility of anti-dumping threats and thus their leverage in future calls for CEEC self-constraint. On 1 June 1992, EUROFER asked the Commission to examine the possibility of applying the safeguard clause under the EAs in particular against Czechoslovak imports (*Financial Times*, 02.06.92: 6) and the following day, the ECSC Consultative Committee demanded that anti-dumping and anti-subsidy procedures should start as soon as possible (*Together in Europe*, 15.06.92: 1). The Commission representatives still tried to use the conciliation mechanism envisaged by the EAs before starting an investigation. However, the assurances from CSFR representatives in the ECSC Contact Group on 20 July did not satisfy the Commission representatives (*Together in Europe*, 01.09.92: 3).

The Commission's resistance to safeguard measures appeared broken and the producers successfully convinced key member state governments to formally present their complaints at the EU level. In late July, the German and French representatives formally requested the Commission to apply the safeguard clause to imports from the CFSR (*Together in Europe*, 01.09.92: 3). German economics minister Möllemann in particular pushed for such measures, as the East German steel industry underwent a deep crisis and he had taken unpopular decisions about closures.[16] Only two member states, the UK and the Netherlands, voiced their general opposition to invoking the safeguard clause.

In the absence of a unanimous agreement in the Council, the final decision rested with the Commission. On 28 July, it emerged that the Commission planned to finally take such measures (*Agence Europe*, 29.07.92:

8). Since the initiative was supported by two central member states, the Commission found it very difficult to uphold its resistance. DG I-D and Bangemann particularly were sympathetic to the industry's case.[17] Andriessen's resistance was weakening. The Brittan *cabinet* suspected that the initiative was deliberately timed to coincide with the holiday period. The timing made it hard to prepare a case against it; rather than preventing them, Brittan had to concentrate on limiting the effect of the measures.[18] While the German and French governments had demanded the application of the safeguard to all ECSC steel products from the CSFR, the Commission limited the measures to three product categories and three member states, and fixed their duration until the end of 1992 (*Agence Europe*, 08.08.92: 4). On 14 August, the Commission authorised Germany, France, and Italy to limit the imports of certain steel products from the CSFR within a quota set at twenty per cent above their 1991 levels. The restrictions concerned exports of bars and rods to Germany, cold rolled sheets to France, and hot rolled wide coils to all three countries. The German producer association welcomed the Commission's decision as 'a clear warning to all east European steel exporters', which would 'help them to understand the need to control volumes exported and the need to sell at the appropriate prices' (*Agence Europe*, 22.08.92: 4).

This episode underlines that informal pressure during the implementation of the EAs presented a considerable threat to unconditional market access for CEEC producers. Parts of the Commission initially resisted such pressures, but once member state governments presented the industry's interests, the advocates of the CEECs' preferences in the Commission were unable to prevent the use of safeguard measures and only managed to limit their magnitude. The change of the structure of the policy process from the EA negotiations made it much harder for these policy advocates to influence policy. The fragmentation of the policy process largely insulated policy-making from broader concerns about EU policy towards CEECs. The implementation of policy gave a much greater role to the sectoral policy-makers in DG I-D, DG III, and the member states' ministries of industry or economics. The political leadership of these departments especially, for example Bangemann in the Commission, or Möllemann in Germany, seemed particularly susceptible to political pressures from industry. By contrast, among the officials who were experts in the steel sector, concerns about the longer term implications for EU steel policy appeared to make them more inclined to consider the merits of the non-intervention paradigm.

The external element of the 1993/94 restructuring plan for the EU steel industry

The debate about the renewal of the Czechoslovak quotas was complicated by the separation of the country in 1993 and by the completion of the internal market, which made it impossible to apply the arrangements to only three member states. However, the issue became primarily entangled with a

Commission initiative for a coordinated restructuring of the steel industry. Although this new restructuring plan was much less interventionist than the Davignon Plan, it presented a key reassertion of the managed restructuring paradigm. It exercised strong pressures for a wholesale reorientation of steel trade policy towards the CEECs for the purposes of internal restructuring. At the same time, the debate about the restructuring plan coincided with the attempts to reinforce policy towards the CEECs that cumulated in the Copenhagen European Council in 1993.

The deepening crisis of the EU steel industry during 1992 started a debate about an EU restructuring plan. Initially some producers demanded that the Commission declared a 'manifest crisis' to use its wide-ranging interventionist powers, but the majority of producers did not share this view. EUROFER proposed instead a voluntary programme to reduce overcapacities, but called on the Commission to use its powers under the ECSC treaty to coordinate the restructuring measures and to support them through financial aid and commercial policy (EUROFER 1992).

The Commission's proposal for a restructuring plan sought a commitment from the industry to cut a minimum of nineteen million tonnes of capacity for hot rolled products during the period 1993–95. The Commission's special envoy, Fernand Braun, a former Director General of DG III, had identified these quantities in confidential consultations with individual producers. Braun obtained some concrete pledges, mainly from public enterprises in Italy and Spain. The remainder was left for the producers to agree among themselves. As an incentive to undertake these capacity cuts and to facilitate them, the Commission offered accompanying measures. The internal measures consisted primarily of the financing of social support measures for redundancies and guidance on market developments. The external measures would prevent imports from disturbing the restructuring effort, but their concrete content was precisely the most contentious aspect of the restructuring plan.

EU producers pressed for comprehensive protection from potentially disruptive imports, in particular from the CEECs and the former Soviet Union. A EUROFER memorandum and statements by its director general, Dietrich von Husen (*Financial Times*, 14.10.92: 2), and the chairman of British Steel, Brian Moffat (*Financial Times*, 17.11.92: 1) presented these demands. The ECSC Consultative Committee most explicitly called for the 'strengthening of peripheral control measures in order to prevent unfair imports in particular from third countries where steel and steel processing industries do not respect the requirements of fair competition. Quantitative solutions must be found immediately in order to prevent injury caused by imports from East Europe and the former USSR' (*Together in Europe*, 01.12.92: 10).

In the Commission, a certain consensus on the need for external accompanying measures emerged, but their nature was contested. Some officials in

DG I reportedly suggested initially that the CEEC governments should be asked to impose an export tax, but other DG I officials considered this at odds with the general thrust of policy towards the CEECs (*Agence Europe*, 16.11.92: 3). The differences within the Commission were epitomised in the confrontation between the commissioners Bangemann and Brittan, who had obtained the external relations portfolio from Andriessen in the third Delors Commission. Bangemann, who had the overall responsibility for the restructuring plan, in coordination with Karel van Miert (competition policy), advocated external measures that provided protection against imports from eastern Europe (*Agence Europe*, 19.11.92: 8). His position was firmly embedded in the managed restructuring paradigm's perspective on trade policy, but also appeared to reflect a particular sympathy for the concerns of the German steel industry (*Times*, 20.03.93). Bangemann argued that the EU was 'prepared to allow products produced in [the CEECs] on to our markets, but at the same time it has been clearly stated that fair conditions should be applied' (*Financial Times*, 19.11.92: 24). 'Additional measures' to curb cheap imports would be discussed with Poland and Czechoslovakia in particular; without external protection as many as four or five of the leading EU steel producers could be forced out of the market, as 'the current price level [was] disastrous for everybody' (*Financial Times*, 17.02.93: 2). Bangemann proposed to ask the CEEC governments to impose minimum prices during a three-year period and to sanction breaches with anti-dumping duties. He also considered extending the quantitative restrictions imposed on Czech and Slovak exporters in 1992 to other CEECs. Such a combination of quantitative and price restraints came very close to some form of VRA arrangement and would have amounted to a full-scale change of the steel trade regime.

Bangemann's proposals were most strongly opposed by Brittan, whose position reflected both his strong personal commitment towards the CEECs and his advocacy of the non-intervention paradigm for EU steel policy. Brittan argued that providing EU producers with stable conditions to complete their restructuring should not undermine the EU's commitment to assist the transformations in CEE (*Financial Times*, 17.02.93: 2). He insisted that any protective measures needed to be justified case-by-case on their economic merits. He thus firmly rejected any price constraints or the extension of tariff quotas in place with the Czechs and Slovaks to other CEECs. At the same time, Brittan sought to use the emergence of a high-level political commitment to a reinforced association policy at the Edinburgh European Council to influence the decisions on steel trade policy:

> It is rightly an essential part of the Community's strategy that trade should play a major part … in the Community's approach to our eastern neighbours. Indeed I would go as so far as to say that the development of trade is the most … valuable contribution we can make towards helping them. […] I recognize that this is a difficult economic time for … sectors such as agriculture, steel and textiles … Nonetheless, we have to ask ourselves: Is the Community merely paying lip-

> service to the need to help our eastern neighbours, or is the commitment real? I
> am sure that it is a genuine one. A real commitment to bring this about is bound
> to involve making difficult choices. (*Together in Europe*, 01.02.93: 2)

Brittan lost the argument at the commissioners' meeting, but while the
Commission's proposals for the external measures envisaged an extension of
tariff quotas to the other CEECs, Bangemann's proposal for additional price
constraints failed (*Agence Europe*, 18.02.93: 5). The Commission proposed
'negotiations with the CEECs of tariff quotas for "sensitive products" (rods,
coils and cold rolled sheet from former Czechoslovakia; rods and heavy plate
from Poland) for the period from 1993 to 1995, on the basis of the 1991 level
of imports plus a certain percentage increase to be determined' (*Agence
Europe*, 24.02.93: 5).

Among the member states, the UK representatives stated their opposition
to the proposals, which in their view contradicted the conclusions of the
Edinburgh European Council. By contrast, Germany, Italy, and Spain particularly favoured greater protection against cheap imports (*Financial Times*,
24.04.93: 5). The German Steel Federation had presented a memorandum to
economics minister Rexrodt, in which it called for protection against cheap
imports from CEE and the former Soviet Union, in particular on long products, through volume restrictions, at twenty per cent over the 1991 level,
rather than minimum prices, which were considered too easy to circumvent
(*Financial Times*, 22.04.93: 2). The ECSC Consultative Committee (1993:
4–5) unanimously urged the Commission to negotiate an extension of tariff
quotas to all sensitive products and to all CEECs.

The Industry Council was generally favourable to the restrictive line in
the Commission's proposal. However, the UK delegation maintained its
strong opposition and insisted on inserting a statement into the Council
conclusions that declared that the EU duly take into account the commitment
of the Edinburgh Council concerning its support for political stability and
economic growth in the CEECs.[19] Although the majority of the other delegations favoured the Commission's proposal, the Council was unable to agree
on the restrictive measures. The determined opposition of the British delegation and the cracks in the Commission's support for the restrictions, which
reappeared in the Council meeting, prevented the insulation of the issue
within the framework of the steel restructuring plan.

The Commission reverted to Brittan's position of applying tariff quotas
only on a case-by-case basis, which thus averted a blanket extension of restrictions to all CEECs and all sensitive products (*Agence Europe*, 26.02.93: 5–6).
In turn, Brittan and the UK delegation conceded to seek an agreement with
the Czech and Slovak governments to extend the tariff quotas already in force
against their producers for the duration of the restructuring plan. Brittan thus
gave up his attempts to prevent a renewal of the 1992 safeguards, which in any
case would have been difficult, as Andriessen had endorsed a renewal in principle during the last days of December 1992 (*Together in Europe*, 01.02.93: 1).

However, the Commission's proposals for the content of the tariff quotas remained locked in a protracted dispute between Brittan, who sought a thirty-five per cent increase in the quotas, and Bangemann (*Agence Europe*, 24.03.93: 8; 14.04.93: 8). In April, the Commission reached a compromise on quota increases that differentiated between product groups, with coils treated more generously than the other products. On the whole, Brittan appeared successful with his demands on the quota increase for 1993, while Bangemann obtained a tightening of quotas for 1994 and 1995 (*Financial Times*, 23.04.93). In late May, meetings of the Joint Committees with the Czech Republic and Slovakia approved the arrangements.

In 1994, however, the agreement on the external measures notwithstanding, the Commission decided to abandon the restructuring plan (see e.g. Vanderseypen 1995). As the situation in the EU steel market improved, it became clear that in particular the privatised steel companies were unable to agree the necessary capacity reductions on which the Commission had made its support conditional. With the steel plan terminated, the EU had to decide the future of the external element, i.e. the arrangements that had been agreed for 1995 on the assumption of its full implementation. The Commission recommended eliminating the tariff quotas in force toward Czech and Slovak producers. Van Miert argued that the EU could not demand a continuation of the export restrictions, which also contradicted the EU's general political objectives towards the CEECs. Bangemann also supported abandoning the measures (*Agence Europe*, 05.11.94: 10). However, to abandon the measures required unanimity in the Council and the Industry Council was far from reaching such a decision (*Together in Europe*, 15.11.94: 4). The measures thus stayed in force until the end of 1995.

In sum, despite strong pressures from the industry and from within the Commission and among member states, the advocates of the CEECs' preferences prevented a reversal of the EAs' liberalisation as part of the restructuring plan for the EU steel industry. The trade restrictions through the external element of the restructuring were much more limited than the wholesale regulation of trade that this powerful coalition of actors intended.

The initial agreement on a new internal restructuring plan for the steel industry was a final reassertion of the managed restructuring paradigm for EU steel policy. The internal measures were much less interventionist than the Davignon Plan, which already indicates the extent to which the dominant ideas had changed. However, the arguments relating to external policy and in particular the notion that exports from the CEECs were 'unfair', reflect that this element of the paradigm was still deeply entrenched. For a majority of sectoral policy-makers, the legitimate function of trade policy towards the CEECs was thus to facilitate internal restructuring. However, the ultimate failure of the restructuring plan precipitated the demise of the managed restructuring paradigm (see also Dudley and Richardson 1999: 243).

The structure of the policy process was a key factor that facilitated a stronger assertion of sectoral policy-makers pressing for trade restrictions. In the context of the restructuring plan, sectoral steel policy-makers had the lead, which put them into a strong position to influence steel trade policy. However, a number of factors limited their ability to generate a highly restrictive policy. Leon Brittan, as the new external relations commissioner, became strongly involved in the detail of policy, on which he and his cabinet had significant expertise. The move towards a closer relationship with the CEECs between the Edinburgh and Copenhagen European Councils allowed Brittan and the UK government to situate steel trade policy within the broader objectives of the association policy and the unanimity requirement for commercial policy under the ECSC treaty facilitated opposition to a restrictive regime. Crucially, despite the strong influence of sectoral policy-makers in the strongly fragmented policy process, the policy advocates could find allies among the sectoral policy-makers, such as some experts in DG III, who had converted to the non-intervention paradigm and did not fully support the pragmatic protectionism of Bangemann.

Conclusions

In the case of steel trade policy, the influence of societal interests on EU policy was much more limited than a materialist rationalist analysis would predict. Despite strong and unified pressures from the EU steel industry for protection from CEEC exports, the EU liberalised trade within the existing framework in 1990 and 1991; essentially liberalised steel trade under the EAs; and resisted pressures for a wholesale re-introduction of a highly regulated regime as part of the restructuring plan.

A crucial factor in this case was the emergence of an alternative policy paradigm for EU steel policy, especially inside the Commission, in which the role of trade policy is much more compatible with the preferences of the policy advocates among the macro-policy-makers. The rise of the non-intervention paradigm enabled the policy advocates to build strategic alliances for trade liberalisation with sectoral policy-makers, who had converted to the new non-intervention paradigm – in contrast to their political leadership that appeared more receptive to interest group pressure.

The changing structure of the policy process at different stages of policy development had an important impact on policy outcomes. Policy in the steel sector usually took place in a fragmented policy process, which gave sectoral policy-makers considerable influence during various stages of policy development. The insulation of negotiations on the renewal of the VRA regime for 1990 and 1991 led to some liberalisation within the quotas, but the regime as such remained unchallenged.

The context of the EA negotiations enabled the policy advocates in the Commission to place policy firmly in the context of the new relationship with the CEECs and to reduce the autonomy of sectoral policy-makers in the policy process. Through horizontal coordination, they obtained a cross-sectoral agreement on substantive liberalisation in the steel sector and thus the abolition of the VRAs. However, during the decentralised drafting of the negotiating directives, sectoral policy-makers from the member states inserted the reference to the possibility of re-introducing VRAs. Nonetheless, the negotiation framework induced the shadow of hierarchical intervention in the policy process. The negotiations allowed the CEECs to raise objections to the possibility of re-introducing the VRAs. When this question emerged as a major contentious issue, the Commission and the Council presidency could engineer a centralisation of decision-making that forced high-level policy-makers to negotiate the issue. These policy-makers were much more receptive to accommodating the CEECs' preferences in order to conclude the negotiations than the sectoral policy-makers.

The influence of sectoral policy-makers increased significantly during the implementation of the EAs. The fragmentation of the policy process made it much harder for the advocates of the CEECs' preferences to oppose interest group pressures for re-establishing a certain level of protection through the use of trade defence instruments. The debate on the restructuring plan for the steel industry gave the lead in the policy process to sectoral policy-makers and threatened to place steel trade policy towards the CEECs firmly at the service of internal policy. Still, interest group pressures did not succeed in reintroducing a comprehensive protective regime, partly because of the strong personal involvement of Leon Brittan in the detail of policy, partly because of the extent to which the non-intervention paradigm for steel policy had acquired a dominant position.

Notes

1 Interviews, British Steel, 01.09.95; UK Department of Trade and Industry, 01.09.95; German Steel Federation, 01.02.95.

2 Interviews, EUROFER, 03.02.95; German Steel Federation, 01.02.95; French Steel Federation, 31.10.95; British Steel, 01.09.95; Usinor Sacilor, 11.07.96.

3 Interviews, French National Steel Traders Association (SNCPS), 27.06.96; Spanish Association of Private Common Steel Producers (Siderinsa), 19.06.96; Spanish Steel Trader Association, 21.06.96; Commission DG III, 31.01.95; UK Department of Trade and Industry, 01.09.95.

4 Interviews, German Ministry of Economy, 21.12.95; Commission DG III, 31.01.95.

5 Interview, Commission DG I, 27.10.95.

6 'les dispositions ci-dessus n'affecteront pas les actuels arrangements d'autolimitation négociés et ceux qui pourraient éventuellement y succéder'; interview, French Permanent Representation, 02.02.95; also quoted in Torreblanca 1997: 574.

7 Interview, Spanish Permanent Representation, 03.02.95.

8 Interview, Spanish Permanent Representation, 03.02.95.

9 Interviews, Spanish Permanent Representation, 03.02.95; French Permanent

Representation, 02.02.95.
10 Interviews, Spanish Permanent Representation, 03.02.95; French Permanent Representation, 02.02.95.
11 Interview, French Permanent Representation, 02.02.95.
12 Interview, Spanish Permanent Representation, 03.02.95.
13 Interview, Spanish Permanent Representation, 03.02.95.
14 Interview, Spanish Permanent Representation, 03.02.95.
15 Interview, Commissioner's *cabinet*, 02.02.95.
16 Interviews, German Permanent Representation, 03.02.95; German Ministry of Economy, 21.12.95.
17 Interview, Commission DG III, 31.01.95.
18 Interview, Commissioner's *cabinet*, 02.02.95.
19 Interview, UK Department of Trade and Industry, 01.09.95.

7

Regulatory alignment with the internal market

This chapter analyses the EU's policy for the regulatory alignment of the CEECs with the internal market. In the EU, the objective of regulatory harmonisation is the elimination of non-tariff barriers (NTBs) to trade that remained a main source of market segmentation after the completion of the customs union. Divergent national product specifications, or safety standards for products, may reflect differences in taste and specific concerns about public policy objectives. However, especially during the 1970s, governments also used them deliberately to protect their industries. The EU's Single Market programme thus focused precisely on these technical impediments to the free circulation of goods. The creation of the single market also has major implications for enlargement. Regulatory alignment – the adjustment to the rules of the internal market – presents a key challenge for prospective members. As Young and Wallace (2000b: 112) observe, the internal market has 'limited the scope of derogations that can be granted to new members to ease their transitions. In this sense the threshold for full membership has been raised much higher'.

The second section of this chapter identifies *selective alignment* as a key preference of the CEEC governments with regard to regulatory alignment. More generally, selective alignment means that the CEECs are free to set their own regulatory priorities during the pre-accession process, which implies that the EU does not impose binding conditions prior to their accession. Moreover, selective alignment relates to the substance of rules to which the CEECs are asked to align. Specifically, the CEECs have an interest in delaying alignment with regulations that concern the production *process* – as opposed to *product* characteristics – until post-accession transitional periods. Key areas of such process regulations concern EU environmental and social policy.

In the third part of this chapter, I examine the balance of interest group pressures in the EU concerning this question. EU interest groups strongly oppose selective regulatory alignment and favour early and strict alignment of the CEECs. Early alignment facilitates their access to the CEECs' markets and, crucially, reduces the competitive advantages that CEEC firms might enjoy through lower production costs.

The fourth section analyses to what extent the ideas that underpin the EU's internal market are compatible with selective regulatory alignment. I argue that the EU's internal market paradigm forms an additional obstacle to selective alignment by the CEECs, since it includes the acceptance of the 'level playing field' argument and the belief that the internal market does not only serve the objective of economic competition, but also the promotion of social and environmental public policy objectives.

Sections five and six analyse the development of the EU's regulatory alignment policy towards the CEECs. The analysis focuses on the Commission's White Paper (WP) on the preparation of the candidates for their participation in the internal market that the Cannes European Council adopted in June 1995 and its follow-up in the Accession Partnerships, the Commission's Regular Reports and in accession negotiations. It examines to what extent the main explanatory factors in the analysis – interest group pressure, structure of the policy process and policy paradigms – affected the ability of the advocates of the CEECs' preferences in the Commission to influence policy outcomes. I conclude that despite the unfavourable configuration of interests on the EU side, the EU essentially followed a selective approach to regulatory alignment. This outcome resulted from the strong coordinating role of DG XV (Internal Market) in the drafting of the WP and the receptiveness of these policy-makers to an alternative, 'economic competition' paradigm for the internal market, at least with regard to allowing selective alignment temporarily. A remaining puzzle is the variation between environmental policy, the clearest example of the selective approach, and social policy, which did not follow this approach.

CEEC preferences concerning regulatory alignment

Adjustment costs

The key challenges of regulatory alignment for the CEECs are different from those encountered in the implementation of the single market programme and in the EFTA enlargement. The challenge for the CEECs is not only to replace incompatible regulations, which in their case often related to the CMEA or stemmed from the 1920s and 1930s. A more fundamental task is the very establishment and operation of regulatory regimes to enforce an entirely new set of rules. The legacy of central planning meant that in many areas of economic activity, regulatory regimes were a novelty in the CEECs (see e.g. Winters 1995b). One type of adjustment cost for the CEECs thus arises from the need to develop the institutional and administrative infrastructure to implement EU rules. At the most basic level, CEEC legislators and administrators have to understand the purpose of regulations. They then have to establish mechanisms for the transposition of regulations into national law and set up enforcement agencies that ensure the implementation of legislation. Procedures are required through which the potential beneficiaries of EU rules can file complaints against improper application. Laboratories for certification and testing of products have to be set up, staffed and equipped. Yet in the context of economic transformation, the necessary financial, administrative, and human resources are all in short supply.

Another type of adjustment cost is direct investment costs. Governments have to bear some of these costs. For example, the World Bank (2000) estimated that over twenty years, Poland would need to spend between three and seven per cent of current GDP in order to implement EU environmental policy. In relative terms, the costs in Hungary and the Czech Republic are even higher – an estimated €1,306 and 1,437 per capita respectively (Mann 1997: 14). Most of the regulatory costs are borne directly by CEEC businesses (see e.g. Orlowski and Mayhew 2001). The implementation of technical standards for production conditions – such as sanitary standards in the food industry, health and safety regulations for the workplace, or pollution controls – require investment to upgrade production facilities. The additional costs of compliance with higher EU standards affect the competitive position of CEEC businesses and their ability to compete on the basis of low production costs.

Sanitary standards even created major problems in the EFTA enlargement. In Austria, for example, the investment costs necessary to conform to EU standards for abattoirs led to a large-scale closure of facilities. In Poland, standards stem from the 1930s and most abattoirs are located in inner city areas, which means that in most cases they might have to be demolished and rebuilt outside cities.[1] In environmental policy, rules existed in the CEECs and often even stipulated rather high levels of protection, but the command economies' reliance on extensive growth meant that these rules were never enforced.[2] Likewise, most CEECs have extensive laws governing working conditions, but national administrations rather tended to offer workers higher pay to work under unhealthy or dangerous conditions (Coss 1997: 14).

Potential benefits of unilateral alignment

Although the CEECs' key incentive for regulatory alignment is EU membership, even unilateral alignment might entail certain benefits for the CEECs. The creation of regulatory systems, standards and enforcement agencies are key elements of establishing the foundations of a functioning market economy (Smith et al. 1996: 1; Winters 1995b). Alignment with the EU's regulatory framework can therefore support the broader process of economic transformation. Indeed, CEEC policy-makers regularly underline the need to modernise their economies through the implementation of a functioning regulatory framework independently of accession.[3]

However, the appropriateness of the EU's regulatory regime as a model for countries in economic transformation can be challenged. The EU's 'regulatory state' (Majone 1996) reflects a specific stage of economic development in Western Europe. More appropriate in the particular context of the CEECs might be a much more interventionist 'developmental state' (Johnson 1982) that directs foreign investment, domestic finance and trade policy to the development of specific target sectors (McGowan and Wallace 1996: 564).

Even if the appropriateness of the EU's regulatory model is not challenged at this fundamental level, the suitability of specific EU rules might be questionable. For example, Holmes and Smith (1997) argue that EU competition policy is not only aimed at promoting economic efficiency, but economic integration for its own sake. A more relaxed competition and state aids regime might therefore fit better with the specific priorities of the CEECs in the context of economic transformation. Another example are intellectual property rules. US regulations that provide high protection of intellectual property abroad, but low protection domestically, might suit the CEECs better than EU rules.[4]

Regulatory alignment might also provide benefits in its own right by preparing the CEECs' economies for internationalisation. Functioning regulatory systems and standards are an essential requirement for the CEECs to attract foreign direct investment and to create certainty for exporters. Polish officials particularly stress this point.[5] In contrast to the voucher privatisation in the Czech Republic, which transferred previously publicly owned enterprises to the mass population, the emphasis in Poland was on finding owners, rather than shareholders. In view of the limited availability of domestic capital, alignment with the single market was a key strategy to attract foreign investors, not only from the EU, but also from the USA and Japan.

Furthermore, the more CEEC producers become active exporters, the greater the need to comply with regulatory requirements on foreign markets. Government regulations occupy an increasingly important role on the international trade agenda and are the focus of a growing number of international trade disputes. Agreements between the US and the EU on regulatory policies and procedures have developed de facto into global standards (Vogel 1997: 3). Regulatory alignment with the EU might thus improve market access for the CEECs to international markets more generally, and not only to the EU.

Examples of regulatory sources of trade problems in EU–CEEC trade relations include the politically highly charged case of the EU's blanket ban on CEEC live cattle in 1993. The EU justified the ban with the discovery of cattle infected by foot-and-mouth disease in Italy, which had been imported from Croatia via Hungary (*Euro-east*, 23.04.1993: 26). While the CEEC denounced the measure as blatant protectionism, the EU pointed at the deficiencies in CEEC regulations concerning customs controls, certification, and veterinary standards. More generally, trust in the regulatory capacities of the trading partner is an important underpinning of trade relations (see e.g. Previdi 1997).

The application of the same competition rules across countries can make the use of the traditional trade defence instruments unnecessary (see e.g. Smith et al. 1996: 19). If the CEECs align themselves with EU regulations on cartels, monopolies, and state aids and enforce a competition regime compatible with those of the EU, then there are no grounds for the use of trade defence measures. However, there is no automatic link; it would require an explicit commitment on the side of the EU and the establishment of a legal regime that bestowed on the Commission the necessary powers to enforce compliance in the CEECs.

Selective alignment

Regulatory alignment might thus provide benefits for the CEECs in its own right, when EU rules provide useful templates for economic transformation or facilitate trade and investment. However, as this is not the case in all policy areas, a selective approach to alignment with the EU is preferable to the CEECs. The prospect of future EU membership can provide a rationale for CEEC alignment even in those areas, or with those specific rules, for which there is no independent rationale in market-making or trade-creation. The benefits of membership might outweigh the opportunity costs of adopting or maintaining rules that are incompatible with EU regulations.

However, even if the goal of membership ultimately limits the scope for selective alignment, there is still a crucial distinction between the pre-accession phase and actual accession. Membership requires that EU rules are applied and enforced only upon accession, but not before. Thus, one key goal for the CEECs is that regulatory alignment remains non-binding prior to accession. Furthermore, in certain areas, the case can be made for temporarily tolerating selective application of EU rules even after accession, i.e. for alignment to take place in post-accession transition periods and with full application only at the end of those transition periods.

In this respect, a particularly strong case can be made for EU legislation that regulates production *processes*. Such process regulations are particularly prominent in environmental and social policy, for example regarding pollution levels from stationary sources or health and safety requirements at the workplace. Such regulations do not directly affect the nature of the *products* traded and therefore do not constitute NTBs. Since they do not impede the free circulation of goods in the internal market, they are therefore not essential for its functioning (Smith et al. 1996).

Furthermore, CEEC policy-makers point out that high levels of environmental, social and consumer protection are a characteristic of relatively affluent societies and certain levels of economic development. Along these lines, CEEC policy-makers have argued, for example with regard to environmental policy, that their countries must have the opportunity to 'become wealthier before becoming cleaner'.[6]

While the interests of CEEC firms and wider publics have been only weakly articulated, the main preferences of the CEEC governments with regard to regulatory alignment is thus to ensure that they only have to apply process regulations after long post-accession transitional periods, let alone prior to accession. Such selective alignment would not only allow the CEECs and their firms to delay costly regulations. Their objective of 'early accession and long transition periods' focuses on becoming full members as soon as they have implemented all the measures of the *acquis communautaire* that are essential for the functioning of the internal market.[7]

EU interest group preferences

Business interests

In general, EU producers benefit from the regulatory alignment of the CEECs, as it allows them to operate in the CEECs within a regulatory framework similar to that of the internal market (see e.g. Young and Wallace 2000a: 119–20). However, this picture changes with regard to the question of selective alignment that allows the CEECs to postpone the implementation of process-related environmental and social policy regulations to post-accession transition periods. The majority of EU producers would be expected to oppose the CEECs' demands for selective alignment. Opposition should be strongest from companies in sectors where environmental and social standards are an important part of the cost structure, namely polluting industries, such as chemicals, and labour-intensive industries, such as textiles. A strict and early alignment of the CEECs with EU regulations in those critical areas would mean a reduction in the competitive advantages that the CEEC firms enjoy through lower wages.[8]

However, EU producer groups have not been very active during the development of the EU's regulatory alignment policy.[9] To the extent that business articulated their positions, they did not focus on the detail of the CEECs' regulatory alignment (see e.g. BDI 1996, CNPF 1997, DIHT 1995). After the publication of the Commission White Paper and with the start of accession negotiations approaching, regulatory alignment attracted more attention. A position paper by the Union of Industrial and Employers' Confederations of the European Communities (UNICE) (1997) reflects that while producers generally welcomed enlargement, they insisted on strict and extensive application of EU rules and standards as early as possible. The demands included the contested areas of social and environmental process standards and, significantly, also those CEECs that were not expected to start negotiations in the near future.

> It is important that extended transition periods or exceptions are avoided, even if, as a consequence, full membership is delayed. (1997: 5)

> European business is in principle against long transition periods or exceptions in the area of the Internal Market *acquis*. The *acquis communautaire* should also be fully implemented in the social policy field and no 'opt-outs' permitted. Adjustment measures should be carried out before accession, not after. (1997: 7)

> Effective means should … be used to secure … compliance with Internal Market disciplines also from those candidate countries, which cannot start negotiations for full membership at this stage. UNICE also proposes that the EU should start immediate negotiations with the remaining candidate countries to introduce essential elements of the Internal Market, including … common safety and health regulations. (1997: 19)

On the other hand, EU businesses that invested in production facilities in the CEECs in order to enjoy the lower production costs could be expected to advocate selective alignment allowing the CEECs to maintain lower environmental and social policy standards. Their voices were, however, largely absent from the policy process. Companies' investment motives differ according to the country of origin, the type of investment and the sectors concerned. For example, German companies have invested more in production and UK companies primarily in distribution. In general, those EU companies that undertook greenfield investment in the CEECs and saw their investment as a long-term operation used technology that conforms with EU standards in anticipation of the CEECs' eventual accession.[10]

Trade unions and NGOs

Trade unions might be expected to be particularly concerned about social policy and health and safety at the workplace in particular, as well as about the lower production costs in the CEECs more generally. However, the European Trade Union Congress (ETUC) has mainly focused on strengthening the role of workers' representation in the CEECs through developing the social dialogue and has warned that some governments attempt to use the accession process to justify regressive social policies (ETUC 1998, 2000). While trade unions did not articulate detailed positions on regulatory alignment, ETUC seemed less concerned about 'social dumping'. In its position paper on the EAs, ETUC (1993: 4) stated that 'there is obvious social dumping going on, like importing labour force from some countries for construction projects etc. [however] ETUC and the European trade union movement must ensure that no irrational protectionist tendencies gain the upper hand over this debate.'

With regard to environmental standards, environmental NGOs stressed the need 'to keep up pressure on governments and business in these countries to implement the environmental *acquis* fully and completely upon accession.'

(EEB 2001: 7). However, with the possible exception of the question of nuclear safety, in which environmental groups and broader publics mobilised to use EU accession as a lever to push for higher standards, such environmental concerns were not very strongly articulated.

In sum, EU business associations clearly opposed the preference of CEECs' governments for selective pre-accession alignment. EU businesses demanded strict and early compliance with the EU's *acquis* during the pre-accession stage and the minimising in accession negotiations of possible transitional periods, which allow CEEC companies to produce under less stringent conditions. The preferences of other societal interest organisations in the EU converge with the preferences of industry, in particular with regard to social policy and environmental standards. The balance of societal interests inside the EU should thus exert pressure on public policy-makers to insist on a strict and early application of EU rules by the CEECs, especially on process-regulations. If policy-makers acted primarily according to the interests of the most powerful societal groups, we would expect little scope for selectivity in the CEECs' alignment.

Policy paradigms underpinning the EU's internal market

The flexibility of the EU's regulatory alignment policy is severely circumscribed by the assumptions underpinning EU accession negotiations: the EU treaties are not subject to negotiations; new members have to accept all of the *acquis*, without exception. These procedures reflect the EU's deliberately defensive stance in response to the UK's first membership application, but they established an orthodoxy that remained in place, despite the differences in nature and approach of subsequent candidates (Ruano 2002). Transition periods that allow new members to phase in their compliance with certain rules by a date agreed during the negotiations are possible, but strictly limited in time and scope (see also Avery 1995: 5). The insistence on unilateral adjustment by the candidates has become part of the 'classical enlargement method' (Preston 1997).

These assumptions ultimately limit the scope for selective regulatory alignment after accession. However, the receptiveness of EU policy-makers to demands for selective alignment during the *pre-accession phase* depends on the compatibility between these demands and the ideas underpinning the EU's internal market. The internal market programme is based on certain shared beliefs among EU policy-makers that relate to their understanding of its functioning and its objectives. Two related components of the EU's 'internal market paradigm' are incompatible with selective alignment with product regulations.

The first component is the general acceptance in the EU of a specific 'level playing field' argument. According to this argument, an elimination of NTBs is not sufficient to ensure fair competition in the internal market. In order for firms to compete on a level playing field, a harmonisation of rules regulating the production process is also necessary. The argument is based on the belief that competitive advantages that result from lower production costs through diverging regulatory requirements for the production process – for example concerning pollution levels or health and safety at the workplace – are unfair. With regard to social policy, this argument is expressed in concerns about 'social dumping' that allows firms that operate where social wages are low to undercut their competitors, which will force them to go out of business, relocate or force their governments into 'regulatory competition' to lower social protection standards (see e.g. Leibfried and Pierson 2000: 284)

The establishment of the single market induced a growing belief that a certain convergence in such process regulation is an essential component of economic integration in the EU. Young and Wallace (2000b: 110) point out:

> As products came to move more easily, attention also focused on the process and conditions under which goods and services were produced and provided. Irrespective of other arguments for European policies on environmental and social issues, the preoccupation of entrepreneurs with operating on a 'level playing field' turned attention to the relevance of these other factors for costs, competition, and profitability.

However, the crucial point is that despite the widespread acceptance of the 'level playing field' argument in the EU, the assumptions underpinning it are by no means generally accepted. Rather, the argument draws on a specific understanding and interpretation of economic competition and economic integration. While divergent regulations of the production process undoubtedly affect the competitive positions of firms, many economists argue that there is nothing 'unfair' about competition between companies that produce according to different environmental or social regulations. In this perspective, there is thus no economic case for harmonisation in those areas, since these regulations do not create non-tariff barriers to the free circulation of goods (see e.g. Begg et al. 1993). It can be argued that workers and citizens should be free to choose whether 'to create competitive advantages for themselves by accepting lower environmental quality or poorer social protection' and thus 'the balance of cash and non-cash rewards they receive' (Smith et al. 1996: 5). Disarmament agreements on investment incentives are more appropriate for addressing the danger of excessive deregulatory competition between governments than harmonisation requirements (1996: 6). In sum, the validity of the 'level playing field' argument for the internal market is thus one distinctive set of ideas that underpin the internal market, rather than an obvious or objective fact.

The other component of the EU's internal market paradigm that runs counter to a selective alignment with product regulations is the broad acceptance of high levels of environmental and social protection as public policy goals in their own right. As with the 'level playing field' argument, this component also initially resulted from a bargaining process. EU policy-makers saw the need for social, environmental and cohesion policies as correctives to market-building measures in order to gain acceptance from broader publics and those who feared the increased competition in the internal market. However, the agreement on such flanking measures has become linked to the notion of a distinctive European model of economic integration. This 'European model' is based on the belief that the rationale of the internal market is not purely to increase economic competition, but also to promote broader public policy objectives. As Laffan (1997: 7) points out:

> the dynamics of integration have led to demands for regulation beyond the narrow confines of the economic sphere to include important areas of social and environmental legislation. Arguments about efficiency were never enough to persuade governments and other social forces about the desirability of the internal market. ... Although the EU is not built on an agreed 'European model of society', it is predicated on a *belief* that economic integration must go beyond the market. (Emphasis added)

Mario Monti (1995: 1–2, 5), the internal market commissioner, expressed this view of the internal market most poignantly:

> The Internal Market could not, however, be designed with purely economic goals in mind. It is only one aspect of a Union which has wider objectives: balanced and sustainable growth respecting the environment, high levels of employment and social protection, better standards of living and quality of life and economic and social cohesion. ... It is also a key feature of the Internal Market that competition between the economic operators within in takes place, so far as possible on a level playing field. ... it also depends on rules which ensure that measures which are designed, for example, to protect the environment do not have the undesired effect of distorting competition. [...] The Internal Market cannot be isolated from the objective of high social and environmental protection standards contained in the Union Treaty. And the Internal Market can only function properly on the basis of fair conditions for competition, which is part of the purposes of much social and environmental legislation at the Community level.

The policy paradigm underpinning the EU's internal market thus militates strongly against demands by the CEECs for a selective alignment with product regulations, while keeping lower process regulations until the end of post-accession transition periods. The areas where such selectivity is most salient – environmental and social policy regulation – have become firmly established elements of the internal market. Arguably, the agreement to harmonise production processes and on high levels of protection was initially the result of bargaining between high-cost and low-cost countries and between business and other societal interests. However, this agreement has achieved acceptance at a much more fundamental level as a component of the internal market paradigm. The legitimacy that the internal market paradigm assigns to stringent process regulations renders it more difficult to argue that the EU should temporarily exempt the CEECs from these requirements. The issue at stake is not simply whether the EU compromises vested interests, but the feasibility of challenging shared understandings of fair competition and legitimate public policy goals.

However, despite its wide acceptance, this internal market paradigm is not uncontested. For example, the Conservative Party in the UK has been a key advocate of a much more deregulated internal market. In this perspective, environmental and social process standards must not be regulated at the EU level, but left to the member states. Such an alternative paradigm of economic integration is much more in line with demands for selective regulatory alignment. The primary focus on economic competition suggests that only regulations that constitute NTBs need to be harmonised. It suggests a clear hierarchy between different parts of the internal market *acquis*: process regulations might be desirable elements of the internal market, but as long as they do not constitute NTBs, they are not essential for the functioning of the internal market. This alternative internal market paradigm has, however, not been able to seriously challenge the dominant paradigm. The accession of the EFTA countries and the change of government in the UK have further bolstered the dominant paradigm.

In sum, in addition to interest group preferences in the EU, the policy paradigm underpinning the internal market is firmly biased against the accommodation of the CEECs' preferences for selective alignment. However, I will argue below that a key factor that nonetheless facilitated such an accommodation was that the views of policy-makers in DG XV (internal market), who played a key role in the development of the EU's regulatory alignment policy, were much more amenable to the narrower, competition-focused view of the internal market.

The Commission White Paper on regulatory alignment

The Europe Agreements contained the first elements of regulatory alignment. Article 68 stipulated that '[the CEEC] shall use its best endeavours to ensure that future legislation is compatible with Community legislation'. However, apart from more specific obligations for legislative approximation in the area of competition policy, the agreements merely provide a rather broad list of priority areas for harmonisation, including, for example, protection of workers at the workplace. The EAs's progress with legislative approximation remained therefore limited.

Regulatory alignment moved to the centre stage of the enlargement policy with the debate on the pre-accession strategy. EU policy evolved in three main stages. The first stage was the Commission's White Paper that the Cannes European Council endorsed in June 2005 and that provided the framework for the CEECs' regulatory alignment with the internal market. The second stage were the Accession Partnerships (APs) and the Commission's regular reports through which the EU monitored and assessed the CEECs' accession preparations. Finally, the accession negotiations reached binding decisions on the possibility of post-accession transitional periods for alignment and their duration.

Chapter 5 described in more detail the considerations that led the advocates of the CEECs' preferences in DG I and the Brittan *cabinet* to identify regulatory alignment with the internal market as the economic core of the EU's pre-accession strategy. Regulatory alignment would provide the CEECs with immediate benefits in trading relations with the EU, e.g. by reducing the threat of anti-dumping measures. In the medium term, preparations for participation in the internal market – the core of EU membership – would accelerate the CEECs' accession.

A key challenge for such a strategy was to establish what alignment with the internal market *acquis* actually entailed. Until then, no systematic attempt had ever been made to draw up a complete inventory of all single market legislation in the various policy areas. The team around DG I and the Brittan *cabinet* therefore consulted DG XV (internal market) for advice on which parts of the *acquis communautaire* were essential for participation in the internal market.[11] Initially, DG XV was rather sceptical about a plan to incorporate the CEECs into the internal market, but became increasingly enthusiastic. After the completion of the single market in 1992, DG XV had acquired a lower profile and such a programme provided an opportunity to assert a central role in the evolving enlargement process. DG XV thus conceived the idea of organising the CEECs' alignment around a Commission White Paper. This WP would identify and explain the key measures necessary for participation in the single market and advise on a logical sequencing in adopting these measures in the various areas.[12]

Initially, the DG I team had certain reservations about such a WP. Their concern was that certain member state governments could abuse such a concrete list of measures to delay enlargement. If the WP was turned into a hard checklist of stringent regulatory pre-accession requirements, it would deprive the CEECs of any flexibility to organise their alignment selectively according to their own priorities. The DG I team came around to accepting that a WP could be a useful instrument, but insisted that it must not become a legally binding yardstick of accession criteria, but strictly remain a tool of technical advice.[13] The Commission's proposal for a pre-accession strategy in June 1994 thus emphasised strongly that the CEECs should be free to drawn up their own programmes for alignment. The Commission (1994a: 5) proposed:

> To enable the associated countries to integrate progressively in a wider European market [...] each associated country should draw up a programme of priorities and a timetable in fields such as the approximation of legislation, and the imple-

mentation of competition and state aids policies which are transparent and compatible with those of the Union. After consultation with the associated countries, the Commission will prepare a White Paper, setting out a programme for meeting the obligations of the internal market which can be followed by each associated country and monitored by the Union.

The Essen European Council in December 1994 endorsed this proposal and called on the Commission to prepare the WP for the Cannes European Council in June 1995. The acceptance of regulatory alignment, organised around a Commission WP, was relatively uncontroversial in the Council, because of different implicit assumptions about what the WP would entail. As its concrete content was left open, it appeared that it could serve quite different purposes. Those member states favourable to enlargement, such as the German government, welcomed it as a strategy to advance the enlargement process. Yet it also appeared to address a key concern in the French government that a politically-motivated, hasty and insufficiently prepared accession would create major problems for the functioning of the internal market after enlargement.[14] As the member states perceived regulatory alignment largely as a purely technical process, the Council did not debate the content of the WP. The initiative was firmly in the hands of the Commission and the drafting process of the WP had to determine the purposes that the WP would serve and to what extent it would accommodate the CEECs' preferences for selective alignment.

The preparation of the WP in time for the Cannes European Council put the Commission under considerable time pressure, given the novelty of the task of establishing such a guide to the internal market legislation. At the same time, this time pressure was part of DG I's strategy to limit the extent to which the Council would be able to discuss the detail of the WP before presenting it to the European Council.

Through the reorganisation of Commission portfolios at the beginning of 1995, Leon Brittan and his *cabinet* lost their direct influence on policy, although some of the policy-makers from the former DG I initially continued their work for DG IA. Furthermore, the overall responsibility in the Commission for organising the EU's regulatory alignment policy shifted to DG XV. After an initial struggle with DG IA, DG XV obtained the task in recognition of its superior technical expertise with regard to the internal market. However, while the van den Broek *cabinet* did not pay detailed attention to the WP, the original advocates of the pre-accession strategy in the team around DG I-E and the Brittan *cabinet* undertook to influence the approach that DG XV would adopt. Building on their extensive previous consultations with DG XV and their economic expertise, they were able to persuade DG XV to adopt a selective approach to regulatory alignment in the WP.[15]

The ability of the policy advocates in DG IA to convince DG XV that a selective approach was the most suitable for the CEECs was facilitated by the prevailing ideas about the internal market in DG XV. These ideas departed from the EU's dominant internal market paradigm to the extent that for a majority of policy-makers in DG XV, the main purpose of regulatory harmonisation was the removal of NTBs. They were therefore much more inclined to draw a distinction between essential and merely desirable elements of the internal market *acquis*. This inclination made them receptive to considering it acceptable in the particular case of the CEECs to temporarily postpone alignment with process regulations. As a result of the agreement on a selective approach with DG IA, DG XV thus acted as an advocate of the preferences of the CEECs towards sectoral DGs in the process of drafting the WP.

The policy process for the drafting of the WP was characterised by centralised coordination through DG XV. Key factors that strengthened the coordinating role of DG XV were the time pressure and the novelty of the exercise, in combination with the general recognition by the sectoral DGs of DG XV's expertise. Initially, DG XV held inter-service consultations with representatives of the different DGs. These meetings explained the rationale of the WP and outlined the logic according to which the DGs should choose which measures in their policy areas to include. In late January, the DGs sent lists with the selected regulations to DG XV, which examined whether these sectoral *fiches* complied with the parameters set for the choice of measures. Most *fiches* went back and forth several times, but by and large the sectoral DGs complied with the selective approach as suggested by DG XV and an overall draft was ready in April.[16] The WP consisted of two parts. A shorter paper explained its purpose and the logic underpinning its selection of measures. The 438-page Annex outlined in detail the concrete legislation in the various areas and suggested a logical sequencing of legislation within policy areas.

At a general level, the WP embraced a selective approach to the CEECs' alignment. It distinguished the parts of legislation that 'create and maintain the internal market' and are thus 'essential' for its functioning (Commission 1995a: 6–7) from other parts of internal market legislation. The WP identifies the former as

> the Treaty articles and secondary legislation ... which *directly* affect the free movement of goods, services, persons or capital. It is legislation without which obstacles to free movement would continue to exist or would reappear. Other legislation which *indirectly* affects the operation of the single market, for example because it affects the competitive situation of firms, has not been covered in the detailed presentation. (1995a: 19; emphasis added)

The selective approach is most striking in the area of environmental policy. The WP only covers the product-related measures based on Article 100a or Article 130s and excludes process-related legislation, such as rules on pollution from stationary sources, or legislation on air and water pollution, nature protection, and horizontal measures. The selective approach was not uncontested in DG XI (environment). Statements by the then Environment Commissioner, Yannis Paleokrassas, clearly resonated with the internal market paradigm. He insisted that 'European law vis-à-vis environmental standards [and] practices ... will have to be implemented step by step in the candidate countries. ... Unfair competition on the basis of dramatically low environmental standards – and therefore to the detriment of the environment – should be avoided' (quoted in Rouam 1994: 646). Nonetheless, DG XI was receptive to a selective approach in the specific context of the CEECs.[17] However, it insisted that while it accepted that pre-accession alignment could be reasonably expected to remain more limited, in the event of membership, all parts of the environmental *acquis* would be important.

> The present exercise concerning the internal market will ... need to be complemented by a more comprehensive approach in the environmental field ... [Pre-accession alignment only includes] legislation that directly affects the free movement of goods and services, *leaving out legislation which relates ... to processes rather than products and which therefore relates only indirectly to the internal market.* (Commission 1995a: 20, emphasis added)

> [Such measures, although] a very important part of environmental legislation, fall outside the scope of the White Paper, and are therefore not included in the annex (1995b: 215).

However, in contrast to environmental policy and the WP's general approach, the section on social policy did not follow the selective approach. The WP included measures on the coordination of social security schemes; equal treatment of men and women; health and safety at work; and certain aspects of labour law (collective redundancies, transfer of undertakings, insolvency of employers, working time, protection of young people at work, information and consultation of workers). DG V (social policy) was concerned that selective alignment by the CEECs would implicitly downgrade the importance of social policy in the EU (*Financial Times*, 16.03.95: 2; 04.05.95). These concerns intensified when it became clear that the UK government – a strong opponent of EU-level social policy – was the member state most receptive of CEEC demands to delay alignment in this area.[18] Although the team around DG I-E and the Brittan *cabinet* team had tried hard to convince van den Broek to strictly oppose exceptions from the general product/process distinction in the WP, van den Broek appeared not to fight very hard at the level of commissioners.[19] The *college* of commissioners thus decided to include the process-related measures of social policy into the WP.[20] Monti (1995: 5) acknowledged: 'The White Paper was never intended to cover the whole *acquis communautaire.* This did not prevent a lively debate within the Commission, however, about what was internal Market legislation and what was not. It was not easy to find the right line in areas such as social and environmental legislation.' The signs of this political compromise between the generally selective approach and the exception for social policy are apparent in the fudged language in the WP's outline of its approach that papered over the resulting inconsistencies:

> The White Paper's presentation of internal market related legislation includes those parts of social legislation which affect the functioning of the internal market *or which are a necessary complement to other measures identified as key instruments* ... (Commission 1995a: 20, emphasis added)

> Legislation which *only* [original emphasis] indirectly affects the operation of the Internal Market by, for example, affecting the competitive situation of firms has *for the most part* [emphasis added] been excluded from consideration. (1995b: v)

Apart from the notable exception of social policy, DG XV was thus to a large extent able to defend the selective approach initially advocated by the team around DG I and the Brittan *cabinet* team. DG XV also prevented the WP's menu being turned into binding conditions, but retained it as an indicative guide. However, the other side of the coin was that the WP did not commit the EU to reciprocating successful alignment of the CEECs with the WP's measures with membership. While some of the CEECs would have preferred a clearer link, the WP strongly emphasised that its selection of measures did not indicate possible areas for transition periods in the accession negotiations.

> As an element in the pre-accession strategy, the White Paper is not part of negotiations for accession and does not prejudge any aspect of such negotiations, including possible transitional arrangements. (Commission 1995a: 6).

> Every piece of Community legislation is important in principle, and ... accession to the Union can only be achieved by taking over the entire body of Community legislation ... (1995a: 22)

> Alignment with the internal market is to be distinguished from accession to the Union which will involve acceptance of the *acquis communautaire* as a whole. (1995a: 38)

The Council did not discuss details of the WP until a very late stage. During the drafting process, the Commission had sent some sectoral 'mini *fiches*' to the member states for comments, which they could then distribute to the relevant line ministries and sectoral interest representations. This procedure provided the member states and interest groups with a feeling of consultations, without however constraining the Commission.[21] The Commission timed its draft in such a way that the Council could not discuss details of the WP, let alone ask for a re-draft. The Council and COREPER had only one general discussion that mainly praised the Commission's efforts. The only point that was more controversially debated was the WP's approach to environment and social policy. The Luxembourg delegation, with support from the Danish, Swedish, Belgian, Irish and Italian delegations, suggested an amendment to include a stronger reference to the importance of alignment with social, environmental and consumer policy. However, this initiative failed, because of the opposition of the Commission, as well as the UK, German, Dutch and Spanish representatives (*Agence Europe*, 06.06.95: 8; *European Report*, 07.06.95: 12).[22] The member states agreed not to enter into negotiations over the detail of the WP and restricted themselves to underlining explicitly that the WP did not prejudge any aspect of accession negotiations.

The Cannes European Council in June 1995 endorsed the WP (Council 1995a). The annex to the presidency conclusions expressed the agreement in the Council on the WP's status (Council 1995b: 1). The WP's selection did not 'anticipate or prejudge the future negotiations on accession', since upon accession they would 'subject if need be, to transitional periods – adopt the whole "acquis" covered by Community legislation'. Nor did it 'lay down further conditions for those negotiations'. The European Council confirmed that 'the associated countries themselves, in the light of the White Paper and their national contexts and priorities, [have] to define and implement their programmes for preparing for integration into the internal market'. The WP's purpose was to 'guide and assist' this process by outlining the measures that the Commission regarded as 'essential' for it.

In sum, the WP largely accommodated the CEECs' preference for selective alignment with product regulations, with the notable exception of social policy legislation. A key factor was that the view of the internal market that prevailed in DG XV was – in contrast to the EU's internal market paradigm – amenable to a selective alignment of the CEECs during the pre-accession period. The advocates of the CEECs' preferences could thus persuade DG XV to take a selective approach to the single market *acquis* in the WP. The strong role of DG XV in horizontal coordination for the drafting of the WP set clear parameters for sectoral DGs about what types of measure to include within their policy areas. The instrumentalisation of time pressure and DG XV's ability to present the drafting of the WP as a boring technical exercise limited the discussion in the Council and the attention paid by interest groups at this stage. The absence of interest group pressure at this stage of policy developments makes it hard to explain the strong resistance of DG V to a selective approach through a focus on interest group pressures. DG V defended the role of social policy within the internal market and the presentation of its arguments in terms of the internal market paradigm limited the grounds for counter-arguments with reference to the special circumstances of the CEECs.

Implementation of the regulatory alignment policy

While the non-binding character of the Commission's WP thus largely accommodated the CEECs' preferences for a selective regulatory alignment during the pre-accession period, much depended on whether this approach would be maintained during the implementation of the EU's regulatory alignment policy.

In the Commission, the implementation of the WP was carried out by a new team of policy-makers in DG IA. The new Director General of DG IA was a former member of the Delors *cabinet* who had been closely involved in the original single market programme. This previous experience with the internal market led to a more technical and legalistic approach of DG IA to regulatory alignment of the CEECs. This approach was more detached from the specific situation in the CEECs and the economic costs of alignment, which might prevent the CEECs from delivering on their commitments in certain areas. DG IA thus focused on establishing clear commitments for alignment and relying otherwise on the possible use of non-compliance procedures if problems with alignment should emerge after accession.[23]

The implementation of regulatory alignment and the WP proceeded trough two related frameworks. The Commission's Agenda 2000 proposed bilateral 'Accession Partnerships' (APs) that committed the CEECs to indicative timetables for implementing particular parts of the *acquis*. The APs were complemented by 'Regular Reports' of the Commission on the CEECs' progress with alignment. The Commission's opinions on the individual applicant countries in Agenda 2000 were the first such comprehensive assessment. Following the Luxembourg European Council in December 1997, the Commission committed itself to continue assessing the CEECs' progress on an annual basis. Binding decisions on the extent to which alignment in certain areas could be carried out during post-accession transition periods were taken during the accession negotiations. Essentially, although the APs initially reduced the flexibility of the CEECs by making regulatory alignment more binding than the policy advocates in the Commission had hoped, the outcome of accession negotiations confirmed that the WP had successfully set the parameters for flexible alignment. In particular in the area of environmental policy, the CEECs obtained rather long transition periods for post-accession alignment.

The Accession Partnerships

The Accession Partnerships (APs) were developed by the new team in DG IA. They reflect the legalistic perspective on regulatory alignment dominating DG IA and the positive experience with setting a clear timetable in the original single market programme.[24] As a result, the APs proposed in Agenda 2000 significantly tightened the CEECs' flexibility (see also Grabbe 1999).

For each AP, the candidates would establish in cooperation with the Commission a national programme for the adoption of the *acquis*. The programmes commit the CEECs to a precise timetable for the implementation of EU legislation, especially in those areas where the Commission opinions have identified shortcomings. EU financial assistance depended on the progress made in achieving these objectives (Commission 1997a: 63). Furthermore, the Commission's recommendations to start accession negotiations were conditional on the applicants' progress with meeting the targets set out in the APs (Commission 1997a: 64; 1997b: A-4). Thus, the nature of regulatory alignment seemed to shift between the WP and the framework of the APs. The APs significantly reduced the CEECs' ability to approach regulatory alignment selectively, as the start and progress of accession negotiations and financial assistance were made conditional on progress with meeting binding deadlines during the pre-accession stage.

DG IA had attempted to prevent sectoral DGs and the member states from subverting the APs by emphasising their technical nature and maintaining a central role in the drafting process. However, this strategy backfired. The attempt by DG IA to limit the input of sectoral DGs to the provision of information on shortcomings with alignment in their respective areas generated growing suspicions among the sectoral DGs, including DG XI, about the role of DG IA in the process.[25]

Likewise, DG IA tried to reduce the influence of the member states by arguing that the APs related primarily to decisions about the allocation of financial assistance that were exclusively in the competence of the Commission. However, this attempt precisely alerted the member states. Their fear was that the Commission might be staging a '*coup institutionel*' to strengthen its role vis-à-vis the Council in accession negotiations: if the APs established deadlines for applying the *acquis* in specific areas, this might prejudge the outcome of accession negotiations.[26] The Council therefore insisted on concluding the APs as a Council regulation on the basis of Art. 308 TEU (ex-235 EEC).

The main effect of this change in the legal status was to make regulatory alignment a 'quasi-legal obligation by establishing a control procedure and system of sanction' (Grabbe 1999: 16). At the same time, the content of the APs did not cause much controversy in the Council (see also Grabbe 1999: 31). The APs distinguished between short-term measures (to be completed or taken on in 1998) and medium-term priorities. Process-related measures were included in both categories and thus established binding obligations for pre-accession alignment. In 1999, the AP with Poland, for example, included among the short-term priorities for environmental policy industrial pollution control and industry-related directives and water quality directives; medium-term priorities in the area of social policy included legislation on occupational health and safety (Commission 1999a).

Commission monitoring of regulatory alignment

While the APs thus established a much tighter regulatory conditionality, Council Regulation 622/98, their legal basis, left it open how the EU would assess whether 'progress towards fulfilment' of these conditions was 'insufficient'. The implementation of the APs thus gave the Commission significant leeway in assessing the CEECs' progress with regulatory alignment, and thus with accession negotiations.

The Commission's 1997 Opinions contained the first assessment of the CEECs' alignment with the internal market. The different DGs assessed primarily the time necessary for a full implementation of the various parts of the *acquis*, distinguishing between the medium term, the long term or very long term. The opinions indicated that for all candidates alignment with process-related regulations, such as environmental policy, might take a very long time. However, this assessment did not prevent the Commission from recommending opening accession negotiations with some of the CEECs, which implies that these shortcomings were not considered an obstacle for a candidate country's prospects to join in the medium term. The opinions did not pass judgement on the salience of alignment with process regulations for membership. Nor did they comment on whether shortcomings in these areas might either lead to a delay of membership, or to a granting of transition periods. For example, the opinion on Poland merely states that

> effective compliance with a number of pieces of legislation requiring a sustained high level of investment and considerable administrative effort (e.g. urban waste water treatment, drinking water, aspects of waste management and air pollution legislation) could be achieved only in the long term. It will necessitate increased levels of public and private investment. (Commission 1997c: 87)

The subsequent Regular Reports from November 1998 made a much clearer link between progress with alignment and progress in accession negotiations, or eligibility to start them. However, while the reports criticised a lack of progress with certain process regulations – for example that in 1999 'none of the candidate countries are very far advanced in the transposition of environment laws' (Commission 1999b: 26) – such criticism did not appear to affect the Commission's overall assessments of a candidate's progress.

Accession negotiations

As the accession preparations became increasingly tied up in accession negotiations, differences emerged between DG IA, which was more favourable to transition periods for process-related legislation, and sectoral DGs and certain member states. With regard to social policy, the differences were most pronounced. While the EU's official position confirmed DG Social Policy's insistence on strict pre-accession alignment, DG IA informally indicated to the CEECs that a lack of progress would not be considered an obstacle to concluding negotiations. Thus, DG IA advised the CEECs not to ask for formal transition periods, but that it would instead not be too strict in assessing compliance (Sissenich 2005). Still, for regulations on health and safety at the workplace, the EU granted Latvia, Poland and Slovenia transition periods until the end of 2005, 'recognising the need to provide businesses with sufficient time to adapt to the requirements of EU legislation' (Commission 2003: 33).

With regard to environmental policy, most CEECs asked for long transition periods for process-related regulations, such as water or air quality. Even before negotiations of the chapter started, it emerged that there was a widespread acceptance among the member states' governments of long transition periods in view of the massive investment required. Nonetheless, this acceptance was far from uncontested. For example, Environment Commissioner Margot Wallström criticised that the CEECs did not take environmental policy seriously enough and the Finnish Environment Minister Satu Hassi insisted on the implementation of all environmental legislation prior to accession (Taylor 1999: 18).

However, DG IA successfully defended its approach to transition periods that was essentially based on the WP's selective approach to regulatory alignment. It thus stressed that while transition periods would not be granted for 'essentials of the internal market (all product-related legislation)', as well as on framework legislation and new installations, they could be considered where substantial investment in infrastructure and technology is required. Such measures would 'allow the future Member States to deal with the legacy of the past but not to attract new investments with lower environmental standards' (Commission 2002: 60–1). As a result, the CEECs obtained in part extensive transition periods on a broad range of process-related regulations, such as Poland for air pollution from large combustion plants (until 2017), or Slovenia for integrated pollution prevention and control (until 2011).

In sum, while the APs and the Commission's regular assessments significantly reduced the flexibility of the CEECs' regulatory alignment, the outcome of accession negotiation largely confirmed the precedent established through the WP's selective approach to regulatory alignment, especially with regard to certain process-related regulations in the area of environmental policy.

Conclusions

Materialist rationalist approaches that focus primarily on interest group pressure cannot fully explain the outcome of the EU's regulatory alignment policy. EU interest groups – including business, trade unions and environmental NGOs – are strongly opposed to accommodating the CEECs' preferences for selective alignment during the pre-accession phase that allows them to implement the internal market legislation that regulates production processes only after post-accession transition periods. However, the Commission White Paper, on which the EU's regulatory alignment policy is based, largely followed a selective approach that separates product from process regulations. The clearest example of this approach was environmental policy, while social policy was the notable exception. The implementation of the WP through the Accession Partnerships and the Commission's regular reports appeared to reverse this approach by making alignment more binding and including process-related regulations into pre-accession preparations. However, the outcome of accession negotiations, which granted the CEECs some extensive transition periods for environmental legislation, confirmed the WP's selective approach to regulatory alignment.

At first glance, the alternative explanatory factors also do not seem to fare much better in explaining this policy outcome. The conditions both with regard to the access to the policy process for the Commission's advocates of the CEECs' preferences and the compatibility of these preferences with the EU's internal market paradigm appeared unfavourable. The internal market paradigm includes the acceptance of the 'level-playing field' argument and the belief that economic integration does not only serve to create and enhance economic competition, but also to promote broader public policy objectives, notably high standards of environmental and social policy. The reorganisation of portfolios in the Santer Commission ended the direct responsibility of Leon Brittan for enlargement and there was not much continuity in the personnel of the new DG IA.

However, a closer analysis of the evolution of the EU's regulatory alignment policy reveals that these two factors have significant explanatory power. The initial team of policy advocates around DG I was able to overcome the problem of access through establishing close relations with DG XV which played a key role in organising the EU's regulatory alignment policy. A crucial factor that enabled the DG I team to persuade DG XV to take a selective approach to alignment was the view of the internal market that prevailed in DG XV. In contrast to the dominant internal market paradigm, DG XV's view was much more amenable to distinguishing between those parts of the *acquis* that are essential for the functioning of the internal market and those that are not, as they do not constitute NTBs. DG XV was thus receptive to the argument that in view of the specific circumstances of the CEECs, pre-accession alignment could prioritise product-related regulations, while temporarily postponing harmonisation of process regulations.

DG XV's presentation of the WP as a technical, non-binding, guidance document limited the access of the member state governments and interest groups to the policy process. The main conflicts occurred thus within the Commission, but DG XV's strong role in the central coordination of the WP's drafting process allowed it to ensure that most sectoral DGs complied with the selective approach. During the implementation of the WP, the policy process, as well as the personnel and approach in DG IA changed. As a result, policy shifted towards a more binding and less flexible approach, notably through the Accession Partnerships. Nonetheless, the WP's introduction of an entirely novel language about regulatory alignment appears to have opened a window of opportunity for accession negotiations. The WP's language challenges the dominant internal market paradigm by indicating a hierarchy within the EU's regulatory *acquis*. As this hierarchy attaches less importance to those parts of the *acquis* that regulate processes and therefore only indirectly affects the functioning of the internal market, it created a basis for the CEECs to demand long transition periods for process-related regulations in the accession negotiations.

However, although the EU's regulatory alignment policy thus largely maintained a selective approach, the exception of social policy seems to confirm the prediction of approaches focused on interest group preferences. However, such an approach cannot explain why DG V opposed selective alignment in social policy during the drafting process of the WP, before interest groups articulated their preferences. It is difficult to explain the conflicts about selective alignment in the Commission with competing material pressures from different client groups. Competing ideas about the internal market inside the Commission provide a more plausible explanation. DG V's opposition to a selective approach was based on the perception of this approach as incompatible with, and a threat to, the dominant internal market paradigm. In turn, as DG V presented its arguments with reference to the internal market paradigm, it was very difficult for DG XV to question their legitimacy.

Bureaucratic politics might provide an alternative rationalist explanation. Policy-makers' concern with the status of their departments and their area of activity could explain why the policy-makers in charge of environmental or social policy are highly reluctant to acknowledge a certain hierarchy within the internal market *acquis* that bestows a less privileged status on their policy areas. While such an explanation appears more plausible than mere interest group pressure, it is not altogether convincing either. It is not obvious that considerations of status and turf motivated policy-makers' insistence on the relevance of regulatory alignment with their area, rather than a sincere conviction of the importance of their particular public policy objectives. They might perceive genuine benefits of alignment for the CEECs and conversely, genuine dangers from relegating the importance of these areas in the EU. In this sense, opposition to selective alignment is less due to bureaucratic self-interest, than to the influence of the dominant policy paradigm that prevents policy-makers from acknowledging a special case for CEECs that could justify selective alignment, or indeed that such an approach is feasible. Crucially, if their opposition to selective alignment was purely based on bureaucratic self-interest, it would be much easier for other policy-makers to oppose their arguments. It is precisely the legitimacy that the internal market paradigm bestows to their position that made it so difficult contest. The main puzzle thus appears rather why the EU did follow a selective approach with regard to environmental policy. The concluding chapter will return to a possible explanation of the variation in environmental and social policy.

Notes

1   Interview, Commission, DG IA, 16.10.97.
2   Interview, Polish Mission to the EU, 13.10.97.
3   Interview, Polish Mission to the EU, 13.10.97.
4   Interview, Commission, DG XV, 25.10.95.
5   Interview, Polish Mission to the EU, 13.10.97.
6   Interview, Polish Ministry of Finance, 12.03.95.
7   Interview, Polish Mission to the EU, 13.10.97.
8   For 1996, the *Financial Times* stated the following wage levels for manufacturing workers (USD per hour): Germany: 30.33; Belgium 27.98; Austria 25.58; Sweden 23.95; Italy 23.89; Czech Republic 17.40; Hungary 8.61; Poland 5.20. However, hourly manufacturing wages in the Czech Republic were just below Spain (18.85) and above the Netherlands (13.79), the UK (13.63) and Ireland (12.17) (FT Survey, 05.11.97: III).
9   Interviews, German Association of Industry and Commerce, 20.12.95; French National Employer Association, 08.07.96; UK Permanent Representation to the EU, 31.01.95; UK Department of Trade and Industry, 10.10.97.
10 Interview, UK Department of Trade and Industry, 10.10.97.
11 Interview, Commission, DG I, 24.10.95.
12 Interview, Commission, DG I, 24.10.95.
13 Interview, Commission, DG I, 24.10.95.
14 Interview, French Foreign Ministry, 10.07.96.
15 Interview, Commission, DG I, 24.10.95.
16 Interview, Commission, DG XV, 25.10.95.
17 Interview, Commission, DG I, 24.10.95.
18 Interview, Commission, DG XV, 25.10.95.
19 Interview, Commission, DG I, 24.10.95.
20 Interview, Commission, DG XV, 25.10.95.
21 Interview, Commission, DG XV, 25.10.95.
22 Interview, German Ministry of Economics, 15.12.95.
23 Interview, Commission, DG IA, 16.10.97.
24 Interview, Commission, DG IA, 16.10.97.
25 Interview, Commission, DG IA, 16.10.97.
26 Interview, Commission, DG IA, 02.12.97.

8
Political Dialogue on foreign policy

This chapter analyses the evolution of the EU's Political Dialogue with the CEECs on foreign policy. The member states have traditionally used 'Political Dialogue' as an instrument to regularly inform particular non-member states about their common foreign policy activities. Political Dialogue consists usually of meetings between foreign ministers or Political Directors, in which the EU[1] representatives inform their counterparts of their positions on international affairs. While Political Dialogue is thus not as such a new instrument, the EU developed it into a novel institutional framework for foreign policy cooperation with the CEECs. The EAs included provisions for bilateral Political Dialogues, but they developed quickly into a multilateral framework, in which EU representatives meet representatives from all associated CEECs.

The CEECs' main preference is that the Political Dialogue goes beyond the standard practice of a one-way provision of information by the EU about positions agreed in the framework of the Common Foreign and Security Policy (CFSP).[2] The CEECs want the Political Dialogue to develop into an institutional framework that establishes a two-way channel of consultations and thus provides them with an opportunity to influence CFSP.

These preferences converge to a large extent with those of EU foreign policy-makers. Clearly, EU policy-makers are against any obligations to accommodate the CEECs' positions, let alone grant them a formal veto right. However, a closer involvement of the CEECs in the CFSP allows the EU to exercise something akin to 'hegemonic socialisation' (Ikenberry and Kupchan 1990). Support from the CEECs is an asset for CFSP. The CEECs' membership aspirations generate pressure for the candidates to align themselves with CFSP positions, but more effective than overt coercion is their socialisation into CFSP through closer involvement.

In contrast to the other meso-policies analysed in this book, societal interest groups are not a constraint on the accommodation of the CEECs' preferences in this policy area. EU foreign policy-makers have considerable autonomy concerning the Political Dialogue. Given the large extent of convergence between EU and CEEC preferences, rationalist materialist approaches would thus expect that an accommodation of the CEECs' preferences is more likely than in the other policy areas analysed in this book.

However, the evolution of the Political Dialogue is difficult to explain from such a perspective. On the one hand, the institutional framework of Political Dialogue with the CEECs has developed much further than the dialogue with other non-members. A crucial element of institutional innovation is the establishment of a mechanism for consulting the CEECs, rather than merely providing information on pre-established CFSP positions. On the other hand, however, this possibility was never put into practice in the actual conduct of the Political Dialogue. Despite mutual dissatisfaction, the EU nonetheless persisted with these arrangements until after the start of accession negotiations, when it replaced the Political Dialogue with the much less ambitious 'European Conference', as the official (and mainly symbolic) multilateral forum for high-level discussions on a broad range of issues with states aspiring to accession (especially Turkey).

I argue that the failure of the Political Dialogue to accommodate the CEECs' preference for substantive consultations – despite largely converging with member state preferences – can be explained through a focus on the structure of the policy process and the policy paradigm underpinning the Political Dialogue and CFSP.

The preferences of the CEECs were promoted inside the EU by the Andriessen *cabinet* (and subsequently the van den Broek *cabinet*) through the idea of a 'European Political Area' (EPA) which would grant the CEECs full participation in CFSP prior to full EU membership. As decisions on the Political Dialogue were kept among the macro-policy-makers, the structure of the policy process facilitated access and influence of these advocates of an EPA to decisions on the dialogue's institutional set-up. The institutional arrangements thus largely accommodated the CEECs' preferences by establishing a mechanism for consultations. However, the structure of the policy process changed for the actual conduct of the dialogue.

The Political Dialogue was conducted by policy-makers from political departments of the member states' foreign ministries, rather than the EU departments. These policy-makers' perception of the extent to which substantive consultations through the Political Dialogue are not only desirable, but also feasible, is shaped by the policy paradigm underpinning the Political Dialogue. This policy paradigm aims to preserve the integrity of the CFSP decision-making process by drawing a sharp distinction between full members and non-members. The incompatibility of this paradigm with the notion of an EPA explains why – despite the potential of the institutional framework – the practice of the Political Dialogue did not accommodate the preferences of the CEECs for consultations on CFSP.

The structure of this chapter is as follows. The next section examines the EU's preferences with regard to the Political Dialogue. I argue that self-interest might lead the EU side to accommodate the CEECs' demands for consultations on CFSP. The second section identifies the ideas that shape CFSP policy-makers' attitudes towards using the Political Dialogue as a forum for consultations. The dominant paradigm for the Political Dialogue should strongly disincline CFSP policy-makers from extending internal consultations to external partners. The following two parts of the chapter analyse the development of the Political Dialogue. First, I examine the evolution of institutional framework, in particular the formal rules and procedures that affect the possibility of the CEECs to influence CFSP. I then review the experience with the conduct of the Dialogue in practice.

EU preferences for the Political Dialogue

To analyse the preferences of EU policy-makers with regard to the Political Dialogue with the CEECs, it is useful to consider the nature of foreign policy cooperation in the EU. The establishment of foreign policy cooperation among the member states was based on a recognition of the benefits of the possibility of coordinating their positions on international affairs. Common positions would carry greater weight internationally and coordination might even allow them to use their collective economic muscle to achieve shared foreign policy goals. At the same time, most member states insisted that foreign policy cooperation in the EU should not constrain their ability for unilateral action. European Political Cooperation (EPC) thus developed in the 1970s outside the treaty framework and its intergovernmental character was preserved after the inclusion of CFSP in the EU framework through the Maastricht Treaty.

CFSP therefore entails no binding legal obligations for common action. Cooperation is voluntary and complementary to independent national foreign policies. The instruments at the disposal of CFSP are thus limited. The Maastricht treaty added 'joint actions' and 'common positions' to the repertoire, which might be further increased with ongoing discussion about a common defence policy. However, the main instruments remain joint declarations, expressing the EU's position or expectations towards third countries and international issues, and diplomatic demarches towards particular countries. The number of demarches and joint declarations has grown steadily to over 300 and 200 respectively per year by 2002 (Council 2003: 60). In order to agree on such joint declarations or further reaching coordination of diplomatic activities, cooperation in the CFSP framework revolves around sharing information and extensive consultations.

Political Dialogue has a long tradition as the main instrument for establishing formal relations between CFSP and third countries (Edwards and Regelsberger 1990; Monar 1997; Regelsberger 1990). The growing visibility of CFSP increased third countries' interest in obtaining regular information about CFSP positions. The member states generally responded positively to requests for formal links with CFSP, not least as they presented welcome acknowledgements of the importance of CFSP. In special cases, such as Turkey or the US, the EU has attempted to create a particularly close relationship through the Political Dialogue. But even in these cases, it remained limited to a one-way flow of information and has stopped short of consultations that might allow non-members to influence CFSP decisions.

Are there any reasons why self-interest might lead the member states to depart from this general pattern and to accommodate the CEECs' demands for a further-reaching inclusion in CFSP? Rationalist approaches would expect the EU generally to oppose granting the CEECs influence on CFSP decisions through the Political Dialogue. Any requirements to accommodate additional voices might further constrain the ability to agree consensual positions. The incumbents should thus be reluctant to grant the CEECs any *formal* say and veto power over CFSP decisions prior to their accession. Nevertheless, self-interest might lead the member states to involve the CEECs to a certain extent in CFSP decision-making through the Political Dialogue, namely to include them in consultations.

Apart from the CEECs' specific foreign policy assets that can increase the effectiveness of particular CFSP policies, EU policy-makers might grant the CEECs consultations and a certain degree of influence in order to obtain their support for CFSP positions. Support from the CEECs is an asset for CFSP, as it enhances its weight internationally. At a minimum, the EU has an interest in avoiding an openly contradictory position, as the negative example of the lack of a common position between member states and CEECs on US policy towards Iraq in February 2003 underlined most spectacularly.

There are clear analogies between the benefits of consultations with the CEECs and cooperation among the member states. While CFSP ultimately aims at 'positive integration' (formulating common approaches to international issues), arguably its main success consists of 'negative integration' (preventing divergent national preferences from developing into openly contradictory international positions and actions that undermine each other) – sporadic failures, such as over Iraq, notwithstanding. What has allowed the member states to achieve such 'negative integration' and even an extent of 'positive integration' are the consultation norms contained in CFSP. In principle, these norms might be also effective if extended to consultations with the CEECs through the Political Dialogue.

The TEU commits the member states to consultations and solidarity in international affairs:

> The Member States shall support the Union's external and security policy actively and unreservedly in a spirit of loyalty and mutual solidarity. They shall refrain

> from any action which is contrary to the interests of the Union as a whole or likely to impair its effectiveness as a cohesive force in international relations. (Art. 11 (ex-J.1) 2)

> Member states shall inform and consult one another within the Council on any matter of foreign and security policy of general interest in order to ensure that the Union's influence is exerted effectively as possible by means of concerted and convergent action. (Art. 16 (ex-J.2))

Independently of such formal rules, evolving habits and practices have established a culture of consultation in foreign policy cooperation. The continuous process of meetings and intensive communication, in which officials share information and attempt to reach common assessments, has led to a mutual interpenetration of national foreign ministries (Foster and Wallace 1996: 416). At the same time,

> Cooperation within the EPC/CFSP framework is also a socialisation process. Representatives from national bureaucracies become acquainted with one another and develop expertise on substantive issues. They hear and accept the same arguments repeatedly, twisted and turned from various national points of view; they use the same words and may even create their own words, abbreviations, meanings and understandings. Maybe they develop personal sympathies, and not to be forgotten is the fact that a common institutional memory is created. (Müller 1995: 16)

Participants are socialised into an 'automatic reflex of consultation brought about by frequent personal contacts with opposite numbers from the other Member States' (Nuttall 1992: 312). This 'true consultation reflex' leads them 'to consult [each other] before adopting formal positions or launching national initiatives on important international questions of mutual concern' (de Bassompierre 1988: 49). According to Nuttall, this socialisation effect 'oils the wheels of EPC' (1992: 14); 'there is no doubt that the phenomenon is real' and generates a 'feeling of solidarity' (1992: 312). CFSP has thus 'both *preempted* the formation of fixed national foreign policy preferences on an expanding number of issues and *socialized* its elite participants into articulating common European policy on those issues' (Smith 2004: 99–100; original emphasis).

In principle, this socialisation process could be extended also to the CEECs – with all the resulting benefits for the weight of CFSP in international affairs – if the EU used the Political Dialogue to engage them in substantive and regular consultations. Moreover, the CEECs should be particularly susceptible to socialisation. First, the CEECs' desire to join the EU creates implicit pressures for them to support CFSP positions in order to demonstrate the compatibility of their foreign policy orientations. Even without explicit requirements to do so, the EU can exercise a 'passive leverage' (Vachudova 2001) on the CEECs which results in their 'anticipatory adaptation' (Nicolaïdis 1993: 236). Indeed, many commentators emphasise that the

CEECs were keen for an opportunity to align themselves with CFSP in order to express their credentials (Dunay et al. 1997: 319; Johansson-Nogues 2004: 88; Regelsberger 2000: 311).

While the CEECs' accession goal might create such pressures to support CFSP positions even without any concessions on the EU side to involve the CEECs, granting consultations can greatly enhance the likelihood and sustainability of such support. In the long term, coercion is more costly than consensual decision-making for a hegemonic power to obtain an ally's support (Martin 1992; Risse-Kappen 1995a: 17–20). Likewise, socialisation through involvement in consultations can be more effective in obtaining the CEECs' support than coercion (Ikenberry and Kupchan 1990). The CEECs are more likely to support EU positions if they have participated to an extent in their establishment, which increases their perceived legitimacy (Checkel 2001: 563). At the same time, given the large extent of prior compatibility of the CEECs' foreign policies (see e.g. Regelsberger 2000: 310), involving them in consultations should be relatively cost-free, as the risk of preference-outliers among the CEECs is small.

The CEECs' desire to join might also facilitate socialisation independently of the EU's (implicit) conditionality. If the CEECs identify with the EU and if the EU represents an in-group to which they want to belong, conditions are conducive for socialisation (Checkel 2001: 563; Johnston 2001: 499). At the same time, the complete re-orientation of the CEECs' foreign policies following the 1989 regime changes that make them more receptive to socialisation also points to a further incentive for the EU to foster such socialisation through involvement in the Political Dialogue. Apart from obtaining the support of the CEECs for particular CFSP positions, the end of the Cold War presented the EU with an opportunity to fundamentally shape the broader orientation of the CEECs' emerging foreign policies.

Indeed, interviews confirm that CFSP policy-makers consider the Political Dialogue as an opportunity to shape early on the development of the CEECs' foreign policy cultures, interests, and machineries. Interviewees stress the benefits of closer involvement of CEEC policy-makers, especially while the CEECs are in the process of redefining their foreign policy objectives and when the prospect of membership provides incentives to demonstrate the compatibility of their foreign policies with those of the EU. For example, Commission officials saw the Political Dialogue as an instrument to provide the EU with influence over the CEECs' foreign policy orientations that they did not consider irreversible at the beginning of the 1990s.[3] German foreign policy officials underlined the Political Dialogue's potential to embed a particular foreign policy culture and orientation in the CEECs. Regular contacts and sustained exposure of CEEC policy-makers to EU foreign policies in the Political Dialogue would provide the EU with a *cordon sanitaire* of 'friendly states'.[4]

In sum, self-interest on the EU side might lead CFSP policy-makers to accommodate CEEC interests for the Political Dialogue policy to a certain extent. By involving them more fully in consultations and deliberations, the EU might be able to tie the CEECs' emerging foreign policies to CFSP positions. Rationalist approaches would expect the EU to stop well short of granting the CEECs a formal voice in CFSP decision-making and much influence on CFSP decisions. However, the EU would invest in institutional arrangements that allow involving the CEECs to a sufficient degree for them to become socialised into supporting CFSP positions and considering them before defining their own foreign policy positions. Given the high autonomy of CFSP from interest groups compared to other EU policies (see e.g. Smith 2004: 97), the significant degree of convergence between EU and CEEC preferences with regard to the Political Dialogue should thus enable a significant accommodation of the CEECs' preferences for consultation on foreign policy.

The EU's Political Dialogue policy paradigm

The EU's Political Dialogue practice is underpinned by specific ideas that affect the possibility of developing it into an instrument to involve the CEECs in consultations about CFSP policies. EU policy-makers' ability to conceive of the Political Dialogue as a forum that enables the CEECs to influence CFSP, relates to ideas about how CFSP functions, or should function, and thus to its decision-making rules and procedures. Such rules constitute a 'procedural' policy paradigm, if they are embedded in unquestioned collectively held beliefs about the role of Political Dialogue within CFSP and its relationship to internal CFSP decision-making. Such a procedural paradigm specifies for policy-makers the relationship between insiders and outsiders, the extent to which non-members can be involved in consultations, and also the very meaning of 'consultation' – whether it is conceived of in merely formal terms or whether it includes a presumption that efforts will be made to include others' preferences in one's own preference formation. This procedural CFSP paradigm affects how EU policy-makers view not only the desirability, but indeed the very feasibility of accommodating the CEECs' demands to influence CFSP through consultation in the Political Dialogue. An overview of the EU's practice towards third countries reveals that the Political Dialogue draws a sharp distinction between insiders and outsiders. The procedural policy paradigm that underpins the Political Dialogue is an 'information paradigm', as opposed to a 'consultation paradigm'. It strongly disinclines CFSP policy-makers to extend internal consultations to external partners, to the extent that they cannot conceive of involving the CEECs in consultations that would allow them to influence CFSP decisions.

EPC did not have a clear philosophy about the organisation of the Political Dialogue and created procedures *ad hoc* on a case-by-case basis (Nuttall 1992: 282). Dialogues with different third countries thus vary according to a number of characteristics that reflect the intensity of the dialogue and establish a hierarchy among the dialogues with different non-members (see e.g. Monar 1997; Regelsberger 1990). Dialogues vary according to the decision-making levels involved (e.g. heads of state/government; foreign ministers; Political Directors; or officials at the working group level); the format in which the EU side is represented (presidency, Troika, or all member states); the frequency of meetings, as well as the types of issues covered. Despite these differences, a shared characteristic feature has emerged. The conduct of the Political Dialogue reflects its purpose as an instrument to inform non-members and a strong resistance to any forms of joint decision-making. The EU representatives can only transmit pre-established positions and cannot conduct negotiations with the external partners.

In very few cases has the EU made particular efforts to create an institutional framework that allows for a more far-reaching participation of non-members. A special case are impending accessions of new members. Other cases concern the United States and Turkey. Both countries are highly relevant for EU foreign policy, either because of their overall weight in international politics or their strategic importance in a specific geographical region. In the case of Turkey, the EU also has been keen to convey a particular closeness of relations. However, even in these cases, the EU stopped well short of granting non-members consultations and influence on CFSP decisions.

In between the signing of accession treaties and the official date of accession, the EU usually allows prospective members to participate in all meetings. However, the experience of the first enlargement in the 1970s, in which Norway was already involved in the EPC mechanism prior to the failed referendum, caused a rethinking on the EPC side. In the accession of Greece, EPC was therefore highly reluctant to grant full participation prior to actual accession and debated possible forms of relations for the interim period (Nuttall 1992: 172–4). The result was an arrangement by which the Council presidency transmitted in advance the agenda of Political Committee meetings and subsequently circulated Greek comments to the member states. Two months prior to accession, Greek representatives were allowed to attend Political Committee and ministerial meetings as observers.

The prospect of Greek accession prompted EPC to ponder a format for an 'external, but special, relationship' with Turkey (Nuttall 1992: 173). The Turkish government demanded in particular consultations on questions relating to the eastern Mediterranean. The UK and Germany pragmatically supported formal consultations on these sensitive issues, while France opposed any formula that could give the impression of a de facto membership (Nuttall 1992:173). As a result, Turkey was denied consultation meetings with the Nine, but received information in meetings with the Troika.

In 1973, the United States put EPC under strong pressure to take account of US concerns at an early decision-making stage, by holding, for example, consultations at the level of EPC working groups (Nuttall 1992: 284–7). Concerns among the member states about the integrity of the EPC decision-making caused considerable controversy and opposition to a formal dialogue. The EU found a formula for informal communication. The US ambassador in the presidency's capital received advance notice of ministerial and Political Committee meeting agendas, and subsequently provided the presidency with the state department's views on specific agenda items. In 1990, against the background of the changed geopolitical situation, a formal dialogue was institutionalised, creating the most sophisticated framework for a Political Dialogue. It formalised contacts at the ministerial and Political Committee level, but crucially also included, for the first time in the history of the Political Dialogue, meetings at the level of heads of state/government and at the working group level.

This overview shows that in particular cases the EU made considerable efforts to create special institutional arrangements for the Political Dialogue to allow greater involvement of non-members in CFSP. However, although some member states supported these attempts, the EU has been extremely reluctant to blur the formal distinction between insiders and outsiders and to jeopardise the integrity of the internal decision-making process. A majority of member states feared that any involvement of non-members would exacerbate the fragility of intergovernmental cooperation and undermine internal consensus. Yet despite the deepening and strengthening of CFSP over the years, CFSP policy-makers continue to regard its decision-making system as requiring special protection. The sharp distinction between insiders and outsiders has become deeply embedded in CFSP (see also Lippert and Becker 1998: 344; Regelsberger 2000: 322). The rigidity of the EU's insistence on this distinction reflects the belief that safeguarding the 'integrity' of the internal decision-making framework is an important objective in its own right, independent of its utility in specific cases. This shared belief has shaped CFSP policy-makers' views on the Political Dialogue: the policy paradigm underpinning the dialogue is an 'information paradigm'.

This paradigm is expressed in the rules and procedures that regulate the conduct of the Political Dialogue. The EU's representatives are only authorised to communicate positions that were internally defined beforehand; they cannot reveal individual positions in the internal decision-making process, let alone conduct negotiations with dialogue partners. The paradigm has thwarted any attempts to open the Political Dialogue as a forum for consultations on CFSP policy. It has precluded the provision of information at early stages of the EU decision-making process, or dialogue meetings with all member states, rather than just the presidency or the Troika. It has ruled out participation of non-members in internal EU meetings, even as observers.

The 'information paradigm' underpinning the Political Dialogue is an important obstacle for a more far-reaching accommodation of the CEECs' interest in shaping CFSP decisions through the Political Dialogue. The notion of an EPA that allows for a full participation of the CEECs in CFSP prior to their full EU membership challenges the fundamental assumptions on which the Political Dialogue is based. A focus on policy paradigms thus suggests that an accommodation of CEEC preferences with regard to the Political Dialogue is unlikely – despite a considerable extent of convergence with EU preferences and the absence of countervailing interest group pressure – because of their incompatibility with the prevailing 'information paradigm' of the Political Dialogue.

Evolution of the Political Dialogue's institutional framework

The Political Dialogue with the CEECs developed into a multilateral format in which the EU side meets with all CEECs. Its institutional framework achieved a sophistication that puts them into a clearly privileged position among non-members (see also Dunay et al. 1997; Lippert and Becker 1998; Regelsberger 1995, 2000). The dialogue is conducted with all levels of the CFSP decision-making hierarchy – heads of state/government, Political Directors, European Correspondents, and crucially, CFSP working groups. Discussions cover all areas of foreign policy (except if they concern specific foreign policy actions of individual CEECs). The Political Dialogue also provided the template for the 'structured dialogue' with the CEECs in other areas of EU activity under the pre-accession strategy, but it remained far more intensive in the area of foreign policy. Crucially, the institutional framework reflected important elements of institutional innovation that go far beyond the standard features of the Political Dialogue. A significant novelty is the possibility for the CEECs to participate in the implementation of CFSP output. The most remarkable innovation is the creation of an institutional mechanism that allows the input of the CEECs on such issues. This institutional framework developed in an incremental process, driven by the strong advocacy of the Commission.

Political Dialogue in the EAs
In the wake of the normalisation of relations with the CMEA, the EU started rather standard bilateral Political Dialogues with Poland and Hungary in 1989 and Czechoslovakia in 1990 (see Regelsberger 1995: 256–7). The provisions for Political Dialogue in the EAs were not only an important novelty of the agreements. They also spelled out far-reaching goals that indicate that it might serve as a forum for consultation. Still, the EAs do not establish any obligations, let alone formal rules or procedures, for consultation.

In the EA negotiations, the CEECs did not press for concrete rules to provide for their involvement in CFSP. Instead they aimed at a more subtle change in terminology, to replace the term 'political dialogue' with 'political cooperation' (Jezek 1995: 267). While in CFSP terminology 'dialogue' refers to relations with non-members, 'cooperation' is between insiders. However, for precisely this reason, the member states refused such a change of terminology. Yet, as a concession, the member states agreed to a formulation whereby the EAs would establish a 'regular political dialogue', while subsequently referring to 'political dialogue *and cooperation*' (EA Poland, Article 2, my emphasis).

On the EU side, the Commission was the main advocate of the CEECs' demands that the Political Dialogue should create an opportunity for their specific foreign policy concerns to be considered in CFSP decision-making. The Commission argued that the Political Dialogue could thus make a crucial contribution to reducing remaining barriers and overcoming the CEECs' sense of isolation (*Agence Europe*, 05.09.91). In particular the German, French and UK governments welcomed the establishment of a link between the Political Dialogue and the foreign policy processes of the two sides, in view of the potential of the Political Dialogue to influence the CEECs' foreign policies.[5] However, all member states opposed any arrangement that could oblige them to consider CEEC positions in their internal consultation process and undermine the integrity of CFSP decision-making.

As a result, the EAs stipulated that the dialogue would 'bring about better mutual understanding and an increasing convergence of positions on international issues, and in particular on those issues likely to have substantial effects on one or the other Party' and 'enable each Party to consider the position and interests of the other in their respective decision-making processes' (EA Poland, Article 2). While these goals were thus rather ambitious and had potentially far-reaching implications, the EAs did not commit either side to actual consultations, let alone the accommodation of the other side's interests in their foreign policy decisions. Nor did the EAs specify rules and procedures on how the Political Dialogue should bring about such a 'convergence' of positions. At the same time, an evolutionary clause allowed the use of 'any … means which would make a useful contribution to consolidating, developing and stepping up this dialogue' (EA Poland, Article 4). This scope for further pragmatic development, without any automatism, satisfied both sides.[6]

Enhancing the Political Dialogue: towards a European Political Area?

The main advocates of a fuller participation of the CEECs in CFSP through the Political Dialogue were the Andriessen *cabinet*, and from the start of 1993, the van den Broek *cabinet*, in which the same official was responsible for external relations. The debate gathered momentum when Andriessen (1991a: 4–5) floated the idea of an 'affiliate membership' of the CEECs through a European Political Area (EPA) that

> would provide membership rights and obligations in some areas, while excluding others, at least for a transitional period. It would give the affiliate member a seat at the Council table on a par with full members in specified areas …. [One of the two] areas in which affiliate members could become active at an early date [is]

> political cooperation … . As 'like-minded countries', affiliate members could
> take part fully in foreign policy decisions coming within the Community sphere.

Concrete initiatives of the Andriessen *cabinet* to strengthen the Political Dialogue focused on extending contacts to experts at the working group level, as well as 'soft' forms of participation in CFSP working groups. The initiative could draw on separate, but not uncoordinated initiatives by the CEECs and the British Council presidency.

The Visegrád memorandum of September 1992 (Visegrád 1992) endorsed the idea of an EPA as a 'superior, different kind of relationship … even before accession'. The CEECs proposed the 'gradual incorporation of the most stable new democracies in Central Europe into the political cooperation of the European Communities, especially via direct linking to the Common Foreign and Security policy as of 1 January 1993'. Specifically, *ad hoc* working groups should be created to discuss issues of mutual interest, and the Political Dialogue should involve EPC working groups and the 'actual official in charge of preparing decisions'.

The UK presidency in the second half of 1992 aimed to move the EU in this direction. It organised an informal dialogue meeting at the ministerial level, between all twelve foreign ministers and their three CEEC counterparts, as well as a meeting at the highest political level between the presidents of the European Council and the Commission and the CEEC heads of state. Furthermore, the UK presidency made considerable efforts to produce joint declarations that could trigger an enhancement of the Political Dialogue, at each meeting. The ministerial declaration on the Political Dialogue acknowledged that 'it could be envisaged to extend it to other areas, forms and mechanisms at different levels' (Council 1992b; my translation[7]). However, the cautious language of this paragraph reflected the reluctance of most member states towards innovations that might affect CFSP decision-making; and it was not included in the joint declaration of the heads of state.

The Andriessen *cabinet* pushed further with concrete proposals for CEEC involvement in CFSP. The first draft of the Commission's report for the Edinburgh European Council suggested not only the extension of the Political Dialogue to the working group level, but also some soft forms of participation of the CEECs (Commission 1992b). On an 'ad hoc and pragmatic basis', CEEC representatives could be invited to participate as observers in certain EPC working groups and 'to make oral or written contributions at the beginning of the meetings' of working groups and the Political Committee. The final report dropped these concrete proposals, but suggested explicitly that the EU should 'increasingly involve [the CEECs] in the process of European political cooperation' (Commission 1992c).

The Commission's report for the Copenhagen European Council argued that if the CEECs were to be given the perspective of membership, the traditional assumption of the Political Dialogue structure – that the partners would remain in a position of third countries – was no longer sustainable in their case. The rigid distinction between insiders and outsiders inherent in the Political Dialogue thus had to be overcome (Commission 1993a: 5). The Commission reaffirmed the proposal for an EPA through the inclusion of the CEECs in enlarged European Council meetings and ministerial Councils, and reiterated that CEEC representatives should be given observer status in CFSP working groups 'where there are special reasons for their participation', such as the *ad hoc* group Yugoslavia, the EC Monitoring Mission and sanctions enforcement. Furthermore, it suggested extending the dialogue to the level of European Correspondents, to prepare the meetings of the Political Directors.

The Copenhagen European Council agreed the inclusion of the working group level into the Political Dialogue, with one meeting per presidency for the working groups in question. The format changed from the bilateralism envisaged in the EAs to multilateral meetings with all CEECs, which had already been practised informally. The broader framework of the 'structured dialogue', which also involves regular contacts at the ministerial level in various areas of the Community pillar, created the possibility for the CEEC heads of state/government to meet all Twelve EU counterparts – a novelty in the history of the Political Dialogue – and meetings with all EU foreign ministers. However, the member states rejected the extension of the Political Dialogue to the European Correspondents and the possibility of CEEC observers in CFSP working groups. Most member states insisted on maintaining a clear distinction between full members and non-members, and between CFSP and the Political Dialogue. Even the delegations that had been otherwise supportive of the Commission's proposals – the UK, Denmark, Germany and the Netherlands – joined in warning the Commission against any form of institutional experimentation that might indicate some form of partial membership.[8]

A large majority of member states was also concerned that dialogue meetings between the full Council at ministerial level could lead to some form of joint decision-making, and that dialogue at the working group level could threaten the integrity of CFSP decision-making by influencing internal preparations of CFSP positions. To rule out any such developments, they thus insisted on stating explicitly in the presidency conclusions that 'these meetings will be of an advisory nature. No decisions will be taken. ... The meetings will be prepared for internally by the usual procedures . ... They will also be the subject of preparatory contacts with the CCEE' (Council 1993).

CEEC involvement in CFSP outputs

However, in the process of implementation the European Council decisions, the institutional framework of the Political Dialogue developed further. The Hurd-Andreatta initiative by the British and Italian foreign ministers in December 1993 was designed to ensure a substantive implementation of the Political Dialogue and resonated with earlier proposals of an EPA.[9] Their joint letter to the Council President, Jean-Luc Dehaene, requested the EU to draw up 'substantive proposals' in the first half of 1994 to 'develop new links between the associated countries and the work of the two intergovernmental pillars of Maastricht. ... Such links would enable the associated countries to align their policies more closely with those of the EU, and thus help to prepare them for eventual accession' (*Agence Europe*, 22.12.93: 6).

The Hurd-Andreatta initiative and continued advocacy from the van den Broek *cabinet* resulted in substantial concessions to the CEECs in the General Affairs Council's decisions on the implementation of the Political Dialogue in March 1994. While most member states had previously opposed that the Political Dialogue could produce joint outputs, now this was even an explicit goal. For ministerial meetings, 'the agenda will be thoroughly prepared in order to cover matters of common interest with a view to arriving as far as possible at common operational conclusions and to accommodating specific concerns of the Associated countries' (Council 1994a: 1). The major development was the creation of the opportunity for the CEECs to align themselves with CFSP outputs. 'In appropriate cases', the CEECs could be invited 'through an agreed mechanism publicly to align themselves jointly with European Union declarations on a particular subject' (Council 1994a: 2). Similarly, they could support demarches and associate themselves jointly with the implementation of joint actions. Although such CEEC involvement only envisaged a unilateral alignment with predetermined CFSP positions, it is an entirely novel form of associating non-members with CFSP. The unilateral form of alignment was a precondition for most member states to agree on this possibility. However, the possibility of an association with CFSP outputs created a window of opportunity for a subsequent debate on whether, and in which form, the CEECs might have an opportunity to influence such CFSP outputs.

This opportunity was seized by the CEECs. In particular Polish and Hungarian officials argued that the implementing arrangements should provide scope for 'decision-shaping' by the CEECs. The Commission supported these demands and in particular the British, Italian and German governments were open to greater involvement of the CEECs in CFSP.[10] As a follow-up to the Hurd-Andreatta initiative, the foreign ministers Hurd and Martino suggested in a joint letter to the German presidency the development of going beyond a mere unilateral alignment of the CEECs with CFSP activities.[11] However, most other member state governments were adamant that the internal CFSP decision-making mechanism had to be protected.[12]

In view of this opposition, the key challenge was thus to invent an arrangement for such 'decision-shaping' without the direct participation of the CEECs in CFSP decision-making. In recognition of the considerable expertise of the Council secretariat in the procedures of CFSP and the Political Dialogue, the German European Correspondent asked officials in the Council secretariat dealing with relations with the CEEC to draft concrete proposals. The German presidency strongly supported the proposal that the Council secretariat presented and after a difficult debate, the Political Directors endorsed the guidelines in October 1994.[13]

The Political Committee guidelines specify how the CEECs should be informed of planned CFSP activities, how their contributions could be considered by the EU, and the concrete modalities of their association with CFSP outputs (Council 1994c). For declarations and demarches, where time pressures are strongest, the Council Secretariat and the CEEC missions in Brussels are the main interlocutors in the consultation process. The secretariat informs the CEEC missions of the main thrust of the planned declaration or demarche. The CEECs then indicate to the secretariat if – in principle – they intend to be associated and which issues they want the EU to take into account in the internal drafting process. Once the EU side has agreed a final draft, the secretariat communicates it to the CEEC missions, who in turn confirm whether they want to be associated with the specific text.

Yet while the Political Committee thus established the principle that the CEECs should have an opportunity to shape the CFSP outputs with which they associate themselves, the proposal granted the more reluctant member states the safeguard of the possibility to veto such CEEC involvement. First, the EU side explicitly retains the right to derogate from these guidelines 'when this is warranted by the urgency of the matter or other overriding concerns'. Second, there is no automatic offer for association, but the EU decides for which issues this should be the case. Third, the EU side only commits itself to considering CEEC comments in the drafting process 'to the extent possible'. Finally, each CEEC government only has a very short time for their own internal consultations about the initial intention of association with a certain declaration, suggestions for its content, and the decision about association with the final text, which has to be communicated 'with a deadline … that will depend on the urgency of the matter, but ideally 24 hours'.

These guidelines were revised twice. In October 1995, the Political Committee took account of a key CEEC criticism.[14] It reversed the underlying assumption about their participation, by making CEEC involvement the rule, unless there was explicit opposition among the member states (Council 1995c). The member states maintained a veto, but the onus shifted by requiring an intervention to stop, rather than to enable, CEEC involvement. The revision of May 1996 codified the association of the CEEC with two further CFSP activities: 'common positions' – broad guidelines for EU policy on a specific issue or a particular country – and cooperation in the UN General Assembly. For activities in the UN framework, this primarily sanctioned previous informal practice. The association of the CEECs with common positions was more controversial. The member states considered this instrument very sensitive and there had been opposition to including it in the decision of March 1994.[15] Agreement on its inclusion was facilitated through the precedent established by the Italian presidency that invited the CEECs during a ministerial political dialogue meeting to associate themselves with a common position on arms exports to former Yugoslavia. Still, in contrast to CEEC association with declarations and demarches, the member states could not agree a formal mechanism that would allow the CEECs to influence CFSP positions in these two areas. CEEC involvement remained therefore limited to unilateral alignment.

A final – and ultimately unsuccessful – attempt to further enhance the role of the CEECs in CFSP through the Political Dialogue was a joint Polish–Lithuanian 'non-paper'. The paper proposed a right of initiative for the CEECs, which would allow them to submit draft proposals for CFSP declarations, demarches, joint actions, and common positions. The initiative failed due to the opposition of most member states, but also because of its poor coordination with potential supporters in the EU, as well as with other CEECs and even the missions in Brussels.[16] At the same time, with the start of accession negotiations looming, many CEECs thought that pressing for enhanced participation in CFSP could become counterproductive. Some member states might take the granting of such a form of partial membership as a pretext to delay moves towards full membership.[17]

In sum, the institutional framework of the Political Dialogue with the CEECs developed far beyond the standard format with other non-members. Some observers even deem it as creating 'an intermediate position between that of third countries and that of the member states' (Dunay et al. 1997: 322). Entirely novel features are the possibility of the CEECs participating in CFSP outputs, and crucially, the invention of a mechanism that allows the CEECs to feed their preferences into the CFSP decision-making process. The incremental development of the institutional framework has been constrained by the strong resistance among the member states to an involvement of the CEECs in the CFSP process. The uninhibited access of the Commission to the decision-making process on the broader framework for relations with the CEECs allowed it to advocate strongly the concept of an EPA. The institutional framework, which softens the distinction between insiders and outsiders, thus nonetheless accommodates the CEECs' preferences significantly. However, the structure of the policy process changed in practice of the Political Dialogue. CFSP officials played the dominant role in the conduct of the dialogue, which determined whether the potential of the ambitious institutional framework was fully used for meaningful consultations with the CEECs.

Conduct of the Political Dialogue in practice

General conduct of meetings

Although some teething problems were inevitable, and despite a learning process that led to a number of pragmatic improvements in the conduct of the dialogue, both sides were largely disappointed with the practice of the Political Dialogue.

Meetings generally took place once per presidency at each level of the CFSP hierarchy, back to back with meetings of the EU bodies – at the margins of the European Council, after the General Affairs Council, the Political Committee or individual CFSP working groups. The conduct of these meetings is similar. On instruction of the presidency, the Council secretariat communicates the agenda to the CEECs. At the meeting, the presidency or a Troika member introduces an agenda item, outlining the EU's assessment and position. Then each of the CEECs presents their views. A general criticism was that especially at the early stage the character of the meetings was far too general and involved little substantive discussion (see also Dunay et al. 1997: 322; Regelsberger 2000: 314). In allusion to the EU's official name for the multilateral dialogue – 'structured dialogue' – some participants dubbed the meetings an 'unstructured monologue'.

The EU side mainly attributed this problem to the nature of the CEECs' contributions, which often consisted of the reading out of long, pre-arranged, and rather general statements that did not relate the EU's position or the interventions of other CEECs. To overcome the problem, the EU asked the CEECs to coordinate their interventions. However, for most CEECs a main shortcoming of the multilateral dialogue was precisely that it did not differentiate sufficiently between individual CEECs. Most CEEC delegations thus rejected, for example, an experiment by the Dutch Council presidency in 1997 with a single CEEC 'keynote speaker' on specific agenda items, who would present the position of their country, while the following discussion would allow the other CEECs to point out where their positions diverged.[18]

The CEECs identified as a key problem the insufficient preparation of meetings. A number of initiatives attempted to alleviate this problem. In 1994, the Commission and the German presidency improved the long-term planning of dialogue meetings, by committing the presidencies to present a timetable of meetings at the beginning of each year. An initiative in 1997 established the early communication of annotated agendas to the CEECs.[19]

The inclusion of lower levels of the CFSP hierarchy also improved the dialogue at the level of foreign ministers. The extension of meetings and contacts to CFSP working groups, European Correspondents, CFSP counsellors in the Permanent Presentations and the Council secretariat improved the preparation of meetings and the flow of information. Still, participants described the early meetings at the working group level as extremely cumbersome[20] and it took some time to improve the division of labour between the different decision-making levels.[21] Meetings remained limited to updates on the subjects discussed in the previous meeting. The EU encouraged the CEECs to bring up their own subjects, which was taken up during the second half of 1997. Communication flows again were a constraint. In order to react, the EU needs to know in advance the issues that the CEECs would raise, as the presidency can only present pre-established EU positions, or respond purely in a personal capacity. Still, observers note a development from an initial EU monologue, to first reactions by certain CEECs, to much more active participation and substantive contributions of CEEC representatives,[22] leading to a 'substantive and effective dialogue' (Dunay et al. 1997: 322).

The lack of a continuous flow of information in between meetings presented another key problem. The CEECs therefore asked that the COREU network, the main secure communication channel for CFSP between the national foreign ministries, should be opened to them (see e.g. Visegrád 1992). Inclusion in the COREU network could also ensure timely information about the agendas of meetings and a meaningful consultation on CFSP activities with which the CEECs were to associate themselves. However, given the secrecy of COREU communications the member states opposed access prior to the CEECs' full membership. In early 1996, after sustained pressure from the associates, the EU agreed to establish an encoded e-mail link between the Council secretariat and the CEECs' Brussels missions. On instruction of the presidency, the CEECs could receive some non-confidential COREU communications, and the presidency could in turn feed the CEECs' views into the COREU system.

However, the quality of information depended crucially on the goodwill of the respective presidencies.[23] Some CEECs complained about being flooded with very general information on subjects they were not particularly interested in.[24] Many CEECs also encountered practical problems that led to the system never becoming fully operational. Some CEECs had problems receiving communications in their Brussels missions and asked for the information by fax, raising questions about the security of communication.[25] Other CEEC missions experienced problems with their own communication systems linking them to their capitals.[26] A subsequent initiative envisaged a protected communication link between the Council secretariat and the CEECs' foreign ministries. Although some member states raised concerns about security and the budgetary costs,[27] the Political Committee agreed to an 'Associate COREU network' (ACN), which was established at the end of 1999 (see also Regelsberger 2000: 316). While the access of the CEECs was thus still selective, it provided for a continuous and rapid flow of information.

The Italian presidency during the first half of 1996 achieved pragmatic practical improvements in the conduct of meetings, which contributed to making the contributions more focused and substantive.[28] The agenda was reduced to only three or four items for each meeting and the presidency made it clear that it would not accept any reading out of statements. However, for CEEC officials, a key structural limitation remained. They considered a lack of substance and focus inevitable, as long as meetings were not geared towards producing joint outputs, such as common assessments or recommendations for action at higher levels.[29]

The possibility of joint outputs emerged in spring 1997, when the presidency and the secretariat committed themselves in the Political Dialogue with the US to draw up non-binding conclusions at the end of meetings, and the Political Committee recommended extending this possibility to the dialogue with the CEECs.[30] However, this recommendation was not put into practice.[31] Its implementation depended on the commitment of the desk officers for individual working groups in the Council secretariat, who mostly considered the nature of discussions not conducive to drawing up conclusions.[32] The Council secretariat generally circulated informal summaries of the meetings to the member states that were not part of the Troika, but the member states feared that circulating them to the CEECs would lead to negotiations over their wording.[33]

Participation of the CEECs in CFSP activities

In view of the shortcomings of the dialogue meetings, it is not surprising that participation of the CEECs in CFSP activities did not realise the potential of the institutional framework and fell short of the CEECs' expectations. From a formal point of view, the association of the CEECs with CFSP outputs improved considerably, especially after the revised Political Committee guidelines made their participation automatic, in the absence of explicit opposition. Table 8.1 indicates that association with CFSP declarations and common positions has steadily increased. However, such figures are not necessarily a useful indicator.

Table 8.1 Association of the CEECs with CFSP outputs

	Declarations		Common positions	
	total	%	total	%
1995	27/106	25.5	0/13	0
1996	30/110	27.3	6/9	66.7
1997	35/122	28.7	2/13	15.4
1998	57/162	35.2	19/22	86.4
1999	73/130	56.2	9/9	100
2000	131/199	65.8	9/15	60
2001	133/192	69.7	10/20	50
2002	131/202	64.9	9/22	40.9
2003	125/132	94.7	8/12	66.7

Source: Council 1999b–2004; Regelsberger 2000: 318; 320.

On the one hand, non-participation does not necessarily reflect substantive disagreement. As a rule, the EU did not invite the CEECs' participation on issues that directly affected one or more of the associates, nor on particularly sensitive issues. Non-participation often also resulted simply from the time constraints for confirming participation. On the other hand, while both sides generally considered the CEECs' participation a useful experience, participation does not necessarily indicate a mutual adjustment of attitudes on key issues. Much of the CEECs' association with CFSP activities does not concern their key areas of interest, but the EU's specific priorities, such as human rights violations in the Asian-Pacific region, South/Central America, or Africa. The common position on arms exports to former Yugoslavia was even an attempt by the EU to constrain certain associates suspected of such exports.[34]

Cooperation on practical security issues, such as on anti-personnel mines, the revision of the UN conventional weapons agreement, or the extension of the nuclear non-proliferation treaty, are generally regarded as very positive experiences. EU officials considered the CEECs' support as an important factor for the success of the EU's joint action on the NPT. They suggest that the Political Dialogue has served as a learning process for the CEECs, similar to the CFSP process for the member states, in which regular explanations of the EU's position and its approach induced common views.[35] Yet in these cases, the association of the CEECs also primarily strengthened the EU's international position, rather then presenting key concerns of the CEECs.

EU policy towards Russia and other successors of the former Soviet Union is a key area of interest for the CEECs, but their influence on CFSP outputs remained marginal.[36] Especially in the earlier period of the dialogue, the CEECs complained about their lack of involvement in EU activities. For example, the EU did not invite the CEECs to participate in the 1995 declarations on Chechnya.[37] The EU feared that an association of the CEECs with a declaration critical of Russian policy might further antagonise Russia and appear to confirm her fears that closer relations with the CEECs would be directed against her.[38] At same time, some member states were concerned that many CEECs were tougher towards Russia than the EU. The CEECs were thus invited, for example, to associate themselves with the presidency statement on the Russian elections in December 1995, but not on Russia's accession to the Council of Europe in October 1995, of which many CEECs were critical. In general, EU officials suggest that after substantial initial differences, the political dialogue has induced a shift in the CEECs' positions towards the EU's and a much more relaxed and pragmatic attitude towards Russia.[39] The mechanism for the CEECs' association with declarations also appears to function fairly well. After relations with Russia became less delicate, reservations against CEEC association in this area have disappeared. The few exceptions seem to have been purely based on time constraints on the EU side.[40]

A key disappointment with regard to the participation of the CEECs in CFSP outputs is that the impact of the special arrangements for the CEECs to influence such CFSP activities remained in practice extremely limited. This failure stemmed partly from practical problems, namely the time constraints that even affect internal CFSP decision-making and are exacerbated in the case of the CEECs, without their access to COREU. If the CEECs' comments were not received at a very early drafting stage by a sympathetic presidency, their scope to prompt changes was extremely limited. Most member states rejected any renegotiation that such changes would require. Despite the establishment of arrangements for consultations, most CFSP policy-makers thus consider the possibility of the CEECs' participation as a 'take-it-or-leave-it' offer for unilateral alignment with a given CFSP text.[41] CEEC officials predominantly share this impression and in practice amendments upon initiatives from CEECs have been limited to a few technical changes,[42] such as – according to an anecdote – the spelling of Chechnya in the national language.

The one key area that both the EU and the CEECs consider as a highly positive experience for the Political Dialogue concerns the cooperation in international fora, in particular in the UN General Assembly.[43] Cooperation in the UN developed well, largely independently from the general framework of the Political Dialogue, due to the pragmatic attitudes of officials on the ground and their positive experience with practical cooperation. The political environment in the UN is generally more open and information is more easily accessible than in CFSP generally,[44] but officials attribute the contrasting experience to other areas mainly to the nature of contacts in this area of cooperation. Instead of sporadic meetings between officials in Brussels who discuss broad lines of policy, day-to-day contacts between permanent representatives based at the UN headquarters in New York and Geneva focus on cooperation on concrete issues.[45] Informal, but regular and continuous consultations on voting intentions take place 24 to 48 hours in advance and CEEC representatives actively seek such coordination. Consultations are also not limited to presidency briefings, but include close links with the representatives of individual member states. Officials therefore consider the socialisation between officials as much greater than is otherwise the case within the Political Dialogue framework.[46] Both sides thus undertake considerable efforts to avoid contradictory positions and possibly to establish common positions.

Cooperation in the UN framework has resulted in an impressive convergence in voting behaviour (see e.g. Johansson-Nogues 2004). However, such convergence does not necessarily reflect a particular receptiveness of the EU to the CEECs' preferences. Similar voting patterns usually result from unilateral alignment by the CEECs that are eager to underline that there are few problems with their adoption of the EU's *acquis politique*. The CEECs do not necessarily compromise their own positions, but rather take EU positions as off-the-shelf policies – a pattern that can be also increasingly observed from other third countries, for example in South and Central America and occasionally even Japan.[47] The French presidency encouraged the CEECs to suggest subjects on which the EU might align itself.[48] However, on the few issues on which individual CEECs asked repeatedly for EU support, the EU has refused politely.[49] Examples include the Baltic states' position on Russian minorities, which the EU does not share, or a Bulgarian initiative on compensation for countries negatively affected by the embargo on Yugoslavia, from which the EU feared the financial implications for itself.

Conclusions

While the institutional framework of the Political Dialogue accommodated the preferences of the CEECs for a fuller involvement in CFSP to a significant degree, this was not the case for the conduct of the dialogue in practice. The dialogue developed an increasingly sophisticated institutional framework, which included all levels of the CFSP decision-making system, and was extended to all CFSP working groups. The EU created the possibility for the CEECs to participate in CFSP outputs, and an institutional mechanism to feed the CEECs' input into the CFSP decision-making. However, CFSP policy-makers appeared unwilling to turn the Political Dialogue into a forum to seriously consider the CEECs' specific foreign policy interests. Although the character of meetings improved from an initial 'unstructured monologue', the meetings did not generate joint outputs, beyond previously established positions. The participation of the CEECs in CFSP declarations, demarches and common positions reached a high level, but such participation essentially remained limited to unilateral support of the CEECs for given CFSP decisions.

The limited accommodation of the CEECs' preferences is at odds with the expectations of approaches focused on interest group pressures. The CEECs' preferences for consultations and involvement converge to a significant extent with those of CFSP policy-makers, since a closer involvement of the CEECs allows their socialisation into like-minded foreign policy positions that generate support for CFSP positions internationally. The autonomy of CFSP policy-makers from interest groups should have made the Political Dialogue the most likely case for an accommodation of the CEECs' preferences among the meso-policy areas analysed in this book.

The structure of the policy area goes some way towards explaining the variation in the accommodation of the CEECs' preferences between the institutional framework and the practice of the dialogue. The advocates of a fuller involvement of the CEECs in CFSP – primarily the Andriessen, and later van den Broek, *cabinet* in the Commission, as well as the UK and Germany among the member states – were among the macro-policy-makers. They had privileged access to the decision-making process on the enlargement, and thus to put the development of the dialogue on the agenda – respectively in the Commission's proposals on closer relations with the CEECs or their Council presidencies. This continuous advocacy succeeded in incrementally breaking down resistance to any involvement of the CEECs in CFSP. These initiatives secured an extension of the dialogue to the working group level and while opposition against direct participation of the CEECs in the CFSP decision-making system remained firm, they resulted in the invention of a novel mechanism to feed the CEECs' preferences into the system.

However, the access of these policy-makers to the day-to-day practice and implementation of the dialogue was limited. While the Commission achieved over time its full association with CFSP, the vulnerability of its status was a major constraint on its activism. Particularly after the Copenhagen European Council, DG IA seemed preoccupied with securing the Commission's own role in CFSP. While the initiatives that forged the dialogue's institutional framework thus came primarily from policy-makers not directly involved in CFSP, or, in the case of the member states, high up in the decision-making hierarchy, their influence on the nature of its conduct was limited.

While the structure of the policy process thus explains partly the difference between institutional promise and failure in practice, the policy paradigm underpinning the Political Dialogue explains why CFSP policy-makers involved in its regular practice did not undertake more efforts to involve the CEECs, despite the potential benefits. These policy-makers had internalised the strong differentiation between insiders and outsiders and the objective to preserve the integrity of CFSP decision-making as an end in itself.

Many CFSP policy-makers criticise that the Political Dialogue has created a clumsy machinery that focuses too much on the formal characteristics of the dialogue, but lacks the necessary flexibility for pragmatic discussion and neglects the key structural limitations of the dialogue.[50] For example, officials in individual working groups considered the proposal to draw up non-binding joint conclusions at the end of meetings as a typical initiative by policy-makers too high up in the CFSP hierarchy to fully understand the character of the dialogue at the working group level.[51]

CFSP policy-makers regularly explain the limitations of the dialogue in practice by referring to the status of the CEECs as 'third countries' as a structural constraint, and the legal, financial, procedural, and technical difficulties of involving them more fully. While these difficulties certainly exist, they are in principle not insurmountable (see also Regelsberger 2000: 321). These arguments thus reflect primarily to what extent the policy paradigm underpinning the Political Dialogue has shaped CFSP policy-makers' perception of the structural limitations of the dialogue and what kinds of innovations are possible. As long as the CEECs are third countries, the Political Dialogue is an instrument to advance the EU's foreign policy objectives towards them, rather than to understand and support their foreign policy preferences.

By contrast, as the policy advocates inside the Commission were not closely tied into CFSP, they could conceive of an alternative view of the Political Dialogue as leading towards an EPA. Yet the notion of an EPA presented a minority position; the failure of the policy advocates to present its institutional and legal implications within a coherent concept made it impossible to dislodge the dominant paradigm.

A focus on policy paradigms and the structure of the policy process thus provides a plausible explanation of the patterns of (non-)accommodation of the CEECs' preferences in the Political Dialogue. However, while approaches focused on interest groups are at best indeterminate, there might be an alternative rationalist explanation. The institutional structure of the dialogue could be interpreted as a cheap side-payment to the CEECs, while CFSP policy-makers could achieve a significant level of unilateral alignment of the CEECs without engaging in more 'costly' consultations on CFSP decisions. Thus, the very premise that a fuller involvement of the CEECs in CFSP serves the EU's self-interest could be disputed.

To be sure, it might be difficult to argue, for example, that a fuller involvement of the CEECs would have prevented the disaster for CFSP that European disunity over US policy towards Iraq presented. After all, the 'Wall Street Journal Eight' who diverted from the CFSP common position of 27 February 2003 also included three EU members. Nonetheless, once the CEECs obtained observer status in CFSP after the signing of the accession treaty, their alignment with CFSP declarations achieved almost 100 per cent (see Table 8.1), although at this stage non-alignment could no longer endanger their accession prospects. Moreover, the institutional framework of the Political Dialogue was anything but cheap. On the one hand, it is extremely time-intensive. CFSP policy-makers already complain about the demands on their time that result from the Political Dialogue with third countries in general (see e.g. Monar 1997: 272). These demands are even heavier in the case of the dialogue with the CEECs, with its exceptionally broad range and frequency of contacts. On the other hand, the expectations that the ambitious framework of the dialogue raised with the CEECs made the lack of delivery in practice a constant source of irritation and criticism from the CEECs, causing high cost for the relationship. Finally, if the institutional framework were cost-free, it is difficult to explain why CFSP policy-makers did not immediately agree to create the many features that the policy advocates in the Commission only achieved incrementally through sustained lobbying.

Notes

1   I use the term 'EU' throughout this chapter, although in many instances it would be more appropriate to use 'the member states' or 'the EU and the member states'.

2 For simplicity, I will use the term CFSP also for foreign policy cooperation prior to November 1993.

3 Interview, Commission DG I, 01.02.95.

4 Interview, German Foreign Ministry, 19.12.95.

5 Interviews, Commission DG I, 01.02.95; German Foreign Ministry, 19.12.95.

6 Interviews, Commission DG I, 23.10.95; German Foreign Ministry, 19.12.95; Polish Mission to the EU, 27.10.95.

7 'L'on pourrait envisager à l'avenir de l'étendre à d'autres domaines, formes et mécanismes à different niveaux.'

8 Interview, UK Permanent Representation, 09.07.93.

9 Interview, UK Foreign Office, 20.03.96.

10 Interviews, Polish Mission to the EU, 13.10.97; French Foreign Ministry, 10.07.97; Spanish Foreign Ministry, 14.06.96.

11 Interview, UK Foreign Office, 20.03.96.

12 Interview, Council Secretariat, 14.10.97.

13 Interview, Council Secretariat, 14.10.97.

14 Interview, Polish Mission to the EU, 13.10.97.

15 Interview, Council Secretariat, 14.10.97.

16 Interview, Polish Mission to the EU, 13.10.95.

17 Interviews, Polish Mission to the EU, 13.10.97; Hungarian Mission to the EU, 13.10.97.

18 Interviews, Commission DG IA, 17.10.97; Council Secretariat, 13.10.97; Council Secretariat, 15.10.97.

19 Interview, Council Secretariat, 13.10.97.

20 Interview, Council Secretariat, 15.10.97.

21 Interview, Polish Mission to the EU, 13.10.97.

22 Interview, Council Secretariat, 15.10.97.

23 Interview, German Foreign Ministry, 19.12.95.

24 Interview, Polish Mission to the EU, 13.10.95.

25 Interviews, Council Secretariat, 13.10.97; Council Secretariat, 16.10.97.

26 Interview, Council Secretariat, 14.10.97.

27 Interview, Council Secretariat, 13.10.97.

28 Interviews, French Foreign Ministry, 09.07.96; Spanish Foreign Ministry, 19.06.96.

29 Interviews, Polish Mission to the EU, 13.10.97; Hungarian Mission to the EU, 13.10.97.

30 Interview, Council Secretariat, 13.10.97.

31 Interviews, Polish Mission to the EU, 13.10.97; Council Secretariat, 13.10.97; Council Secretariat, 15.10.97.

32 Interview, Council Secretariat, 16.10.97.

33 Interview, Council Secretariat, 15.10.97.

34 Interview, Council Secretariat, 13.10.97.

35 Interview, French Foreign Ministry, 15.10.96.

36 Interview, Spanish Foreign Ministry, 19.06.96.

37 Interview, Polish Mission to the EU, 13.10.97.

38 Interview, UK Foreign Office, 20.03.96.

39 Interview, Commission, DG IA, 17.10.97.

40 Interview, Council Secretariat, 16.10.97.

41 Interviews, Council Secretariat, 15.10.97; Council Secretariat, 13.10.97; Council Secretariat, 17.10.97.

42 Interviews, Council Secretariat, 13.10.97; Polish Mission to the EU, 13.10.97;

Hungarian Mission to the EU, 13.10.97.

43 Interviews, Polish Mission to the EU, 13.10.97; Council Secretariat, 15.10.97; French Foreign Ministry, 11.07.96; French Foreign Ministry, 10.07.96.

44 Interview, French Foreign Ministry, 11.07.96.

45 Interview, Council Secretariat, 15.10.97.

46 Interviews, Council Secretariat, 15.10.97; French Foreign Ministry, 11.07.96; French Foreign Ministry, 10.07.96.

47 Interview, Council Secretariat, 15.10.97.

48 Interview, French Foreign Ministry, 10.07.97.

49 Interview, Council Secretariat, 15.10.97.

50 Interviews, French Foreign Ministry, 10.07.97; Spanish Foreign Ministry, 14.06.96.

51 Interview, Council Secretariat, 16.10.97.

Part IV

Conclusions

9

Conclusions

EU identity and eastern enlargement

Materialist rationalist approaches, such as liberal intergovernmentalism in EU studies, identify some crucial factors influencing EU enlargement. But they cannot fully account for crucial features in both the macro- and the meso-dimension of the EU's eastern enlargement policy. The overall evolution of the policy, leading to the decision to enlarge, and its various substantive policies accommodate the CEECs' preferences to a greater extent than approaches purely based on material interests and bargaining power would expect. In order to explain these outcomes, we have to take social factors into account.

The central social factor is the EU's discursively constructed collective identity vis-à-vis the CEECs, which includes the notion of a 'special responsibility' towards the CEECs. As the effect of this element of EU identity is uneven across different groups of EU policy-makers, it affected policy primarily through the advocacy by a group of policy-makers who promoted policy options compatible with this identity. These policy-makers identified most closely with this component of EU identity, which formed a large part of their multiple social identities. The policy-makers most receptive to the behavioural prescriptions of this role-identity are those who present the EU externally and interact with the CEECs in this function, as well as identify most closely with the EU in general. The policy advocates were thus based inside the Commission, particularly in the DG responsible for external relations. They promoted an accommodation of the CEECs' preferences not only because of far-sighted self-interest, but as an objective in its own right.

Initiatives for policy to evolve towards enlargement and for improving policy concessions to the CEECs emanated primarily from the commissioners for external relations and their *cabinets*, and from DG I, specifically the unit for relations with the CEECs. The Commission played a key role in the EU's immediate policy responses to the unfolding changes in the CEECs in the late 1980s (the Trade and Cooperation Agreements, coordination of G24 aid, and PHARE). DG I reacted rapidly to the Council's decision to base relations with the CEECs on association agreements by devising quickly a far-reaching framework for 'Europe Agreements'. During the EA negotiations and intra-EU debates on the negotiation directives and their subsequent revision, Andriessen and the officials in DG I-E were consistently the strongest advocates of the CEECs' preferences. They also devised the initiative that moved policy beyond the EAs, by committing the EU to the objective of an eventual accession of the CEECs, and accelerated trade concessions in the sensitive sectors. Leon Brittan, as the new external relations commissioner from 1993, bestowed further momentum on the initiative, leading to the declarations of the Copenhagen European Council. Brittan's *cabinet* and DG I-L conceived of the idea of a pre-accession strategy, which put the principle of the eventual accession of the CEECs on a working footing, and achieved its endorsement in the Council through close cooperation with the German presidency.

The path to the decision to enlarge

The EU's role-identity affected not only the behaviour of the policy advocates. It was also a crucial factor enabling their success. The impact of EU identity was most direct with regard to the decision to enlarge. First, its behavioural prescriptions are most specific with regard to this dimension of policy. Second, the group of policy-makers in charge of this dimension of policy – the macro-policy-makers – were all receptive to this element of EU identity. The member states' foreign ministers and heads of state/government were most frequently the source of statements that affirmed the EU's role-identity, both individually and collectively in the Council or European Council.

While EU identity did not forge a positive consensus on enlargement, it restricted opposition and induced a path-dependence into the policy process. EU identity ruled out opposition to the general principle of enlargement and required justifying concerns about eastern enlargement with competing norms and legitimate goals, but not with material self-interests. Crucially, the policy advocates' initiatives incrementally removed legitimate arguments against enlargement. They thus increasingly narrowed the scope for opposition and confined policy options to a path to enlargement, which became increasingly irreversible.

Legitimate counterarguments included the need to safeguard EU integration, the functioning of the internal market after enlargement, and the functioning of EU institutions. By focusing on questions of principle and previous commitments, the policy advocates were able to strip away these potential objections, one after the other.

In the direct aftermath of the 1989 revolutions, the governments reluctant about the prospect of eastern enlargement could legitimately argue – with regard to the EU's standards of legitimacy – that it was premature to start discussing enlargement while the internal deepening agenda was incomplete, with the IGC on Political Union and EMU ongoing. However, once the ratification of the TEU was achieved, the policy advocates were able to sharpen the agenda to the key question of whether the member states did or did not accept the general legitimacy of the CEECs' desire to join. The question served as a 'fence buster': the reluctant governments could no longer sit on the fence once the question was posed this way; and none of the governments could answer it in the negative.

In turn, once the Copenhagen European Council had acknowledged the legitimacy of the CEECs' claim to eventual membership, it was equally difficult to refuse devising a strategy to prepare the CEECs for enlargement, which would sketch the way from the general principle of membership to accession. Although many governments had expected that the Copenhagen European Council would allow enlargement to be pushed off the medium-term agenda, they endorsed the pre-accession strategy at the Essen European Council.

Once the accession preparations for the CEECs were outlined, the only legitimate objection to starting accession negotiations with those judged to be able to meet the requirements was that the EU itself was not prepared for enlargement. With this requirement stated as an explicit pre-condition, the member states had no legitimate grounds to oppose setting an indicative date for starting accession negotiations at the Madrid European Council. Crucially, although the member states failed to meet precisely this precondition at the 1996/97 IGC, they nonetheless agreed to the start of accession negotiations. The agreement to tackle the question of institutional reform at a later stage, as well as the ability to forge compromises both on institutional reform and on budget allocations through the CAP and structural funds, reflected that they had accepted that the EU could not legitimately refuse to create the conditions to make enlargement possible that were within its powers.

Initially, the knowledge that legitimate counterarguments might serve as 'safety-valves', which left exit options further down the line, made it easier to reach agreement on the earlier steps towards enlargement. However, it turned out that precisely these incremental steps on the path to enlargement made it difficult to use such exit options later. These steps not only invalidated potential legitimate counterarguments, they also made the EU's commitment to enlargement increasingly explicit and concrete, by establishing clearer obligations and firmer deadlines for reaching specific signposts on the path. In this way, the EU's role-identity towards the CEECs and subsequent concretisations of the EU's commitment to enlargement increased the path-dependence of the process.

In a rationalist version of this path-dependency, reluctant governments initially discounted the future material costs of enlargement against the immediate social costs related to their reputation as community members (especially given the remaining safety-valves). However, subsequent moves increased the social costs of opposing enlargement, to the point that a veto in the final stages of the process became prohibitively costly. A constructivist perspective emphasises that the EU's identity entailed initially rather loose behavioural prescriptions, such as supporting the integration of those countries that had been involuntarily excluded from the integration project. Subsequent statements and initiatives considerably increased the specificity of the EU's role by linking it to enlargement. The increasing precision of the evaluative standard narrowed the behavioural options to the point that they were reduced to the path leading to enlargement.

The path to substantive terms of the enlargement policy

However, on substantive policies, the impact of identity and of the policy advocates was less direct. First, concerning this dimension, the behavioural prescriptions of identity were less specific; they only entailed a diffuse notion of accommodating the CEECs' preferences. Second, as enlargement is a composite policy, the role that the macro-policy-makers played in the various meso-policies of enlargement was circumscribed. Yet the sectoral policy-makers who play a considerable role in these meso-policies are much less receptive to this aspect of EU collective identity.

The structure of the policy process, which assigns their respective roles to macro- and meso-policy-makers with regard to specific substantive policies, was thus a significant mediating factor. When the foreign ministers in the GAC or the European Council became involved in the detail of policy, appeals to the EU's identity facilitated an accommodation of the CEECs' preferences. This was the case, for example, in the two revisions of the EAs' negotiation directives; the acceleration of the EAs' timetable for trade liberalisation agreed in a high-level group of foreign ministry officials in the run-up to the Copenhagen European Council; the agreement on economic flanking measures of the pre-accession strategy, agreed by a COREPER *restreint* prior to the Essen European Council; or the preliminary agreement on the budgetary package for the Cologne European Council, agreed by the foreign ministers meeting in a conclave.

However, such instances of involvement of the macro-policy-makers were generally rare. Often they were restricted to the management of crises in relations with the CEECs. On such occasions, the importance of the macro-policy-makers' collective self-perceptions showed when the EU's behaviour appeared in contradiction with their professed role-identity. For example, it was reflected in their sensitivity and vulnerability to the criticism of the lack of accommodation in EAs, although such criticism was not linked to material threats. One the one hand, the shadow of hierarchical coordination once crises in relations with the CEECs emerged increased the incentives for sectoral policy-makers to find (restrictive) agreements at lower levels of the decision-making hierarchy. On the other hand, it made it possible for the policy advocates in the Commission to choose strategies that resulted in the reassertion of hierarchical coordination. The fact that the history of eastern enlargement is to a large extent the history of European Council declarations reflects the importance of engineering a centralisation of the policy process among the macro-policy-makers.

In the national policy formulation processes, foreign ministry officials were also generally inclined to argue for more accommodating policies against their colleagues with sectoral portfolios. An example is the effort by French foreign minister Dumas to obtain a more generous French position in the EA negotiations. By contrast, in the less transparent and less publicly exposed national policy formulation process, some heads of state/government appeared more likely to cede to domestic pressures than either their foreign ministries, or they themselves, were likely to do within the context of the European Council.

In general, however, the formulation and especially the implementation of the enlargement policy was characterised by a fragmented policy process. This book has therefore emphasised the structure of the policy process in a composite policy as one crucial mediating factor that delimits the access of the macro-policy-makers in general, and the policy advocates in particular, to sectoral decisions. However, once the policy advocates have obtained access to decision-making on a meso-policy, they still need to be able to build 'winning alliances' with sectoral policy-makers that are sufficiently powerful to achieve policy changes that accommodate the CEECs' preferences.

Liberal intergovernmentalism, the dominant materialist rationalist approach in EU studies, suggests that the key factor that determines the behaviour of sectoral policy-makers are the preferences of sectoral interest groups, which then determine the scope for alliance-building and the likelihood of an accommodation of the CEECs' preferences. By contrast, I have argued that the preferences of these policy-makers are shaped by sectoral policy paradigms. Compatibility of sectoral policy paradigms with the CEECs' preferences might thus enable their accommodation, even if it is opposed by EU interest groups. Conversely, incompatible policy paradigms present a deeper obstacle to accommodation, possibly in addition to (but irrespective of) interest group pressure. In this sense, sectoral policy paradigms shaped the path to substantive policy outcomes of eastern enlargement.

Table 9.1 Summary: meso-policy cases and outcomes

Cases		Test variables			Policy outcomes
		Interest groups	Policy process	Policy paradigms	
Steel trade liberalisation	EA negotiations	Accommodation unlikely	Accommodation possible	Accommodation possible	Accommodation
	Implementation of the EAs	Accommodation unlikely	Accommodation unlikely	Accommodation likely	Accommodation
Regulatory alignment	Environmental policy (White Paper)	Accommodation possible	Accommodation possible	Accommodation unlikely	Accommodation
	Environmental policy (accession negotiations)	Accommodation unlikely	Accommodation unlikely	Accommodation unlikely	Accommodation
	Social policy (White Paper)	Accommodation possible	Accommodation possible	Accommodation unlikely	No accommodation
	Social policy (accession negotiations)	Accommodation unlikely	Accommodation unlikely	Accommodation unlikely	No accommodation
Foreign policy consultations		Accommodation possible/likely	Accommodation possible	Accommodation unlikely	No accommodation

Interplay of paradigms and process structures in the meso-policies

Table 9.1 (see also Table 1.1, Chapter 1) summarises the conditions with regard to the alternative explanatory variables in the meso-policies – interest group pressure, structure of the policy process, and sectoral policy paradigms – and contrasts their respective predictions about the likelihood of accommodation with the policy outcomes at various stages of the policy process. The pattern emerging from Table 9.1 favours explanations based on policy paradigms and the structure of the policy process over explanations based on interest groups. Explanations that focus only on interest group pressure generally fare poorly; they do not reliably predict the likelihood of accommodation across cases. Predictions based on the compatibility of sectoral policy paradigms with the preferences of the CEECs generally fare much better in cases in which interest group pressure and paradigms pull in opposite directions. The record is more mixed with regard to particular instances of regulatory alignment, to which I will return below; the outcome of accession negotiations for environmental policy presents a puzzle for both interest-based and paradigm-based explanations. Moreover, it is not immediately obvious from Table 9.1 how particular interplays of the structure of the policy process and paradigm compatibility affect accommodation.

Box 9.1 therefore locates the observations from the meso-policy case studies in Chapters 6–8 in the framework of Box 3.1 (Chapter 3), which suggested how variations in the constellation of the structure of the policy process and sectoral policy paradigms affect the likelihood of accommodation, even if interest groups oppose such accommodation. A closer analysis suggests that variation in the configuration of policy paradigms and the structure of the policy process does not only affect the likelihood of accommodation as such, but also its *sustainability*, as well as particular pathways through which accommodation might be achieved in the face of countervailing interest group pressure.

Box 9.1 Mediating factors in the meso-policies

		Policy process	
		Fragmented	Centralised
Policy paradigms	**Compatible**	Implementation of steel trade liberalisation	General approach of WP on regulatory alignment; steel trade liberalisation in EAs
	Incompatible	Implementation of Political Dialogue; environmental and social policy in accession negotiations	Alignment with environmental and social policy in WP; institutional framework of Political Dialogue

Likelihood of accommodation

The predictions are most clear-cut for the lower-left and upper-right cells. In the case of the latter, the favourable conditions with regard to both factors did indeed lead to an accommodation of the CEECs' preferences. In the case of steel trade liberalisation, the paradigm shift in EU steel policy resulted in a greater compatibility with the CEECs' preferences for abolishing the VRAs. The centralisation of the policy process during the EA negotiations allowed this decision to be imposed on those sectoral policy-makers who had not bought into the new ideas, despite vigorous opposition from the Spanish ministry of industry in particular. The case of the Commission's WP on regulatory alignment is similar. The view of officials in DG XV of the internal market, which focused primarily on the elimination of NTBs, was much more compatible with the CEECs' preferences for a selective alignment with product-standards during the pre-accession phase, than the EU's general internal market paradigm. The centralisation of the drafting of the WP in DG XV allowed it to maintain a strong coordinating role in the Commission and limited the involvement of the member states. The WP's general approach thus largely accommodated the CEECs' preferences.

The cases in the lower-left cell also generally appear to conform to expectations: unfavourable conditions for both factors resulted in a lack of accommodation of the CEECs' preferences. With regard to the Political Dialogue, interest group pressure was absent, but an accommodation of the CEECs' preferences for consultations on foreign policy failed due to their incompatibility with the policy paradigm underpinning the EU's political dialogue. The centralised policy process which privileged access of the policy advocates and actors at the highest level of the foreign ministries' decision-making hierarchy resulted in an institutional framework for the dialogue that established a mechanism for consultations. However, the CFSP officials who were in charge of the conduct of the dialogue in practice were much more influenced by the policy paradigm underpinning the Political Dialogue. This paradigm draws a sharp distinction between full members and 'third countries', which made it impossible for CFSP officials to conceive of two-way consultation or a participation of the CEECs in CFSP meetings, let alone joint decision-making.

Likewise, an accommodation of the CEECs' preference for selective alignment with EU social policy was incompatible with the EU's internal market paradigm, which emphasises the importance of a level playing field through harmonising process regulations and high levels of social protection as an end in itself. The fragmentation of the policy process gave social policy-makers the ability to veto proposals for selective alignment in their area. The case that does not conform to predictions is environmental policy. The CEECs were granted long post-accession periods, which are incompatible with the internal market paradigm. I will return to this case below.

Sustainability of accommodation

The key cases to explore the interplay of sectoral paradigms and process structures are the upper-left and lower-right cells. Conditions are mixed; they are favourable for one of the variables, but unfavourable with regard to the other.

The cases in the lower-right cell suggest that a centralised policy process allowed a temporary accommodation of the CEECs' preferences through a hierarchical imposition of such polices on sectoral policy-makers. While the new policy paradigm for EU steel policy was still fragile, the macro-policy-makers imposed the elimination of VRAs for the CEECs on unwilling sectoral policy-makers in the EA negotiations. The institutional framework of the Political Dialogue was agreed among the macro-policy-makers, despite the aversion of CFSP officials to blurring the line between members and non-members. The strong coordinating role of DG XV in the drafting of the Commission's WP on regulatory alignment allowed it to obtain the assent of environmental policy-makers to selective alignment, despite its incompatibility with the internal market paradigm. However, in all these cases, accommodation proved difficult to sustain if the policy paradigm remained incompatible with accommodation. In practice, the Political Dialogue never fully used the possibilities for consultation that its institutional framework offered. Immediately after the signing of the EAs, sectoral policy-makers who had not converted to the 'non-intervention' paradigm for EU steel policy supported the industry's calls for the use of trade defence measures.

The case in the lower-right cell which appears not to fit with expectations is the requirement for the CEECs' regulatory alignment with EU social policy. Here the incompatibility of the CEECs' preference for selective pre-accession alignment and long transition periods appears to have trumped the favourable condition created through a centralised policy process during the drafting of the Commission's White Paper. This case underlines, however, the significance of policy paradigms, rather than societal interests. As Chapter 7 showed, EU interest groups did not attempt to influence the policy process at this stage.

The case in the upper-left cell suggests that compatible policy paradigms may eventually lead to accommodation, even in a fragmented policy process. Furthermore, once such accommodation has been achieved, it is likely to be sustainable. In the case of steel trade liberalisation, the ascendancy of the 'non-intervention' paradigm for EU steel policy, which is compatible with the CEECs' preference for free and unconditional market access, created such conditions. In the renewal of the VRAs prior to the EAs, the new paradigm was not strong enough to lead to more than a moderate accommodation of the CEECs' preferences, which did not challenge the VRAs as such. During the EA negotiations, hierarchical imposition facilitated abolishing the VRAs. Despite the early set-back of the use of safeguards against Czechoslovakia in the implementation process, the growing influence of the new paradigm on sectoral policy-makers cumulated in the failure of attempts to reintroduce a protectionist trade regime as part of the 1993/94 restructuring plan.

Summary: mediating factors in meso-policies
In sum, the evidence of the meso-policy case studies suggests that interest group opposition might only be an effective constraint on an accommodation of the applicants' preferences in those cases in which the policy process is fragmented and sectoral policy paradigms are incompatible with the applicants' preferences. Sectoral policy paradigms are a key variable, concerning both the *likelihood* and *sustainability* of accommodation. Incompatibility between sectoral paradigms and preferences is a key obstacle to accommodation, even in a centralised policy process. In such cases, centralisation might still make accommodation possible, but it is likely to remain temporary.

By contrast, compatibility between paradigms and preferences can lead to accommodation, despite interest group opposition. Compatible paradigms can eventually lead to accommodation, even in a predominantly fragmented policy process. Fragmentation makes it difficult for the policy advocates to gain access to decision-making. However, once access has been achieved, the policy paradigm facilitates alliance-building, which makes accommodation possible and likely to be sustainable. Alternatively, as in the case of steel trade, once a compatible paradigm has achieved a sufficient dominance among sectoral policy-makers, accommodation is possible, even if the policy process remains predominantly insulated at the sectoral level.

Yet the analysis in this book also suggests that cases might be rather rare in which an accommodation of the applicants' preferences is compatible with paradigms but opposed by interest groups. Such cases might primarily concern periods of paradigm shifts, which would make it difficult to systematically test the relative importance of paradigm compatibility and interest group pressure. However, in the previous enlargement round, the negotiations between the EU and EFTA candidates on environmental policy fitted these conditions. The EU allowed the new members to maintain higher environmental standards – which EU firms opposed since they created trade barriers for them – as higher environmental standards are compatible with the EU's internal market paradigm.

Internal and external status of sectoral policy paradigms
The cases that appear to remain difficult to explain on the basis of paradigms and process structures concern the requirements for the CEECs' regulatory alignment with environmental and social policy. In these cases, the key question concerns the likelihood of *temporary* accommodation (such as post-accession transition periods). The contrast between temporary accommodation in the area of environmental policy and resistance to it in social policy is striking. This variation in outcomes is puzzling, since both during the drafting of the Commission's WP and during accession negotiations, the conditions co-varied in the two policy areas. At the WP stage, there was no interest group pressure, the policy process was centrally coordinated and an accommodation of the candidates' preferences was incompatible with the

broader internal market paradigm that underpins both sectors. During the EA negotiations, conditions with regard to interest group pressure and the structure of the policy process changed, but for both policy areas.

A tentative starting point is to investigate more closely the status of the sectoral paradigms. Arguably, while in the EU there is a strong acceptance of high levels of environmental protection, acceptance of a further expansion of social policy is much more contested. In other words, while the respective sectoral policy paradigms are strongly consensual *within* both sectors, their *external* acceptance in the broader context of the EU differs. While the acceptance of high levels of environmental protection outside the sector is high, the external acceptance is much more problematic in the case of social policy.

In turn, external acceptance might make a temporary accommodation of the CEECs' preferences more easily tolerable for environmental policy-makers. By contrast, for social policy-makers, such temporary accommodation might be considered much more of a threat to their sectoral policy paradigm, which could explain the strong resistance to even a temporary accommodation. Box 9.2 summarises these propositions about how the differences in the external and internal status of policy paradigms affect the likelihood of temporary accommodation.

Drawing on the insights of the case studies, Box 9.2 also suggests how the status of these paradigms might structure the strategies that are available to the policy advocates in their attempts to influence policy. In the case of environmental policy, the intra-sectoral consensus made the building of strategic alliances difficult, while the external consensus on the sectoral paradigm enabled the policy advocates to persuade sectoral policy-makers to agree to a temporary accommodation. In the case of social policy, even temporary accommodation was impossible. Persuasion was difficult, as accommodation might threaten the sectoral paradigm, given the lack of external consensus. In cases where the policy paradigm is contested both within the sector and externally (again, typically the case in periods of paradigm shift as in the case of EU steel policy in the first half of the 1990s), persuasion is unlikely to work, but there is scope for strategic alliance-building within the sector.

Policy paradigms thus appear as a central variable not only for the likelihood of accommodation, but also for its sustainability, and for the strategies to achieve it. This is not to suggest that policy paradigms generally favour accommodation. Far from it. Maybe ironically, even in the case of steel, in which a paradigm shift enabled an accommodation of the CEECs' preferences for unconditional market access to the EU during the association period, the shift towards a 'non-intervention' paradigm is likely to make it difficult to accommodate public interventions to restructure the CEECs' steel industries after accession.

Box 9.2 Status of policy paradigms and the likelihood of preference accommodation

Status of policy paradigms within the sector

		Consensual	Contested
External status of policy paradigms	Consensual	Temporary accommodation possible through persuasion (e.g. environmental policy)	
	Contested	Even temporary accommodation unlikely (e.g. social policy)	Accommodation possible through strategic alliance-building (e.g. steel trade, 1990–94)

The upshot is that more often than not, policy paradigms appear to be a crucial obstacle to an accommodation of new members' and candidates' preferences – especially if they are at a different level of socio-economic development from the EU. The ideas that underpin EU policy paradigms have evolved in a particular socio-economic context and do not necessarily fit in different contexts. This means that it is not simply rent-seeking by vested interests, but these different contexts that make so difficult mutual adjustment between incumbents and candidates, and anything more than a temporary accommodation of the preferences of the latter. The taken-for-grantedness of policy paradigms prevents scrutiny of the potential drawbacks of exporting the ideas that underpin them. Even in those sectors – and arguably particularly in those sectors – in which paradigms are contested in the EU, there is strong resistance to considering the viability of their underlying ideas in the context of the candidates.

An important direction for further theoretical and empirical research is thus to explore the conditions which might facilitate a temporary accommodation of candidates' preferences that are incompatible with sectoral policy paradigms. As a starting point, I have suggested that further investigation might focus on the interplay between different actor strategies (persuasion and strategic alliance-building) and differences in the status of sectoral policy paradigms (variations in the degree to which they are contested or consensual, both inside a particular sector as well as in the EU's broader institutional context).

Policy paradigms and transgovernmental politics

Composite policies

The concept of a composite policy has broader applications in EU studies and in research on international institutions and international political economy. Enlargement is a specific type of composite policy, which includes the full range of EU policy areas among its meso-policies. But the concept also allows the analysis of more limited cross-sectoral policies, in which the macro-policy is a policy area in its own right, and which affects one or more other policy areas, such as the links between transport and environmental policy. Composite policies which draw on a more extensive range of meso-policies are most frequent in the EU's external relations, such as trade negotiations. However, composite policies are also found in the EU's internal policies. For example, cooperation in Justice and Home Affairs includes separate meso-policies, such as asylum policy, visas, citizenship, or police cooperation. Armstrong and Bulmer (1998) analyse the internal market as a range of distinctive 'governance regimes', even if they focus primarily on their formal institutional characteristics.

A key insight of the concept of a composite policy is the emphasis on the challenge of policy coordination across policy areas. This focus is also relevant for rationalist material approaches, to the extent that it emphasises the structure of the policy process as an important mediating factor for policy outcomes in specific meso-policies. It also draws attention to questions of the capacities of the General Affairs Council, the European Council, and the commissioners' *college* with regard to coordination, problem-solving, leadership and strategic policy-making.

Policy paradigms

Apart from its potential usefulness in rationalist analyses, a particular strength of the composite policy concept is the focus on institutional effects on the collective preference formation of certain groups of policy-makers at the macro- and meso-policy levels. The concept of sectoral policy paradigms and the uneven impact of 'collective identity' captures the social factors that relate bureaucratic and organisational positions to beliefs about legitimate policy. It can explain the emergence of collective differences between groups of national and Commission policy-makers in specific policy areas, which are in certain cases more pronounced than the nationality cleavage. It emphasises that under certain conditions transgovernmental alliances – rather than inter-state bargaining – characterise the policy debate in the EU.

More generally, a focus on policy paradigms can contribute to understanding policy change and resistance to change in particular policy areas. Policy paradigms draw attention to the fact that influence on policy can be achieved without the material attributes of power. Policy paradigms are particularly relevant in areas that are characterised by technical complexity.

However, the ideas that underpin them are not simply about cause/effect relations and the effectiveness of policy, but just as much about questions of legitimacy. In this sense, policy paradigms can be seen as belief-systems that provide the glue for advocacy coalitions (Sabatier 1988, 1997), in particular in policy domains in which technical issues are dominated by normative and identity concerns (1997: 122).

For the more general analysis of composite policies, a focus on sectoral paradigms pinpoints a challenge to policy coordination that is not easily captured in materialist rationalist analyses. Policy paradigms might either form more deeply embedded obstacles to coordination than domestic interest group pressures, or provide a channel to overcome such pressure. Debates in the policy coordination process are not simply about preserving interests of different client groups, but about communicating to other groups of policy-makers how particular measures might affect the functioning of policy in a specific area. In the end, the key question is whether it is possible to find mutually acceptable definitions of policy problems and legitimate goals. A focus on policy paradigms suggests that opposition from sectoral policy-makers to changes in their area might not simply stem from capture and rent-seeking, but from concerns about dysfunctionalities that an accommodation of the preferences of macro-policy-makers can create in the meso-policy.

Transgovernmental politics

A focus on policy paradigms in cross-sectoral policies also allows us to conceptualise and examine the role of transgovernmental coalitions in the EU and other international institutions. Other analyses of the EU's enlargement policies have also suggested that rather than inter-state bargaining, distinctive 'policy communities' (Ruano 1999) and 'cross-cutting coalitions' (Torreblanca 1998) characterise conflicts over substantive policies. However, while these observations are rarely conceptualised in a broader analytical framework, they fit well with findings in other policy areas. For example, a key cleavage in the Uruguay Round of the GATT was between the collective position of the foreign ministers in the General Affairs Council on the one hand, and the Agriculture Council on the other, rather than between conflicting national positions (Woolcock and Hodges 1996). Lindberg and Scheingold (1970: 160) observed that

> The Ministers of Agriculture … and their aides and advisors … have come to share preoccupations and expertise. They are subject to similar constituency demands, engaged in annual budget battles against their respective Ministers of Finance, and they seek the same general goals of improving the conditions of farmers and of modernizing agriculture. Indeed, in the eyes of many of their colleagues in other governmental ministries, they have come to form an exclusive club, thoroughly defended by impenetrable technical complexities.

The cleavage that these analyses observe is strongly reminiscent of the concept of transgovernmental relations in international organisations (Keohane and Nye 1974). Transgovernmental networks or coalitions are characterised by officials in sub-units of national governments that pursue preferences that are independent from or even contrary to official government policy (see also Risse-Kappen 1995c: 9–10). It is not a recent observation that the EU 'constitutes an almost purpose-built laboratory for examining the impact of transnational actors and relations on policy process. The network of economic relationships and scale of bureaucratic interpenetration necessitated and sustained by the EC's policy responsibilities suggests a hotbed of transnational activity' (Webb 1983: 35). In addition to these formal characteristics of EU policy-making, Risse-Kappen (1995b: 286–7) emphasises that the EU's normative structure is particularly conducive to the emergence of transgovernmental coalitions:

> [In the EU], transnational and transgovernmental coalition-building of like-minded officials bargaining with other alliances within the normative framework provided by the institution appears to better characterize the interaction pattern within highly integrated regimes and organisations. [...] Transgovernmental networks are particularly relevant within the regimes and organizations ... such as ... the EU ... [that] are based on common identities among the actors ... which transcend identities based on national boundaries.

An analysis of the EU's eastern enlargement policy as a composite policy, with its emphasis on the collective differences between the groups of policy-makers that have respectively the primary responsibility for the macro- or one of the various meso-policies, provides conceptual tools to analyse such transgovernmental relations in the EU and international institutions more generally. The focus on sectoral policy paradigms and the uneven effect of specific elements of the EU's collective identity across different groups of policy-makers suggests that distinctive sets of ideational factors influence the collective preference formation of the policy-makers operating within a particular policy sub-system. These factors – in addition to, but separately from, material factors – shape the ability to coordinate policy across sectors and to agree on broader goals of the system of governance.

References

Adler, E. (1997), 'Seizing the Middle Ground: Constructivism in World Politics', *European Journal of International Relations*, 3:3, 319–63.

—— (2002), 'Constructivism and International Relations', in W. Carlsnaes, T. Risse and B. Simmons (eds), *Handbook of International Relations* (London: Sage), 95–118.

Allen, D. (2000), 'Cohesion and the Structural Funds: Transfers and Trade-Offs', in H. Wallace and W. Wallace (eds), *Policy-Making in the European Union*, 4th edn (Oxford: Oxford University Press), 243–65.

Allison, G. (1969), 'Conceptual Models and the Cuban Missile Crisis', *American Political Science Review*, 63:3, 689–718.

Andriessen, F. (1991a), 'Towards a Community of Twenty Four?', speech at the 69th Assembly of Eurochambers, 19.04.1991.

—— (1991b), 'The Integration of Europe: It's Now or Never', *European Affairs*, No. 6, 6–11.

Armstrong, K. and Bulmer, S. (1998), *The Governance of the Single European Market* (Manchester: Manchester University Press).

Aspinwall, M. and Schneider, G. (eds) (2001), *The Rules of Integration: Institutionalist Approaches to the Study of Europe* (Manchester: Manchester University Press).

Avery, G. (1995), 'The Commission's Perspective on the EFTA Accession Negotiations', *Sussex European Institute Working Paper* No. 12.

—— (2004), 'The Enlargement Negotiations', in F. Cameron (ed.), *The Future of Europe: Integration and Enlargement* (London: Routledge), 35–62.

—— and Cameron, F. (1998), *The Enlargement of the European Union* (Sheffield: Sheffield Academic Press).

Bacon, N. and Blyton, P. (1996), 'Re-casting the Politics of Steel in Europe: The Impact on Trade Unions', *West European Politics*, 19:4, 770–86.

Baker, J. (1989), 'A New Europe, a New Atlanticism: Architecture for a New Era', speech at the Berlin Press Club, 12.12.1989, *Europe Documents*, No. 1588, 15.12.1989.

Baldwin, R. (1994), *Towards an Integrated Europe* (London: CEPR).

—— Francois, J. and Portes, R. (1997), 'The Costs and Benefits of Eastern Enlargement: The Impact on the EU and Central Europe', *Economic Policy* 24, 125–76.

—— et al. (1992), *Monitoring European Integration, Vol. 3: Is Bigger Better? The Economics of EC Enlargement* (London: CEPR).

Baun, M. (2000), *A Wider Europe: The Process and Politics of European Union Enlargement* (Lanham: Rowman & Littlefield).

BDI (Bundesverband der Deutschen Industrie) (1996), 'Die Beziehungen der

EU zu den Reformländern Mittel- und Osteuropas – Stand und Perspektiven. Ein Leitfaden aus Sicht der deutschen Industrie', January 1996.

Begg, D. et al. (1993), *Making Sense of Subsidiarity: How Much Centralization for Europe?* (London: CEPR).

Benz, A., Scharpf, F. and Zintl, R. (1992), *Horizontale Politikverflechtung. Zur Theorie von Verhandlungssystemen* (Frankfurt: Campus).

Börzel, T. (1997a), 'Zur (Ir-)Relevanz der "Postmoderne" für die Integrationforschung', *Zeitschrift für Internationale Beziehungen*, 4:1, 125–37.

—— (1997b), 'What's So Special About Policy Networks? An Exploration of the Concept and Its Usefulness in Studying European Governance', *European Integration Online Papers*, 1:16.

Bulmer, S. (1986), *The Domestic Structure of European Community Policy-Making in West Germany* (New York: Garland).

Cadot, O. and Melo, J. (1995), 'France and the CEECs: Adjusting to Another Enlargement', in R. Faini and R. Portes (eds), *European Trade with Eastern Europe: Adjustments and Opportunities* (London: CEPR), 86–122.

Checkel, J. (1998), 'The Constructivist Turn in International Relations Theory (Review Article)', *World Politics*, 50:2, 324–48.

—— (2001), 'Why Comply? Social Learning and European Identity Change', *International Organization*, 55:3, 553–88.

—— (2004), 'Social Constructivisms in Global and European Politics: A Review Essay', *Review of International Studies*, 30:2, 229–44.

—— and Moravcsik, A. (2001), 'A Constructivist Research Programme in EU Studies?', *European Union Politics*, 2:2, 219–49.

Chirac, J. (1996), speech before the Polish Sejm and Senate, Warsaw, 12.09.1996.

Christiansen, T., Jørgensen, K.-E. and Wiener, A. (2001a), 'Introduction', in Christiansen, T., K.-E. Jørgensen and A. Wiener (eds), *The Social Construction of Europe* (London: Sage), 1–19.

—— (eds) (2001b), *The Social Construction of Europe* (London: Sage).

CNPF (Conseil National du Patronat Français) (1997), 'Pour un élargissement ordonné de l'Union Européenne', January 1997.

Cockerill, A. (1993), 'Steel', in P. Johnson (ed.), *European Industries. Structure, Conduct and Performance* (Aldershot: Edward Elgar), 52–74.

Commission (1990a), 'The Development of the Community's Relations with the Countries of Central and Eastern Europe', SEC (90) 194, 01.02.1990.

—— (1990b), 'The Development of the Community's Relations with the Countries of Central and Eastern Europe', SEC (90) 717, 18.04.1990.

—— (1990c), 'Association Agreements with the Countries of Central and Eastern Europe: A General Outline', COM (90) 398, 27.08.1990.

—— (1990d), 'Recommendation for a Council Decision Authorising the Commission to Negotiate a European Agreement with the Republic of Poland, SEC (90) 2122, 30.10.1990.

—— (1990e), 'General Objectives for Steel 1995', COM (90) 201.

—— (1990f), 'Industrial Policy in an Open and Competitive Environment. Guidelines for a Community Approach', COM (90) 556.

—— (1992a), 'Europe and the Challenge of Enlargement', *Bulletin of the EC*, Supplement 3/92.

—— (1992b), 'Towards a New Partnership with the Central and East European Countries', draft report for the European Council in Edinburgh, Brussels, 03.11.1992.

—— (1992c), 'Towards a Closer Association with the Countries of Central and Eastern Europe', SEC (92) 2301, 02.12.1992.

—— (1993a), 'Towards a Closer Association with the Countries of Central and Eastern Europe', SEC (93) 648, 18.05.1993.

—— (1993b), 'Eleventh Annual Report on the Community's Anti-Dumping and Anti-Subsidy Activities (1992)', COM (93) 516, 28.10.1993.

—— (1994a), 'The Europe Agreements and Beyond: A Strategy to Prepare the Countries of Central and Eastern Europe for Accession', COM (94) 320, 13.07.1994.

—— (1994b), 'Follow-up: The Europe Agreements and Beyond: A Strategy to Prepare the Countries of Central and Eastern Europe for Accession', COM (94) 361, 27.07.1994.

—— (1995a), 'White Paper: Preparation of the Associated Countries of Central and Eastern Europe for Integration into the Internal Market of the Union', COM (95) 163, 03.05.1995.

—— (1995b), 'White Paper: Annex', COM (95) 163/2, 10.05.1995.

—— (1996), 'Intergovernmental Conference 1996: Commission Opinion – Reinforcing Political Union and Preparing for Enlargement', COM (96) 90, 28.02.1996.

—— (1997a), 'Agenda 2000. Volume I: For A Stronger and Wider Union', COM (97) 2000, 15.07.1997.

—— (1997b), 'Agenda 2000. Volume II: The Challenge of Enlargement', COM (97) 2000, 15.07.1997.

—— (1997c), 'Commission Opinion on Poland's Application for Membership of the European Union', COM (97) 2002, 15.07.1997.

—— (1999a), 'Poland: 1999 Accession Partnership', December 1999.

—— (1999b), 'Composite Paper: Reports on Progress towards Accession by Each of the Candidate Countries', 13.10.1999.

—— (2002), 'Enlargement of the European Union. Guide to the Negotiations – Chapter by Chapter', November 2002.

—— (2003), 'Report on the Results of the Negotiations on Accession', January 2003.

Coss, S. (1997), '... While Ensuring the Workforce is Healthy and Safe', *European Voice*, 25 September, 14.

Council (1985), 'Ad hoc Committee for Institutional Affairs: Report to the European Council ('Dooge Committee Report')', Brussels, 29–30.03. 1985.

—— (1988), 'European Council in Rhodes, 2–3 December 1988, Presidency Conclusions', SN 4443/1/88.

—— (1989), 'European Council in Strasbourg, 8–9 December 1989,

Presidency Conclusions', SN 441/2/89.

—— (1990a), 'European Council in Dublin, 28 April 1990, Presidency Conclusions', *Bulletin of the EC*, 4–1990.

—— (1990b), 'European Council in Rome, 27–28 October 1990, Presidency Conclusions', SN 304/2/90.

—— (1990c), 'European Council in Rome, 27–28 October 1990, Presidency Conclusions: Part 2', SN 428/90.

—— (1992a), 'Rencontre des ministres des affaires étrangères de la Communauté européenne et des pays de Visegrad – Déclaration commune', Presse 9033/92, 05.10.1992.

—— (1992b), 'European Council in Edinburgh, 11–12 December 1992, Presidency Conclusions', *Bull-EC* 12/1992.

—— (1993), 'European Council in Copenhagen, 21–22 June 1993, Presidency Conclusions', *Europe Documents* No. 1844/45, 24.06.1993.

—— (1994a), 'Council Conclusions. Reinforcement of the Political Dialogue with Central and Eastern European Countries', Doc 5181/94, 07.03.1994.

—— (1994b), 'European Council in Corfu, 24–25 June 1994, Presidency Conclusions', SN 150/94.

—— (1994c), 'Political Committee. Guidelines for Implementation of the Enhanced Political Dialogue with the Associated Central and Eastern European Countries', 25.10.1994.

—— (1994d), 'European Council in Essen, 9–10 December 1994, Presidency Conclusions, Annex IV: Report from the Council on a Strategy for the Accession of the Associated CCEE', SN 300/94, 7–25.

—— (1995a), 'European Council in Cannes, 26–27 June 1995, Presidency Conclusions', *Europe Documents*, No. 1942, 29.06.1995.

—— (1995b), 'Cannes European Council Conclusions of the Presidency, Part B. Preparation of the Associated Countries of Central and Eastern Europe for Integration into the Internal Market of the European Union', *Europe Documents*, No. 1943, 30.06.1995.

—— (1995c), 'Political Committee. Guidelines for Enhanced Political Dialogue with the Central and Eastern European Countries Associated with the Union', 20.10.1995.

—— (1995d), 'European Council in Madrid, 15–16 December 1995, Presidency Conclusions', SN 400/95.

—— (1995e), 'Reflection Group's Report. Second Part: An Annotated Agenda', SN 517/95 (REFLEX 18), 10.11.1995.

—— (1995f), 'Reflection Group's Report. Second Part: An Annotated Agenda', 05.12.1995.

—— (1999a), 'Berlin European Council, 24–25 March 1999, Presidency Conclusions', *Bulletin of the EU* 3–1999.

—— (1999b), 'Annual Report CFSP 1998', 16.04.1999.

—— (2000), 'Annual Report CFSP 1999', 5990/00 PESC, 04.04.2000.

—— (2001a), 'European Council in Laeken, 14–15 December 2001, Presidency Conclusions', SN 300/1/01REV1.

—— (2001b), 'Annual Report CFSP 2000', 7853/01 PESC, 06.04.2001.

—— (2002), 'Annual Report CFSP 2001', 7330/02 PESC, 18.04.2002.

—— (2003), 'Annual Report CFSP 2002', 7038/03 PESC, 07.04.2003.

—— (2004), 'CFSP Statements – 2003'.

de Bassompierre, G. (1988), *Changing the Guard in Brussels. An Insider's View of the EC Presidency* (New York: Praeger).

de La Serre, F. (1994), 'A la Recherche d'une Ostpolitik', in F. de La Serre, C. Lequesne and J. Rupnik (1994), *L'Union Européenne: Ouverture à l'Est?* (Paris: Presses Universitaires de France), 11–41.

Delors, J. (1990), speech at Gent University, 10.05.1990.

—— (1994), 'Voeux à la presse', spokesman's service, 28.01.1994.

DIHT (Deutscher Industrie und Handelstag) (1995), 'Perspektiven für Europa', June 1995.

Dinan, D. (1998), 'The Commission and Enlargement', in J. Redmond and G. Rosenthal (eds), *The Expanding European Union. Past, Present, Future* (Boulder: Lynne Rienner), 17–40.

Dominguez, L. (1988), 'Agriculture and the Third Enlargement of the EC', PhD dissertation, University of Edinburgh.

Dudley, G. and Richardson, J. (1990), *Politics and Steel in Britain, 1967–88. The Life and Times of the British Steel Corporation* (Aldershot: Dartmouth).

—— —— (1999), 'Competing Advocacy Coalitions and the Process of "Frame Reflection": A Longitudinal Analysis of EU Steel Policy', *Journal of European Public Policy*, 6:2, 225–48.

Dunay, P., Kende, T. and Szücs, T. (1997), 'The Integration of Central and Eastern Europe into the Common Foreign and Security Policy of the European Fifteen', in M. Maresceau (ed.), *Relations Between the EU and Central and Eastern Europe* (London: Longman), 316–45.

Dunnet, D. (1991), 'The European Bank for Reconstruction and Development: A Legal Survey', *Common Market Law Review*, 28:3, 571–97.

ECSC Consultative Committee (1991), 'Resolution on the Association Agreements with the Countries of Central and Eastern Europe', OJ C 197, 26.07.1991, 3–4.

—— (1993), 'Resolution Concerning "External measures" – Steel Imports from Countries of Central and Eastern Europe', OJ C 121, 01.05.1993, 4–5.

Edwards, G. (1998), 'The Council of Ministers and Enlargement: A Search for Efficiency, Effectiveness, and Accountability', in J. Redmond and G. Rosenthal (eds), *The Expanding European Union. Past, Present, Future* (Boulder: Lynne Rienner), 41–64.

—— and Regelsberger, E. (eds) (1990), *Europe's Global Links: The European Community and Inter-Regional Cooperation* (London: Pinter).

EEB (European Environmental Bureau) (2001), 'EEB and the EU Enlargement', October 2001.

Elleman-Jensen, U. (1992), 'The New Europe: A Danish View', *NATO Review*, 40:1, 8–11.

Elorza, J. (1997), 'New Members – A Southern View', *Challenge Enlargement*, January 1997, 9–10.

Esser, J. and Fach, W. (1989), 'Crisis Management "Made in Germany": The

Steel Industry', in P. Katzenstein (ed.), *Industry and Politics in West Germany. Towards the Third Republic* (Ithaca: Cornell University Press), 221–48.

ETUC (European Trade Union Congress) (1993), 'Social Dimension of the Association Agreements Between the EC and Some Central and Eastern European Countries', 09.03.1993.

—— (1998), 'European Union Enlargement: Involving Social Partners – Protecting the Welfare State', Executive Committee Resolution, 17.12.1998.

—— (2000), 'Post-Nice Enlargement of the European Union', Executive Committee Resolution, 14.12.2000.

EUROFER (1992), 'Memorandum', October 1992.

Evans, P., Rueschemeyer, D. and Skocpol, T. (eds) (1985), *Bringing the State Back In* (Cambridge: Cambridge University Press).

—— Jacobsen, H. and Putnam, R. (eds) (1993), *Double-Edged Diplomacy: International Bargaining and Domestic Politics* (Berkeley: University of California Press).

Fearon, J. and Wendt, A. (2002), 'Rationalism v. Constructivism: A Skeptical View', in W. Carlsnaes, T. Risse and B. Simmons (eds), *Handbook of International Relations* (London: Sage), 52–72.

Ferner, A., Keep, E. and Waddington, J. (1997), 'Industrial Restructuring and EU-wide Social Measures: Broader Lessons of the ECSC Experience', *Journal of European Public Policy*, 4:1, 56–72.

Fierke, K. and Wiener, A. (1999), 'Constructing Institutional Interests: EU and NATO Enlargement', *Journal of European Public Policy*, 6:5, 721–42.

Finnemore, M. and Sikkink, K. (1998), 'International Norm Dynamics and Political Change', *International Organization*, 52:4, 887–917.

Fischer, J. (2000), 'From Confederacy to Federation: Thoughts on the finality of European integration', speech at the Humboldt University, Berlin, 12.05.2000.

Flemming, J. and Rollo, J. (eds) (1992), *Trade, Payments and Adjustment in Central and Eastern Europe* (London: RIIA).

Foster, A. and Wallace, W. (1996), 'Common Foreign and Security Policy: A New Policy or Just a New Name?', in H. Wallace and W. Wallace (eds), *Policy-Making in the European Union*, 3rd edn (Oxford: Oxford University Press), 411–35.

Friis, L. (1997), 'When Europe Negotiates. From Europe Agreements to Eastern Enlargement', PhD dissertation, University of Copenhagen.

—— (1998) 'The End of the Beginning of Eastern Enlargement: Luxembourg Summit and Agenda-setting', *European Integration online Papers* 2:7.

GATT (1991), *Trade Policy Review: The European Communities, Vol. I* (Geneva: GATT).

Gautron, J.-C. (ed.) (1991), *Les Relations Communauté Européenne – Europe de l'Est* (Paris: Economica).

Ginsberg, R. (1989), *Foreign Policy Actions of the European Community: The Politics of Scale* (Boulder: Lynne Rienner).

Glais, M. (1995), 'Steel Industry', in P. Buigues, A. Jacquemin and A. Sapir (eds), *European Policies on Competition, Trade and Industry: Conflict and Complementarities* (Aldershot: Edward Elgar), 219–67.

Goldberg, H. (1986), *Ailing Steel: The Transoceanic Quarrel* (Aldershot: Gower).

Goldstein, J. and Keohane, R. (1993), 'Ideas and Foreign Policy: An Analytical Framework', in J. Goldstein and R. Keohane (eds), *Ideas and Foreign Policy: Beliefs, Institutions, and Political Change* (Ithaca: Cornell University Press), 3–30.

Grabbe, H. (1999), 'A Partnership for Accession? The Implications of EU Conditionality for the Central and Eastern European Applicants', *European University Institute Working Paper* RSC No. 99/12.

—— (2001), *Profiting from Enlargement* (London: Centre for European Reform).

—— and Hughes, K. (1998), *Enlarging the EU Eastwards* (London: Pinter).

Grunert, T. (1986), 'Decision-Making in the Steel Crisis Policy of the EEC: Neocorporatist or Integrationist Tendencies?', in Y. Mény and V. Wright (eds), *The Politics of Steel: Western Europe and the Steel Industry in the Crisis Years (1974–1984)* (New York: de Gruyter), 222–307.

Guggenbuhl, A. (1995), 'The Political Economy of Association with Eastern Europe', in F. Laursen (ed.), *The Political Economy of European Integration* (The Hague: Kluwer), 211–82.

Haas, P. (1992), 'Introduction: Epistemic Communities and International Policy Co-ordination', *International Organization*, 46:1, 1–35.

Haggard, S., Levy, M. Moravcsik, A. and Nicolaïdis, K. (1993), 'Integrating the Two Halves of Europe: Theories of Interests, Bargaining, and Institutions', in R. Keohane, J. Nye and S. Hoffmann (eds), *After the Cold War: International Institutions and State Strategies in Europe, 1989–1991* (Cambridge: Harvard University Press), 173–95.

Hall, P. (1986), *Governing the Economy: The Politics of State Intervention in Britain and France* (New York: Oxford University Press).

—— (1993), 'Policy Paradigms, Social Learning, and the State. The Case of Economic Policymaking in Britain', *Comparative Politics*, 25:3, 275–96.

—— and Taylor, R. (1996), 'Political Science and the three New Institutionalisms', *Political Studies*, 44:5, 936–57.

Hayes, P. (1993), *Making Trade Policy in the European Community* (New York: St. Martin's Press).

Hayes-Renshaw, F. and Wallace, H. (1997), *The Council of Ministers* (Basingstoke: Macmillan).

Haywood, E. (1993), 'The European Policy of François Mitterrand,' *Journal of Common Market Studies*, 31:2, 269–82.

Hindley, B. (1993), 'Helping Transition through Trade? EC and US Policy towards Exports from Eastern and Central Europe', *EBRD Working Paper* No. 4.

Holmes, P. and Kempton, J. (1997), 'Study on the Economic and Industrial Aspects of Anti-dumping Policy', *Sussex European Institute Working Paper* No. 22.

—— and Smith, E. (1997), 'Trade and Competition Policy in the Europe Agreements: Lessons from the EEA Experience', paper presented at the ECSA conference, Seattle, May.

Hudson, R. (1994), 'Restructuring Production in the West European Steel Industry', *Tijdschrift voor Economische en Sociale Geografie*, 85:2, 99–133.

Ikenberry, J. and Kupchan, C. (1990), 'Socialization and Hegemonic Power', *International Organization*, 44:3, 283–315.

Jachtenfuchs, M. (1996), *International Policy-Making as a Learning Process? The European Union and the Greenhouse Effect* (Aldershot: Avebury).

—— (2001), 'The Governance Approach to European Integration', *Journal of Common Market Studies*, 39:2, 245–64.

Jepperson, R., Wendt, A. and Katzenstein, P. (1996), 'Norms, Identity, and Culture in National Security', in P. Katzenstein (ed.), *The Culture of National Security. Norms and Identity in World Politics* (New York: Columbia University Press), 33–75.

Jezek, K. (1995), 'The Multilateralisation of the Political Dialogue: First Experiences', in B. Lippert and H. Schneider (eds), *Monitoring Association and Beyond* (Bonn: Europa Union Verlag), 267–73.

Jileva, E. (2004), 'Do Norms Matter? The Principle of Solidarity and the EU's Eastern Enlargement', *Journal of International Relations and Development*, 7:1, 3–23.

Johansson-Nogues, E. (2004), 'The Fifteen and the Accession States in the UN General Assembly: What Future for European Foreign Policy in the Coming Together of the "Old" and "New" Europe?', *European Foreign Affairs Review*, 9:1, 67–92.

Johnson, C. (1982), *MITI and the Japanese Miracle* (Stanford: Stanford University Press).

Johnston, A.I. (2001), 'Treating International Institutions as Social Environments', *International Studies Quarterly*, 45:4, 487–515.

Jones, K. (1986), *Politics vs Economics in World Steel Trade* (London: Allen and Unwin).

Jørgensen, K.-E. (1997), *Reflective Approaches to European Governance* (Basingstoke: Macmillan).

Jupille, J., Caporaso, J. and Checkel, J. (2003), 'Integrating Institutions: Rationalism, Constructivism, and the Study of the European Union', *Comparative Political Studies*, 36:1/2, 7–41.

Juppé, A. (1994), speech at the Anglo-American press lunch, Paris, 2 May 1994.

Katzenstein, P. (1996a), 'Conclusion: National Security in a Changing World', in P. Katzenstein (ed.), *The Culture of National Security. Norms and Identity in World Politics* (New York: Columbia University Press), 498–537.

—— (1996b), 'Introduction: Alternative Perspectives on National Security', in P. Katzenstein (ed.), *The Culture of National Security. Norms and Identity in World Politics* (New York: Columbia University Press), 1–32.

—— (ed.) (1996c), *The Culture of National Security. Norms and Identity in World Politics* (New York: Columbia University Press).

—— Keohane, R. and Krasner, S. (1998), 'International Organization and the Study of World Politics', *International Organization*, 52:4, 645–85.

Kassim, H., Peters, G. and Wright, V. (eds) (2000), *The National Co-ordination of EU Policy: The Domestic Level* (Oxford: Oxford University Press).

—— Peters, G. Menon, A. and Wright, V. (eds) (2001), *The National Co-ordination of EU Policy: The European Level* (Oxford: Oxford University Press).

Keohane, R. (1988), 'International Institutions: Two Approaches', *International Studies Quarterly*, 32:4, 379–96.

—— (1991), 'Empathy and International Regimes', in J. Mansbridge (ed.), *Beyond Self-Interest* (Chicago: University of Chicago Press), 227–36.

—— and Nye, J. (1974), 'Transgovernmental Relations and International Organizations', *World Politics*, 27, 39–62.

Kerremans, B. (1998), 'The Political and Institutional Consequences of Widening: Capacity and Control in an Enlarged Council', in P.-H. Laurent and M. Maresceau (eds), *The State of the European Union, Vol. 4: Deepening and Widening* (Boulder: Lynnne Rienner), 87–109.

Klepper, G. (1991), 'The Steel and Metal Industry', in D. Mayes (ed.), *The European Challenge: Industry's Response to the 1992 Programme* (London: Harvester Wheatsheaf), 372–85.

Klotz, A. (1995), 'Norms Reconstituting Interests: Global Racial Equality and U.S. Sanctions against South Africa', *International Organization*, 49:3, 451–78.

Koch, K. (1995), 'The Policy of the EU Members on the Issue of Enlargement: The Case of the Netherlands', paper prepared for the EVROPEVM conference, 10–12 October, Bonn.

Kohler-Koch, B. (2000), 'Framing: The Bottleneck of Constructing Legitimate Institutions', *Journal of European Public Policy*, 7:4, 513–31.

Kowert, P. and Legro, J. (1996), 'Norms, Identity, and Their Limits: A Theoretical Reprise', in P. Katzenstein (ed.), *The Culture of National Security. Norms and Identity in World Politics* (New York: Columbia University Press), 451–97.

Kramer, H. (1993), 'The European Community's Response to the "New Eastern Europe"', *Journal of Common Market Studies*, 31:2, 213–44.

Laffan, B. (1997), 'The European Union: A Distinctive Model of Internationalisation?', *European Integration online Papers*, 1:18.

—— and Shackleton, M. (2000), 'The Budget: Who Gets What, When, and How', in H. Wallace and W. Wallace (eds), *Policy-Making in the European Union*, 4th edn (Oxford: Oxford University Press), 211–41.

Lamers, K. (1995), 'Facing the IGC '96', speech at the Royal Institute of International Affairs, London, 19.10.1995.

Legro, J. (1997), 'Which Norms Matter? Revisiting the "Failure" of Internationationalism', *International Organization*, 51:1, 31–64.

Leibfried, S. and Pierson, P. (2000), 'Social Policy: Left to Courts and Markets?', in H. Wallace and W. Wallace (eds), *Policy-Making in the European Union*, 4th edn (Oxford: Oxford University Press), 267–92.

Lenschow, A. and Zito, A. (1998) 'Blurring or Shifting of Policy Frames? Institutionalization of the Economic-Environmental Policy Linkage in the European Community', *Governance*, 11:4, 415–41.

Lequesne, C. (1991), 'Les Accords de Commerce et de Coopération Communauté Européenne – Pays d'Europe de l'Est', in J.-C. Gautron (ed.), *Les Relations Communauté Européenne – Europe de l'Est* (Paris: Economica), 357–71.

—— (1993), *Paris–Bruxelles: comment se fait la politique européenne de la France* (Paris: Fondation Nationale des Sciences Politiques).

Lindberg, L. and Scheingold, S. (1970), *Europe's Would-be Polity: Patterns of Change in the European Community* (Englewood Cliffs, N.J.: Prentice-Hall).

Lippert, B. (1990), 'EC–CMEA Relations: Normalisation and Beyond', in G. Edwards and E. Regelsberger (eds), *Europe's Global Links: The European Community and Inter-Regional Cooperation* (London: Pinter), 119–40.

—— and Becker, P. (1998), 'Structured Dialogue Revisited: The EU's Politics of Inclusion and Exclusion', *European Foreign Affairs Review*, 3:3, 341–65.

—— and Schneider, H. (1995), 'Association and Beyond: The European Union and the Visegrád States', in B. Lippert and H. Schneider (eds), *Monitoring Association and Beyond* (Bonn: Europa Union Verlag), 25–45.

Lumsdaine, D. (1993), *Moral Vision in International Politics: The Foreign Aid Regime 1949–1989* (Princeton: Princeton University Press).

Majone, G. (1996), 'A European Regulatory State?', in J. Richardson (ed.), *European Union: Power and Policy-Making* (London: Routledge), 263–77.

Mann, M. (1997), 'Giant "Green" Mountain to Climb', *European Voice*, 25 September, 14.

March, J. and Olsen, J. (1989), *Rediscovering Institutions: The Organizational Basis of Politics* (New York: Free Press).

Maresceau, M. (1989) (ed.), *The Political and Legal Framework of Trade Relations Between the European Community and Eastern Europe* (Dordrecht: Nijhoff).

Martin, L. (1992), 'Interests, Power, and Multilateralism', *International Organization*, 46:4, 765–92.

Mayhew, A. (1997), 'Forgotten Dreams Stall Integration', *Challenge Enlargement*, January 1997, 11.

—— (1998), *Recreating Europe: The European Union's Policy towards Central and Eastern Europe* (Cambridge: Cambridge University Press).

—— (2000), 'Enlargement of the European Union: An Analysis of the Negotiations with the Central and Eastern European Candidate Countries', *Sussex European Institute Working Paper*, No. 39.

—— (2002), 'The Negotiating Position of the European Union on Agriculture, the Structural Funds and the EU Budget', *Sussex European Institute Working Paper*, No. 52.

Mayntz, R. and Scharpf, F. (1975), *Policy-Making in the German Federal Bureaucracy* (Amsterdam: Elsevier).

McGowan, F. and Wallace, H. (1996), 'Towards a European Regulatory

State?', *Journal of European Public Policy*, 3:4, 560–76.

Mény, Y. and Wright, V. (eds) (1986), *The Politics of Steel: Western Europe and the Steel Industry in the Crisis Years (1974–1984)* (New York: de Gruyter).

Messerlin, P. (1992), 'The Association Agreements between the EC and Central Europe: Trade Liberalization vs Constitutional Failure', in J. Fleming and J. Rollo (eds), *Trade, Payments and Adjustment in Central and Eastern Europe* (London: RIIA), 111–43.

—— (1993), 'The EC and Central Europe: The Missed Rendez-Vous of 1992?', *Economics of Transition*, 1:1, 89–109.

Michalski, A. and Wallace, H. (1992), *The European Community: The Challenge of Enlargement* (London: RIIA).

Monar, J. (1997), 'Political Dialogue with Third Countries and Regional Political Groupings', in E. Regelsberger, P. de Schoutheete and W. Wessels (eds), *Foreign Policy of the European Union: From EPC to CFSP and Beyond* (Boulder: Lynne Rienner), 263–74.

Monnet, J. (1955), *Les Etats-Unis d'Europe ont commencé* (Paris: Robert Laffont).

Monti, M. (1995), 'Preparing the Countries of Central and Eastern Europe for Integration into the Internal Market', speech at the College of Europe, Natolin, 03.10.1995.

Moravcsik, A. (1993), 'Preferences and Power in the European Community: A Liberal Intergovernmentalist Approach', *Journal of Common Market Studies*, 31:4, 473–524.

—— (1998), *The Choice for Europe: Social Purpose and State Power from Messina to Maastricht* (Ithaca: Cornell University Press).

—— and Vachudova, M. (2003), 'National Interests, State Power, and EU Enlargement', *East European Politics and Societies*, 17:1, 42–57.

Müller, H. (1995), 'European Nuclear Non-Proliferation Policy', manuscript.

Neumann, I. and Welsh, J. (1991), 'The "Other" in European Identity: An Addendum to the Literature on International Society', *Review of International Studies*, 17:4, 327–48.

Niblett, R. (1995), 'The European Community and the Central European Three, 1989–92: A Study of the Community as an International Actor', PhD dissertation, Oxford University.

Nicolaïdis, K. (1993), 'East European Trade in the Aftermath of 1989: Did International Institutions Matter?', in R. Keohane, J. Nye and S. Hoffmann (eds), *After the Cold War: International Institutions and State Strategies in Europe, 1989–1991* (Cambridge: Harvard University Press), 196–245.

Nuttall, S. (1992), *European Political Cooperation* (Oxford: Clarendon Press).

Orlowski, W. and Mayhew, A. (2001), 'The Impact of EU Accession on Enterprise Adaptation and Institutional Development in the Countries of Central and Eastern Europe', *Sussex European Institute Working Paper* No. 4.

Ostry, S. (1993), 'The Threat of Managed Trade to Transforming Economies', *EBRD Working Paper* No. 3.

Paarlberg, R. (1997), 'Agricultural Policy Reform and the Uruguay Round:

Synergistic Linkage in a Two-Level Game?', *International Organization*, 51:3, 413–44.

Patterson, L. (1997), 'Agricultural Policy Reform in the European Community: A Three-Level Game Analysis', *International Organization*, 51:1, 135–65.

Pedersen, T. (1990), 'Problems of Enlargement: Political Integration in a Pan-European EC', *Cooperation and Conflict*, 25:2, 83–99.

Pedler, R. (1994), 'The Fruit Companies and the Banana Trade Regime', in R. Pedler and M.Van Schendelen (eds), *Lobbying the European Union: Companies, Trade Associations and Issue Groups* (Aldershot: Dartmouth), 67–91.

Peers, S. (1995), 'An Ever Closer Waiting Room? The Case for Eastern European Accession to the European Economic Area', *Common Market Law Review*, 32, 187–213.

Pelkmans, J. and Murphy, A. (1991), 'Catapulted into Leadership: The Community's Trade and Aid Policies vis-à-vis Eastern Europe', *Journal of European Integration*, 14:2/3, 125–51.

Peterson, J. (1995), 'Decision-making in the European Union: Towards a Framework for Analysis', *Journal of European Public Policy*, 2:1, 69–93.

Phinnemore, D. (1999), *Association: Stepping-Stone or Alternative to EU Membership?* (Sheffield: Sheffield Academic Press).

—— (2004), 'Institutions and Governance', in N. Nugent (ed.), *European Union Enlargement* (Basingstoke: Palgrave), 118–31.

Pierson, P. (1996), 'The Path to European Integration: A Historical Institutionalist Perspective', *Comparative Political Studies*, 29:2, 123–63.

Pinder, J. (1991), *The European Community and Eastern Europe* (London: Pinter).

—— and Pinder, P. (1975), 'The European Community's Policy towards Eastern Europe', *Chatham House European Series* No. 25.

Pollack, M. (2001), 'International Relations Theory and European Integration', *Journal of Common Market Studies*, 39:2, 221–44.

Powell, W. and DiMaggio, P. (eds) (1991), *The New Institutionalism in Organizational Analysis* (Chicago: University of Chicago Press).

Preston, C. (1997), *Enlargement and Integration in the European Union* (London: Routledge).

Previdi, E. (1997), 'Making and Enforcing Regulatory Policy in the Single Market', in H. Wallace and A. Young (eds), *Participation and Policy-Making in the European Union* (Oxford: Clarendon Press), 69–90.

Price, R. and Tannenwald, N. (1996), 'Norms and Deterrence: The Nuclear and Chemical Weapons Taboos', in P. Katzenstein (ed.), *The Culture of National Security. Norms and Identity in World Politics* (New York: Columbia University Press), 114–52.

Putnam, R. (1988), 'Diplomacy and Domestic Politics: The Logic of Two Level Games', *International Organization*, 42:3, 427–60.

Regelsberger, E. (1990) 'The Dialogue of the EC/Twelve with Other Regional Groups: A New Identity in the International System?', in G. Edwards and E.

Regelsberger (eds), *Europe's Global Links: The European Community and Inter-Regional Cooperation* (London: Pinter), 3–26.

—— (1995), 'Political Dialogue with the Visegrád Group: Only Business as Usual at High Speed?', in B. Lippert and H. Schneider (eds), *Monitoring Association and Beyond* (Bonn: Europa Union Verlag), 251–66.

—— (2000), 'Die schrittweise Integration der Beitrittsländer in die Außen-, Sicherheits- und Verteidigungspolitik der EU – der strukturierte Dialog ungleicher Partner', in B. Lippert (ed.), *Osterweiterung der Europäischen Union – die doppelte Reifeprüfung* (Bonn: Europa Union Verlag), 309–23.

Rein, M. and Schön, D. (1991), 'Frame-reflective Policy Discourse', in P. Wagner, C. Weiss, B. Wittrock and H. Wollmann (eds), *Social Sciences and Modern States: National Experiences and Theoretical Crossroads* (Cambridge: Cambridge University Press), 262–89.

Reinicke, W. (1992), *Building a New Europe: The Challenge of System Transformation and Systemic Reform* (Washington: Brookings).

Rhodes, M. (1989), 'West European Steel – The Prospects to 1992', *Contemporary European Affairs*, 2:2, 69–102.

Risse, T. (2000), '"Let's Argue!" Communicative Action in World Politics', *International Organization*, 54:1, 1–39.

—— (2001), 'A European Identity? Europeanization and the Evolution of Nation-State Identities', in J. Caporaso, M. Cowles and T. Risse (eds), *Transforming Europe. Europeanization and Domestic Change* (Ithaca: Cornell University Press), 198–216.

—— (2004), 'Social Constructivism and European Integration', in A. Wiener and T. Diez (eds), *European Integration Theory* (Oxford: Oxford University Press), 159–75.

—— and Sikkink, K. (1999), 'The Socialization of International Human Right Norms into Domestic Practices: Introduction', in T. Risse, S. Ropp and K. Sikkink (eds), *The Power of Human Rights: International Norms and Domestic Change* (Cambridge: Cambridge University Press), 1–38.

Risse-Kappen, T. (1994), 'Ideas Do Not Float Freely: Transnational Coalitions, Domestic Structures, and the End of the Cold War', *International Organization*, 48:2, 185–214.

—— (1995a), *Cooperation Among Democracies. The European Influence on U.S. Foreign Policy* (Princeton: Princeton University Press).

—— (1995b), 'Structures of Governance and Transnational Relations: What Have We Learned?', in T. Risse-Kappen (ed.), *Bringing Transnational Relations Back In: Non-State Actors, Domestic Structures, and International Institutions* (Cambridge: Cambridge University Press), 280–313.

—— (1995c), 'Bringing Transnational Relations Back In: Introduction', in T. Risse-Kappen (ed.), *Bringing Transnational Relations Back In: Non-State Actors, Domestic Structures, and International Institutions* (Cambridge: Cambridge University Press), 3–33.

—— (1996), 'Exploring the Nature of the Beast: International Relations Theory and Comparative Policy Analysis Meet the European Union', *Journal of Common Market Studies*, 34:1, 53–80.

Rollo, J. and Smith, A. (1993), 'The Political Economy of Eastern European Trade with the European Community: Why so Sensitive?', *Economic Policy*, 16, 139–81.

Ross, G. (1995), *Jacques Delors and European Integration* (Oxford: Oxford University Press).

Rouam, C. (1994), 'L'Union Européenne face aux pays d'Europe Centrale et Orientale: Délocalisations industrielles ou harmonisation des conditions de concurrence?', *Revue du Marché Commune et de l'Union Européenne*, 383, 643–8.

Ruano, L. (1999), 'A Policy Communities Approach to Enlargement: British and Spanish Accession Negotiations in the Agricultural Sector', paper presented at the ECPR joint sessions of workshops, Mannheim, 26–31 March.

—— (2002), 'Origins and Implications of the European Union's Enlargement Negotiations Procedure', *European University Institute Working Papers*, RSC No. 2002/62.

Sabatier, P. (1988), 'An Advocacy Coalition Framework of Policy Change and the Role of Policy-oriented Learning therein', *Policy Sciences*, 21, 129–68.

—— (1997), 'The Advocacy Coalition Framework: Revisions and Relevance for Europe', *Journal of European Public Policy*, 5:1, 98–130.

Sandholtz, W. (1996), 'Membership Matters: Limits of the Functional Approach to European Institutions', *Journal of Common Market Studies*, 34:3, 403–29.

Saryusz-Wolski, J. (1994), 'The Reintegration of the "Old Continent": Avoiding the Costs of "Half-Europe"', in S. Bulmer and A. Scott (eds), *Economic and Political Integration in Europe. International Dynamics and Global Context* (Oxford: Blackwell), 19–28.

Scharpf, F. (1993), 'Positive und negative Koordination in Verhandlungssystemen', in A. Héritier (ed.), *Policy-Analyse* (Opladen: Westdeutscher Verlag), 57–83.

—— (1997), *Games Real Actors Play: Actor-Centred Institutionalism in Policy Research* (Boulder: Westview Press).

Schimmelfennig, F. (2001), 'The Community Trap: Liberal Norms, Rhetorical Action, and the Eastern Enlargement of the European Union', *International Organization*, 55:1, 47–80.

—— (2003), *The EU, NATO and the Integration of Europe: Rules and Rhetoric* (Cambridge: Cambridge University Press).

—— and Sedelmeier, U. (2002), 'Theorizing EU Enlargement: Research Focus, Hypotheses and the State of Research', *Journal of European Public Policy*, 9:4, 500–28.

Schön, D. and Rein, M. (1994), *Frame Reflection Towards the Resolution of Intractable Policy Controversies* (New York: Basic Books).

Sedelmeier, U. (1994), 'The European Union's Association Policy Towards Central Eastern Europe: Political and Economic Rationales in Conflict', *Sussex European Institute Working Paper* No. 7.

—— (1998), 'The European Union's Association Policy towards the

Countries of Central and Eastern Europe: Collective EU Identity and Policy Paradigms in a Composite Policy', PhD dissertation, University of Sussex.

—— (2000a), 'Eastern Enlargement: Risk, Rationality, and Role-Compliance', in M. Cowles and M. Smith (eds), *The State of the European Union, Vol. 5: Risk, Reforms, Resistance, and Revival* (Oxford: Oxford University Press), 164–85.

—— (2000b), 'East of Amsterdam: The Implications of the Amsterdam Treaty for Eastern Enlargement', in A. Wiener and K. Neunreither (eds), *European Integration after Amsterdam: Institutional Dynamics and Prospects for Democracy* (Oxford: Oxford University Press), 218–35.

—— (2001), 'Accommodation Beyond Self-Interest? Identity, Policy Paradigms, and the Limits of a Rationalist Approach to EU Policy towards Central Europe', *Politique Européenne*, 3, 13–37.

—— (2002), 'Sectoral Dynamics of EU Eastern Enlargement: Advocacy, Access and Alliances in a Composite Policy', *Journal of European Public Policy*, 9:4, 627–49.

—— and Wallace, H. (1996), 'Policies towards Central and Eastern Europe', in H. Wallace and W. Wallace (eds), *Policy-Making in the European Union*, 3rd edn (Oxford: Oxford University Press), 353–87.

—— —— (2000), 'Eastern Enlargement: Strategy or Second Thoughts?', in H. Wallace and W. Wallace (eds), *Policy-Making in the European Union*, 4th edn (Oxford: Oxford University Press), 427–60.

Shaffer, M. (1995), 'The Applicability of Three-Level Game Analysis to EC-Visegrad Negotiations for the Europe Agreements', paper presented at the UACES conference, Birmingham, 18–19.09.1995.

Sissenich, B. (2005), 'The Transfer of EU Social Policy to Poland and Hungary', in F. Schimmelfennig and U. Sedelmeier (eds), *The Europeanization of Central and Eastern Europe* (Ithaca: Cornell University Press), 156–77.

Sjursen, H. (2002), 'Why Expand? The Question of Legitimacy and Justification in the EU's Enlargement Policy', *Journal of Common Market Studies*, 40:3, 491–513.

Skalnes, L. (2001), 'Geopolitics and the Eastern Enlargement of the European Union', paper presented at the APSA meeting, San Francisco, 30 August–2 September.

Skogstad, G. (1998), 'Ideas, Paradigms and Institutions: Agricultural Exceptionalism in the European Union and the United States', *Governance*, 11:4, 463–90.

Smith, A. and Wallace, H. (1994), 'The European Union: Towards a Policy for Europe?', *International Affairs*, 70:3, 429–44.

—— Holmes, P., Sedelmeier, U., Smith, E., Wallace, H. and Young, A. (1996), 'The European Union and Central and Eastern Europe: Pre-accession Strategies', *Sussex European Institute Working Paper* No.15.

Smith, E. (1995), 'The European Economic Area as a Transitory Regime', paper presented at the UACES conference, Birmingham, 18–19.09.1995.

Smith, M. (2004), 'Institutionalization, Policy Adaptation and European

Foreign Policy Cooperation', *European Journal of International Relations*, 10:1, 95–136.

Snyder, J. (1991), *Myths of Empire: Domestic Politics and International Ambition* (Ithaca: Cornell University Press).

Spence, D. (1994), 'Structure, Functions and Procedures in the Commission', in G. Edwards and D. Spence (eds), *The European Commission* (London: Longmans), 97–116.

—— (1995), 'The Co-ordination of European Policy by Member States', in M. Westlake (ed.), *The Council of the European Union* (London: Cartermill), 353–72.

Stubb, A. (1997), 'The 1996 Intergovernmental Conference and the Management of Flexible Integration', *Journal of European Public Policy*, 4:1, 37–55.

Suchocka, H. (1992), 'Le passage d'un système à l'autre doit être moins brutal', *Le Monde*, 17.09.1992.

Taylor, S. (1999), 'Environmental "Reprieve" on the Cards', *European Voice*, 10.11.1999.

Thelen, K. and Steinmo, S. (1992), 'Historical Institutionalism in Comparative Politics', in S. Steinmo, K. Thelen and F. Longstreth (eds), *Structuring Politics: Historical Institutionalism in Comparative Analysis* (Cambridge: Cambridge University Press), 1–32.

Torreblanca, J. (1997), 'The European Community and Central Europe (1989–1993): Foreign Policy and Decision-Making', PhD dissertation, Instituto Juan March.

—— (1998), 'Overlapping Games and Cross-Cutting Coalitions in the European Union', *West European Politics* 21:2, 134–53.

—— (2001), *The Reuniting of Europe: Promises, Negotiations and Compromises* (Aldershot: Ashgate).

Tsebelis, G. (2002), *Veto Players: How Political Institutions Work* (Princeton: Princeton University Press).

Tsoukalis, L. and Strauss, R. (1986), 'Community Policies on Steel 1974–82: A Case of Collective Management', in Y. Mény and V. Wright (eds), *The Politics of Steel: Western Europe and the Steel Industry in the Crisis Years (1974–1984)* (New York: de Gruyter), 186–221.

UNICE (1995), Industrial Cooperation with the Countries of Central/Eastern Europe. UNICE Statement, 09.11.1995.

—— (1997), 'UNICE Position on the Implications for Business of EU Enlargement to Central and Eastern European Countries', version 19.11.1997.

Vachudova, M. (2001), 'The Leverage of International Institutions on Democratizing States: Eastern Europe and the European Union', *European University Institute Working Paper* RSC 2001/33.

—— (2005), *Europe Undivided: Democracy, Leverage and Integration After Communism* (Oxford: Oxford University Press).

van den Broek, H. (1994), 'The Challenge of Wider Europe', speech at the Université Libre de Bruxelles, Brussels, 17.03.1994.

Vanderseypen, G. (1995), 'La politique de restructuration sidérurgique: un bilan nuancé', *Revue du Marché Commun et de l'Union Européenne*, No. 386, 160–7.

Vernet, D. (1992), 'The Dilemma of French Foreign Policy', *International Affairs*, 68:4, 655–64.

Visegrád (1992), 'Memorandum of the Governments of the Czech and Slovak Federal Republic, the Republic of Hungary and the Republic of Poland on Strengthening their Integration with the European Community and on the Perspective of Accession', Prague, Warsaw and Budapest, 11.09.1992.

—— (1993), Aide-memoire of the Governments of the Czech and Slovak Federal Republic, the Republic of Hungary and the Republic of Poland, Prague, Warsaw and Budapest, 02.06.1993.

Vogel, D. (1997), 'Regulatory Cooperation Between the European Union and the United States: Introduction', *ECSA Review*, 10:2, 3–7.

Waever, O. (1997), 'Figures of International Thought: Introducing Persons Instead of Paradigms', in O. Waever and I. Neumann (eds), *The Future of International Relations. Masters in the Making* (London: Routledge), 1–37.

Wallace, H. (1991), 'The Europe that Came in from the Cold', *International Affairs*, 67:4, 647–63.

—— and Wallace, W. (1995), 'Flying Together in a Larger and More Diverse European Union', *Netherlands Scientific Council for Government Policy, Working Documents* W87, 9–74.

Wang, Z. and Winters, A. (1993), 'EC Imports from Eastern Europe: Iron and Steel', *CEPR Discussion Paper* No. 825.

Webb, C. (1983), 'Theoretical Perspectives and Problems', in H. Wallace, W. Wallace and C. Webb (eds), *Policy-Making in the European Community*, 2nd edn (Chichester: Wiley), 1–41.

Weber, S. (1994), 'Origins of the European Bank for Reconstruction and Development', *International Organization*, 48:1, 1–38.

Wendt, A. (1992), 'Anarchy is What States Make of It: The Social Construction of Power Politics', *International Organization*, 46:2, 391–425.

—— (1994), 'Collective Identity Formation and the International State', *American Political Science Review*, 88:2, 384–96.

—— (1999), *Social Theory of International Politics* (Cambridge: Cambridge University Press).

Winters, A. (1992), 'The Europe Agreements: With a Little Help from Our Friends', in *The Association Process: Making It Work. Central Europe and the EC*, CEPR Occasional Paper No. 11, 17–33.

—— (1995a), 'Liberalisation of the European Steel Trade', in R. Faini and R. Portes (eds), *European Union Trade with Eastern Europe. Adjustment and Opportunities* (London: CEPR), 201–35.

—— (1995b) (ed.), *Foundations of an Open Economy* (London: CEPR).

Woolcock, S. (1982), 'The International Politics of Trade and Production in the Steel Industry', in J. Pinder (ed.), *National Industrial Strategies and the World Economy* (London: Croom Helm), 53–84.

—— and Hodges, M. (1996), 'EU Policy in the Uruguay Round', in H.

Wallace and W Wallace (eds), *Policy-Making in the European Union*, 3rd edn (Oxford: Oxford University Press), 301–24.

World Bank (2000), 'Poland: Complying with EU Environmental Legislation', *World Bank Technical Paper* No. 4554.

Wright, V. (1996), 'The National Co-ordination of European Policy-Making: Negotiating the Quagmire', in J. Richardson (ed.), *European Union: Power and Policy-Making* (London: Routledge), 148–69.

Young, A. and Wallace, H. (2000a), *Regulatory Politics in the Enlarging European Union* (Manchester: Manchester University Press).

—— —— (2000b), 'The Single Market: A New Approach to Policy', in H. Wallace and W. Wallace (eds), *Policy-Making in the European Union*, 4th edn (Oxford: Oxford University Press), 86–114.

*I*NDEX